Children of the Klondike

Also by Frances Backhouse
Women of the Klondike

Children of the Klondike

Frances Backhouse

whitecap

Cover design by Michelle Mayne
Interior design by Diane (Yee) Robertson, Enthusiastic Elephant Illustration & Design
Edited by Lesley Cameron
Maps by C. Stuart Daniel, Starshell Maps

Printed in Canada

Care has been taken to trace the ownership of copyright material used in the text. The author and publisher welcome any information enabling them to rectify any reference or credit in subsequent editions.

Library and Archives Canada Cataloguing in Publication

Backhouse, Frances
     Children of the Klondike / Frances Backhouse.

ISBN 978-1-55285-950-6

     1. Children—Yukon—Klondike River Valley—History. 2. Klondike River Valley (Yukon)—Gold discoveries. 3. Yukon—History—1895–1918. I. Title.

FC4022.3.B283 2010   971.9'102083   C2009-906420-0

The publisher acknowledges the financial support of the Canada Council for the Arts, the British Columbia Arts Council, and the Government of Canada through the Canada Book Fund (CBF). Whitecap Books also acknowledges the financial support of the Province of British Columbia through the Book Publishing Tax Credit.

 BRITISH COLUMBIA ARTS COUNCIL   Canada Council for the Arts   Conseil des Arts du Canada

The inside pages of this book contain FSC-certified 100 percent post-consumer fibre, are processed chlorine free, and are manufactured using biogas energy. For more information, visit www.environmentalbychoice.com.

 ANCIENT FOREST FRIENDLY

10 11 12 13 14   5 4 3 2 1

To my parents, John and Helen, with love

Contents

Foreword
by Ted Harrison

The little-known world of children who lived through the period of the Yukon gold rush has been well researched by the author of this book.

It was an era of simple homemade entertainments filled with traditional games, which encouraged personal inventiveness and imagination. Radio and television were yet to appear on the scene, but books gave children another insight into other cultures.

The Yukon was a mysterious world to the rest of Canada and the US. However, the children learned to cope with this new world and its unique problems. "Cabin fever" would plague both their elders and themselves, especially if it was a hard winter. Pioneers commenced a rudimentary school system which later became more organized and funded. The childhood memories of senior adults lend a piquancy to the many stories.

Children also had to cope with disease and accidents without specialized care, and many a tiny grave marker still bears testimony to this sad chapter of a Yukon childhood.

I congratulate Frances Backhouse on the depth of her research and on her empathy with the children of that brief exciting time in Canada's history when the world's focus lay on the gold. Those children have waited to come to life in this most interesting book.

Ted Harrison, C.M., B.Ed.
Victoria, BC
July 2009

Ted Harrison is a celebrated artist, author, and teacher who spent a quarter century living in the Yukon, capturing the spirit of the North in his vibrant, whimsical paintings.

Preface

I first became aware of the youngest participants in the world's last great gold rush while writing *Women of the Klondike* in 1994. The women who followed the golden trail to the Yukon were a diverse lot, ranging from dancehall girls to doctors, entrepreneurs to missionaries, and housewives to wealthy tourists. Many of them were also mothers, and through their stories I was introduced to their children. Ever since then I've been intrigued by this younger generation.

I wondered which of the various people who claimed to have been the first white baby born in the Klondike had the right to this title, and I was curious about the Native children whose ancestral lands were overrun by the gold seekers. I wanted to know what it was like to be a lone child on one of the stampede trails, travelling with thousands of gold-crazed adults, or to grow up in boom town Dawson or on the creeks. How did those tender young Southern transplants cope with their first cold, dark Northern winters? What games and amusements kept them entertained through the long days of summer? Did they burn with gold fever like so many of their elders?

In searching out the answers to all these questions and more, I discovered that in the vast body of Klondike literature published since 1896, children are largely ignored or relegated to the sidelines. As in real life during the late Victorian–early Edwardian period, they are seen but not heard.

Nevertheless, deep digging into the letters, diaries, photographs, legal documents, institutional records, unpublished memoirs, academic papers, books, newspapers, magazines, and websites that hold the history of the Klondike gold rush unearthed a wealth of information about children. Even when I had to sift through great quantities of unwanted material to get to the precious nuggets, it was worth the effort. And then came the fun—and the challenge—of melting down the gold and pouring it into my moulds. In the interests of authenticity and accuracy, however, I left some of the ore in its raw state. All the quotes in the book appear with their original spelling and punctuation.

One big decision I had to make early on in my research was how to define *children*. I considered taking my cue from Canada's government of the day, which declared anyone under the age of eighteen too young to obtain a free miner's certificate, but most of the seventeen-year-olds I found in the historical record seemed too mature to count as children. Instead I set my upper age limit at sixteen at the time of arrival in the Klondike. Admittedly, some of the sixteen-year-olds who appear in the book operated rather independently, but their parents and society still clearly viewed them as minors. Then, as now, mid-adolescence was a time of transition.

During the first winter of the gold rush most of the people in the Klondike area who were sixteen or under were Tr'ondëk Hwëch'in children, possibly numbering no more than several dozen altogether. The rest, a mere handful, were prospectors' offspring, including the daughter of one of the men who instigated the stampede to the North that put the Klondike on the map. Over the summer of 1897, a few more non-Native children arrived, and that fall the first gold rush baby was born in Dawson. But at the time of the first official head count in the region, in the late summer of 1899, children still comprised less than five percent of Dawson's population. Not until well into the new century did Dawson's demographics start to resemble those of more established communities elsewhere. Out on the creeks, children were always relatively rare.

Although many of these young Klondikers' names are unrecorded, enough story fragments survive to collectively create a vivid picture of their experiences. Theirs was a unique perspective on a unique and colourful episode in Northern history. It is my pleasure and privilege to finally add their voices to the Klondike narrative.

Acknowledgements

I was fortunate enough to be able to spend nearly three months as writer-in-residence at Berton House Writers' Retreat in Dawson City while working on *Children of the Klondike*. Although Pierre Berton was born a few years too late to be included in this book, I found it inspiring to reread his autobiography while living in his childhood home. I also enjoyed becoming acquainted with the winter side of Dawson and seeing freeze-up for the first time. I'm deeply grateful to the Writers' Trust of Canada, the Klondike Visitors Association, the Dawson City Library Board, and the Canada Council for the Arts for this opportunity. Writers' Trust program manager James Davies did an admirable job of handling all the arrangements for my stay. In the Yukon I was welcomed and made comfortable by dedicated Berton House volunteers Mary Cafferty and Steve Robertson in Whitehorse, and by Kathy Webster, Miriam Havemann, and Betty Davidson in Dawson.

Others who helped make my Yukon stay memorable include Dan Davidson, John and Madelaine Gould, Dan and Laurie Sokolowski (and, by extension, the entire Bombay Peggy's crowd), the members of the St. Paul's ecumenical Christmas choir, and Kathy and Michael Gates (who also gave me a couple good research leads). Sue Carr and her delightful children, Maddy and J.J., deserve special recognition for driving all the way up from Whitehorse on winter roads to brighten one of my weekends.

This book could not have happened without the assistance provided by the staff of the libraries and archives I consulted during my research. I offer particular thanks to Susan Twist, Donna Darbyshire, Clara Rutherford, and Peggy D'Orsay at the Yukon Archives; Laura Mann, Joanna Mazanti, and Katie Fraser at the Dawson City Museum; Jacki Swearingen at the Alaska State Library, Alaska Historical Collections; Rose Speranza at the Elmer E. Rasmuson Library, University of

Alaska Fairbanks; James Stack at Special Collections, University of Washington Libraries; Parks Canada employees Louise Ranger and Paula Hassard (Dawson City) and David Neufeld (Whitehorse); and Susan Parsons and Jody Beaumont of the Tr'ondëk Hwëch'in Heritage Department. The Diocese of Yukon kindly granted me permission to consult certain restricted records from the parish of St. Paul's, Dawson City, held at the Yukon Archives.

Relatives of several Klondike children generously gave me access to family documents and photographs, as well as much-appreciated words of encouragement. Special thanks go to Mary Henderson and Dorris Pooley (the daughters of Bessie and Dorothy Miller, respectively); Mary Kingsley and George Kingsley Bryce (Jim Kingsley's daughter and grandson) and Margo Grant (Charlie Kingsley's daughter); Robert Schuldenfrei (Bertie Schuldenfrei's grandson); Bill and Sharon Gurney (Gibson family relatives); and John McTavish (Emilie Craig's son, contacted in 1999).

Additional research assistance was obligingly provided by Megan Highet of the University of Alberta, *Alaska* magazine editor Tim Woody, author Lael Morgan, and Rick Karp of Whitehorse.

I sincerely appreciate the time Ted Harrison took to read my manuscript and to write the foreword. Thanks also to his biographer and our mutual friend, Katherine Gibson, for putting in a good word for me.

Whitecap Books publisher Robert McCullough embraced this project with enthusiasm. It has been a pleasure to work with Robert McCullough, Taryn Boyd, and other Whitecap staff, as well as Lesley Cameron, a skilled and diplomatic editor. Thanks also to Stuart Daniel for his fine maps.

As always, I greatly appreciate Carolyn Swayze's efforts on the business side of things and the fact that our relationship is not merely businesslike.

Mark Zuehlke kept the home fires burning while I was in Dawson and welcomed me back with open arms, giving me a taste of the separations and reunions that Klondikers experienced when they left loved ones behind in the South. They, however, did not have the benefit of modern telecommunications. I cherish Mark's unwavering love and support, which is always there whether we are together or far apart.

A Klondike Chronology

August 1896   The discovery of gold on Rabbit (Bonanza) Creek precipitates the Klondike gold rush. Over the winter, residents of Forty Mile and Circle City, including a handful of children, converge on Dawson City and the surrounding area, displacing the Tr'ondëk Hwëch'in from their traditional village at the mouth of the Klondike River.

Spring 1897   As word of the discovery reaches coastal Alaska, gold seekers start pouring over the Chilkoot and White Pass trails. Two babies die near Lake Lindeman, the first young casualties of the gold rush.

July 1897   The *Excelsior* and *Portland* steam into San Francisco and Seattle carrying more than $1 million worth of gold and setting off a worldwide stampede.

September 8, 1897   The first non-Native child is born in Dawson; the celebrated baby girl is named Dawson Klondike Schultz. Klondike Timothy Crowley, the town's second gold rush baby, arrives three weeks later.

Spring 1898   Work begins on the White Pass and Yukon Railway (WP&YR) line and paddlewheelers begin running between Bennett and Dawson.

August 1898   The Anglican church builds the Klondike's first schoolhouse in Moosehide and begins holding classes for Tr'ondëk Hwëch'in children. (It will be decades before they are allowed to attend school with non-Natives.)

Fall 1898	St. Paul's Anglican Church offers Dawson's first Sunday school classes and the Combination Theater presents Dawson's first family matinees.
January 6, 1899	In Fort McPherson, Mr. and Mrs. Braund, stampeders who took one of the Edmonton routes to Dawson, become parents of the first baby to be both conceived and born en route to the Klondike.
July 1899	The WP&YR line from Skagway to Bennett is completed. Use of the Chilkoot Trail by stampeders ceases soon afterwards.
November 1899	St. Mary's School, the Klondike's first public school, opens with eighteen students.
July 1900	The WP&YR reaches Whitehorse, greatly facilitating travel to Dawson and contributing to a remarkable influx of women and children over the summer.
Fall 1900	The territorial government opens public schools in Dawson and Grand Forks. The next two years see five more public schools opened on the Klondike creeks.
May 1901	Children play an active role in Dawson's Victoria Day celebrations for the first time.
January 1902	The *Klondike Nugget* introduces a Children's Department to its Saturday edition.
November 1902	Dawson students successfully petition for a children's skating rink.
1904–08	Due to falling enrolment, most schools on the creeks are closed or changed to assisted schools with reduced funding. Dawson schools continue to thrive as the number of children in town increases.

PACIFIC NORTHWEST

Bering Sea

Nome

Akulurak

St. Michael

Yukon R.

Holy Cross

A L A S K A

Arctic Circle

Fairbanks

Circle

Tanana R.

Yukon R.

Dawson

Rampart House

Herschel Island

Fort McPherson

Beaufort

Sea

Great Bear Lake

Mackenzie R.

Gulf

of

Alaska

U.S.A.
CANADA

Y U K O N

Whitehorse

Skagway

Juneau

Glenora

Stikine R.

Wrangell

Liard R.

Great Slave Lake

Port Resolution

Pacific

Queen Charlotte Islands

B R I T I S H

C O L U M B I A

A L B E R T A

Peace R.

Athabasca R.

Fraser R.

Edmonton

Ocean

Vancouver Island

Vancouver

Victoria

Seattle

CANADA
U.S.A.

WASHINGTON

100	200	300	400	500	mi.
0	200	400	600	800	km.

© F. Backhouse, 1995

STARSHELL MAPS

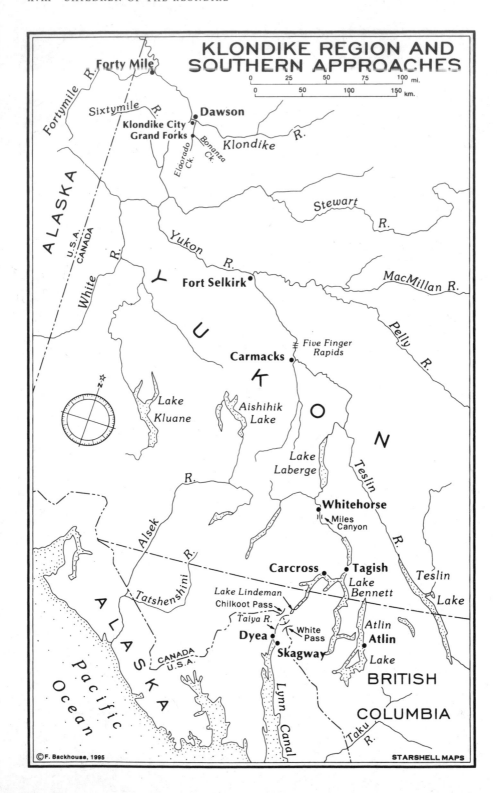

KLONDIKE REGION AND
SOUTHERN APPROACHES

Forty Mile

Sixtymile R.

Dawson

Klondike City
Grand Forks

Klondike R.

Eldorado Ck.
Bonanza Ck.

Fortymile R.

ALASKA

U.S.A.
CANADA

White R.

Stewart R.

Yukon R.

Fort Selkirk

MacMillan R.

Y

Pelly R.

Five Finger
Rapids

Carmacks

U

Lake
Kluane

Aishihik
Lake

O

N

Lake
Laberge

Teslin R.

Alsek R.

Whitehorse

Miles
Canyon

Carcross

Tagish
Lake
Bennett

Teslin
Lake

Tatshenshini R.

Lake Lindeman
Chilkoot Pass

Taiya R.

White
Pass

Dyea

Skagway

Atlin

Atlin

Lake

A L A S K A

CANADA
U.S.A.

BRITISH

COLUMBIA

Pacific
Ocean

Lynn Canal

Taku R.

©F. Backhouse, 1995

STARSHELL MAPS

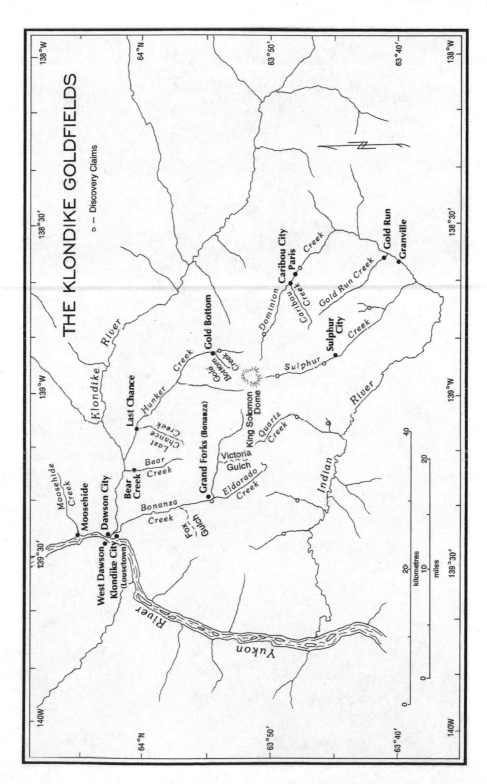

THE KLONDIKE GOLDFIELDS

∘ – Discovery Claims

She must not take
Graphie away. If she does,
I will take her by law.

Chapter 1

The Prettiest Little
Daughter You Ever Saw

At three and a half years old, Graphie Gracie Carmack was too young to fully appreciate the reason for her father's excitement when he returned to camp on August 16, 1896, but she knew the word "gold." Her father, George Washington Carmack, had been in the thrall of the precious metal ever since she was born, and for better or worse it would shape the rest of her life.[1]

George Carmack had first come north in 1885, a footloose young Californian who had been dreaming of gold for most of his twenty-four years. His first prospecting trip took him from Dyea, Alaska, over the Chilkoot Pass, and down the Yukon River as far as Miles Canyon. It yielded only a couple of ounces of gold, but George didn't care. He'd found both a lifestyle and a place that suited him perfectly.

George soon became acquainted with Keish, a tall, powerfully built Tagish packer who traced his ancestry to both the Tlingit and Tahltan peoples, and was invited to spend the winter of 1886–87 with his new friend's family. By spring George had entered into a common-law union with one of Keish's sisters, whom he called Jenny in preference to her now-forgotten birth name. Within months, however, Jenny was dead, one of the many victims of an influenza epidemic that was ravaging Native communities throughout the North.

Another of Keish's sisters, Shaaw Tláa, was widowed around the same time. She had been wed to a coastal Tlingit man, but he too was struck down by influenza, along with their young daughter. At her mother's urging, she returned home to marry George.

For the next couple of years, George and Shaaw Tláa—or Kate, as her new husband dubbed her—stayed in close contact with her family, especially Keish, who had become widely known as Skookum Jim for his strength and prowess as a packer. Working sometimes alone, but more often with his in-laws, George travelled between Dyea and the Yukon interior, packing, trapping, and prospecting.

Kate went with him, supporting his efforts with her valuable knowledge of how to live off the land. When George and Jim had a falling-out in 1889, she dutifully followed her husband north to the Fortymile district, not knowing that it would be another seven years before she saw her people again.

The Carmacks' first and only child was born on January 11, 1893, at Fort Selkirk. Inspired by a character in a novel he'd borrowed from Fort Selkirk's resident Anglican missionary, the Reverend Thomas H. Canham, George had the baby christened Graphie Gracie. From Kate she received a traditional name, Aagé, most likely in honour of Kate's older sister who had also married a white prospector. The senior Aagé never met her namesake—she died two years after Graphie's birth—but her death prompted a reconciliation between Jim and George.

Aagé was the fourth of the family's seven siblings to die in the 1880s and 1890s. As the only surviving son, Jim felt responsible for making sure the long-absent Kate was alive and well. He also missed George and the friendship they'd enjoyed. So, in the early summer of 1896, accompanied by his nephews, K̲áa Goox̱ (who also went by the name Dawson Charlie) and Koołseen (later known as Patsy Henderson), Jim set out to find his sister and brother-in-law.

Travelling down the Yukon River by boat, they finally located the Carmack family in late July, camped near a Hän fishing village at the mouth of the Tr'ondëk, or Klondike, River. It was a happy reunion. They all had many stories to tell and much news to share. Jim met his little niece for the first time and had the pleasure of reporting that he and his wife, Daak̲ux̱da.éit (also known as Mary), had also become parents. Born in 1891, their daughter, Daisy (Saayna.aat, in her mother's Tlingit language), was just two years older than her cousin.

When Jim and his nephews found them, the Carmacks had just come from buying supplies in the nearby mining community of Forty Mile. George had decided to spend some time salmon fishing in the Klondike River and prospecting on some of the many creeks that flowed into it. He urged the three Tagish men to stay for a while and join him.

They all knew they had a decent chance of finding gold in the area. Rumours about the motherlode had been floating around the North for years, sparking minor gold rushes here and there, and fellow prospector Robert Henderson had recently told George of a promising claim he'd staked on a Klondike tributary he called Gold Bottom. But they were equally aware of how devious the gods of fortune could be, constantly taunting prospectors with a few small nuggets here and a spoonful of gold dust there, and never delivering the big payout. For all their dreaming, probably none of them believed deep down that they would be the ones to initiate the greatest gold rush of the century.

The details of what happened on August 16, 1896, are lost in the shadows of history and myth, but what is known for sure is that a member of their party found gold on Rabbit Creek that day. Most versions of the Klondike story credit either Jim or George with making the discovery that launched the gold rush. That initial find—a sizable nugget or two plucked from the shallow water—was exciting enough, but the astonishing abundance of golden flakes that then appeared as they washed out their first trial pans made them ecstatic.

The next day all the men except Patsy, who at seventeen years old was too young to have a free miner's certificate, each staked out a section of the creek. Then George, Charlie, and Patsy headed for Forty Mile to register their claims while Jim started working the ground. George's news, shared shortly after arriving in Forty Mile on August 20, electrified everyone who was on hand to hear it, and by morning the town was practically empty. The stampede was on, with several hundred men in boats muscling their way upstream toward the Klondike. George and his companions didn't linger long at Forty Mile. Even so, by the time they got back to Rabbit Creek it had been renamed Bonanza Creek and was staked from end to end.

At first the spectacular gold strike had little effect on Graphie's life. She was used to moving from place to place and sometimes living in a canvas tent, as her family now did on their Bonanza Creek claim. And when their simple log cabin home was completed, it, too, was familiar. She probably spent most of her time with her mother, largely oblivious to the hundreds of gold seekers who poured

Kate and George Carmack with four-year-old Graphie at their Bonanza Creek cabin in 1897.

into the area over the winter as word of the Klondike discovery spread through Alaska and the Yukon.

Communication with the rest of the world had to wait until spring breakup, when steamboats could once again carry mail up and down the river. Among the letters George sent out after his hard but profitable winter of work was one addressed to his sister, Rose Watson. Besides gleefully informing her of his good fortune, he slipped in a casual remark about his previously unacknowledged family. He hinted that Rose might frown on his wife's background, but he wasn't ready to admit that he'd married across racial lines. "My wife is Irish and talks very broad English," he wrote evasively, "but I have the prettiest little daughter you ever saw."[2]

Come spring, many of the miners who'd flocked to Bonanza Creek and the surrounding country went south to make their debut as Klondike Kings. But George and his companions were content to wait. As the stampede gathered momentum through 1897 and on into the next year, they continued to jointly work their claims, growing increasingly rich. Then, in August 1898, after another lucrative winter, Graphie, Kate, and the four men boarded a boat and began the long journey to Seattle. Of the six of them, only George had ever been Outside and even he hadn't left the North in thirteen years.

The 1898 trip was a mixed success. Initially it was somewhat marred by the Tagish family members' culture shock and George's inability to ease them into his world. Things improved somewhat when they left Seattle and went to visit George's sister and brother-in-law at their ranch in California, but Rose and James Watson were not keen to host the whole group for long. Jim, Charlie, and Patsy soon headed home, and the Carmacks settled in to spend what would turn out to be their last winter together.

In March 1899 George and Kate went back to the Klondike, leaving Rose to look after six-year-old Graphie, a dark-eyed, raven-haired child who, like her mother, would never pass for Irish in person. As promised, George and Kate were not gone long. When they returned to California in late July they brought a companion for Graphie, her eight-year-old cousin, Mary Wilson, daughter of the late Aagé.

Skookum Jim, who had by then adopted the surname Mason, and Dawson Charlie also made a trip south in the summer of 1899, along with their wives, Mary and Annie. Kate was undoubtedly pleased to see some familiar faces when they met in Seattle, but George was soon ready to disown all his Yukon relatives, including his wife. On several occasions the unconventional, eyebrow-raising behaviour of one or more of them led to the publication of sensational news

Graphie Carmack with her parents in California in 1898, the year before George and Kate's bitter parting.

stories, replete with the unfettered racism typical of the time. Although some of the incidents may have sprung from the great cultural divide between the Tagish and the average Seattleite, the newspapers—and George—simply put them down to drunkenness.

"I am disgusted with the whole outfit," he wrote to Rose on July 28, 1899. "If Kates trunks were here I would ship her back to Dyea mighty quick."[3] Instead, he took Kate to spend the winter at the Watsons' ranch with the two girls and her disapproving in-laws while he returned north.

On June 20, 1900, at a Dawson dinner party, George met Marguerite Laimee, a twenty-six-year-old businesswoman whose cigar store may well have been the front for a brothel. Instantly smitten with this voluptuous and outgoing new acquaintance, George proposed to her that evening and she accepted at once. He knew his relationship with Kate had never been sanctified by church or state and so, without the slightest compunction, he renounced the woman he had called "wife" for thirteen years.

In July he wrote to Rose, asking her to tell Kate that he would never live with Kate again. He would send money for Kate to travel to Seattle and meet Jim and Charlie, he said, and would provide an additional sum when she arrived there, but she must leave their daughter behind. "She must not take Graphie away," he wrote. "If she does, I will take her by law."[4]

The ensuing custody battle was long and bitter. Kate refused to abandon her child. George refused to come and negotiate face to face. When the Watsons moved into town in September, taking Graphie and Mary with them, Kate enlisted the help of sympathetic friends and rented the house next door. Because she was illiterate, she relied on others to write letters for her, first to George, and later to the attorneys she hired to represent her when it became clear he had no intention of responding.

Kate's sense of betrayal, her devotion to Graphie, and her confusion about the best way to proceed are evident in her correspondence. In a lengthy missive to lawyer John H. Durst, dictated to Mrs. L. A. Steward on October 15, 1900, Kate complained about Rose's authoritarian ways and false accusations about her being intimate with other men and getting drunk. Her most poignant words addressed her sister-in-law's attempts to separate her from the two girls.

> She . . . has my children to watch me and carry talk, has decoyed my child
> Graphy . . . also my dead sisters little girl my niece [Mary] Wilson—I love her
> as my own daughter Graphy . . . I took a little cottage next door to her yard—
> so I could watch my children. She keeps my children—wont let my little girl
> come over and sleep with me at night when my little daughter ask her she tells
> her I am out. I am not out of nights and I am to lonly. I want my child to sleep
> with. I want my bone, flesh and blood. I dont like her learning my child and
> my niece my dead sisters child queer things and many little things which make
> me trouble.[5]

In a postscript, Mrs. Steward made it clear that not all who knew Kate shared Rose's low opinion of her. "She has made good warm friends among the people of this town and neighborhood and she has been a lady," she noted. "Everyone speaks in her favor."

Durst responded promptly, telling Kate that although she didn't want to terminate the marriage and had refused to sign the divorce papers George had served upon her, she would have to contest his suit. "Otherwise," he wrote, "he will get a judgment of divorce against you. In that event, he will keep all his property, and probably get a judgment giving him charge of your daughter."[6]

For Graphie—the prize for which both parents were desperately fighting— this was an upsetting and bewildering time. Not only was she separated from her mother, she had to rely on her aunt for all communication with her father.

"Tell [Graphie and Mary] that I say they must keep nice and clean and be good Girls, because Christmas is not far of and I know where there are lots of pretty things," George wrote to Rose in October from San Francisco. Yet he seemed uncertain about where the girls' loyalties lay. "What do they say about [Kate]," he asked in the same letter, "does Graphie ever say anything about me. Would she like to come to me if she had a chance." Then, on a more practical note: "do the children need any underwear or anything if they do I will send it to you."[7]

Graphie's letters to George went unanswered because he feared his replies might somehow be used against him in the legal battle that was unfolding. So suspicious was he of Kate and her supporters, whom he dismissed as busybodies and self-interested gold diggers, that he even doubted the authenticity of his daughter's attempts to contact him. On November 13 he told his sister that he had received "a letter supposed to be written by Graphie did she write it or was it another of them tricks, It was a nice little letter, & if she wrote it she is learning fast, I would have answered it only I was afraid someone els might get hold of it."[8]

Two weeks later he further defended his actions. "I know it must seem hard on little Pot that I wont write to her," he wrote to Rose, "but I know she would tell her mother that she got a letter from PaPa then it would get out & then such pumping the child would get & maybe wind up in trouble the less I seem to care for the child the less will be the fight for her, You know Kate does not care a rap for the child but she hates for you or me to get her then I suppose she thinks that by holding on to the child she will be able to get a few dollars more out of mee."[9]

By this time George had married Marguerite, and Kate had countered George's divorce suit by filing her own divorce papers, as well as launching a kidnapping suit against Rose. At the end of November Kate dropped both lawsuits and the two girls were returned to her care, but she remained in California while her lawyer started a new action aimed at winning a maintenance settlement from George. Finally, in July 1901, broke, homesick, and doubtful that she would ever see justice from the US legal system, Kate abandoned the maintenance suit and returned to the Yukon with Graphie and Mary.

When they arrived in Carcross they were warmly welcomed by Skookum Jim, who had a small house built for them and assumed responsibility for their financial support. In 1905, when Graphie had gone as far as she could with her schooling in Carcross, Jim offered to pay the $300 a year it would cost to continue her education in Whitehorse.

In Whitehorse, twelve-year-old Graphie boarded with Anglican Bishop Isaac O. Stringer and his family. On one occasion, Graphie and the bishop's daughter Rowena, who was three years younger, snuck off together to explore the town's red-light district. Amused and charmed by their unusual visitors, the women of the district showered them with sweets and hair ribbons, and placed a large, showy hat on each girl's head before sending them on their way. When the adventurers got home and admitted where they'd been, Rowena's horrified mother threw all the gifts into the wood stove.

In 1909 Graphie received a letter from the father she had not seen for nearly a decade, inviting her to visit him in Seattle. She jumped at the opportunity and, according to some accounts, left without Kate's knowledge. A year later, at the age of seventeen, she married Marguerite's thirty-two-year-old brother, Jacob Saftig. The marriage lasted thirteen years, until conflict over George's will prompted Graphie to leave, taking their three children and moving in with her Aunt Rose. A few years later she married again, this time to a used-car salesman, but that marriage also ended in divorce. After her third husband died, she lived alone, but remained close to her children and grandchildren.

Graphie neither lived in the Yukon again nor mended her broken relationship with her mother, but some part of her heart always remained connected to her Northern roots. To her first son, Ernest Charles Saftig, she gave her uncle's Tlingit name, Keish. And in 1960, three years before her death, she told her father's biographer, James Albert Johnson, that her feet ached and she wished she had a pair of Tagish moccasins.

Being the child of one of the men who started the Klondike gold rush did not bring much joy to Graphie's life, but Daisy Mason, daughter of the other key player on that fateful day at Rabbit Creek, fared even worse. Both were bound to the North by lineages that extended back ten thousand years or more, yet those ties were not strong enough to keep either of them there. The Klondike's most lasting legacy for both cousins was the breakdown of their parents' marriages and their own eventual alienation from their Tagish and Tlingit peoples.[10]

After Skookum Jim left to find Kate and George in 1896, Daisy did not see her father again for many months. When at last Jim did return to tell his wife and daughter about his gold find, he didn't stay long. Mary Mason was little impressed with the spendthrift lifestyle her husband had adopted since striking it rich and was particularly troubled by his drinking sprees. Although she accompanied him to Seattle in 1899, she preferred being at home in Carcross or with her Tlingit people in Alaska. Over the next few years, Daisy's parents were often apart, and she moved back and forth between them.

Until 1904, when he sold his Bonanza Creek properties, Jim made periodic trips to the Klondike, sometimes staying for a while to supervise the crews he hired to work his claims. There's no record of how often Mary and Daisy joined him, but they were at Bonanza Creek for at least part of the summer of 1900. Rose Marek spent that summer working for Jim, her hours divided between helping in the

Daisy Mason, born Saayna.aat. Her life changed dramatically after her father and other relatives made the discovery that launched the Klondike gold rush.

mess hall and giving nine-year-old Daisy reading and writing lessons. Rose had only recently arrived in North America from Bohemia and was still mastering English,[11] which may have limited her effectiveness as a tutor, but there were no other education options for Daisy. The government had yet to establish a school in the Bonanza area, and when they did, it was not open to Native children.

In 1905, after several unsuccessful attempts to reconcile their differences, the Masons split up for good. Mary returned to the coast, taking their younger child, a son named Kał.ens, whose birthdate is unrecorded. Jim and Daisy stayed in Carcross in the large, wood-frame house he had built for his family in 1899. Constructed from expensive, imported lumber and filled with ornate furnishings, it was a striking symbol of his wealth and left no doubt in anyone's mind, especially Daisy's, that she was different from all the other girls in her village, except perhaps Graphie.

Daisy didn't see much of her cousin until 1901. The two Klondike discoverers' daughters got to know each other after Graphie's return from California, but both girls soon left Carcross to attend schools elsewhere—Graphie in Whitehorse and Daisy in Seattle. Jim doted on his daughter and wanted to give her every opportunity to succeed in the world beyond the Yukon. Realizing that his innate

Daisy Mason stands between her mother, Mary, and father, Skookum Jim. Also pictured are Patsy Henderson (far right), a man believed to be George Carmack (far left), and an unidentified man.

generosity and profligate habits were rapidly depleting his Klondike fortune, he established a trust fund in her name in 1904.

Jim's plans for Daisy probably didn't include an acting career, but she became enamoured of the silver screen in her teens and decided to study acting in California. By 1916 she had managed to win some auditions, but no parts, so there was nothing to stop her from heading north immediately when she heard that Jim was critically ill with kidney disease. She spent the spring caring for her beloved father at his home in Carcross and stayed on for another month after he died on July 11. Then she returned south, still hoping for her big break.

On her subsequent, infrequent visits back to Carcross, Daisy sometimes spoke of wanting to marry someone local. However, the few eligible Tagish men considered her foreign and stuck-up. "She acts white lady too much," was how one potential husband put it.[12]

Instead she married a white man, and after they divorced she married another, abandoning her movie star dreams and slipping into alcoholism and poor health along the way. Daisy's second husband was remembered by her relatives as "a real deadbeat," but when she died in 1937, he did find the means to grant her final wish—that her body be brought home to the Yukon and laid to rest beside her father's in the Carcross cemetery.[13]

They throw the money around;
they throw the gold around.

Chapter 2

All Those People
Come for Gold

Although Graphie Carmack's and Daisy Mason's gold rush experiences were uniquely coloured by their family's involvement in this historic episode, they were far from being the only First Nations children whose lives were dramatically altered by it. The end of the nineteenth century was a time of enormous social turmoil for the original inhabitants of the Yukon and Alaska, especially those whose homelands overlapped the Klondike goldfields or the routes that connected them to the outside world. A slow but insidious process of cultural erosion had been undermining the foundations of their societies for nearly a century before the Bonanza Creek strike. With the Klondike gold rush came changes that were unprecedented in both speed and magnitude.

The first non-Natives to enter the Alaska-Yukon region were Russian fur traders who ventured into Alaskan waters around 1740. They were soon joined by Spanish, British, and American traders and explorers. By the early 1800s, European trading posts had been established at key locations on the coast and along the lower Yukon River, reaching the upper Yukon River in the 1840s. Meanwhile, the Hudson's Bay Company and Northwest Company had also extended their inland operations into the northwestern corner of the continent.

Not far behind the fur traders were Christian missionaries, bringing the word of God to a populace whom they saw as being in desperate need of salvation. And trailing behind by about a decade were the prospectors, a motley group of hardy individualists seeking the treasure that was surely buried somewhere in this vast land.

The search for gold in the Yukon River basin began in the 1870s, but relatively few gold hunters came to the area at that time. In 1880 the coastal Tlingits started allowing non-Natives to use the Chilkoot Pass. The improved access to the headwaters of the Yukon River attracted a handful of additional gold hunters, but in the late 1880s a series of promising strikes stirred up excitement within and outside the North and the number of prospectors rose from dozens to scores and then to a few hundred. The creation of small mining communities like Forty Mile and Circle City attracted other outsiders as well, mostly men and women hoping to pocket some second-hand gold, but also a few wives and children.

Despite this growing interest in the North, the number of non-Natives in Alaska and the Yukon remained relatively small, and many Natives had little or no direct contact with them. Indirectly, however, all the Natives were influenced by the introduction of novel trade goods, from guns, iron pots, and steel knives to flour, sewing needles, and calico.

Tragically, they were also affected by exposure to foreign pathogens to which they had no immunity. In the decades following the first interactions between Europeans and Natives, smallpox, scarlet fever, influenza, measles, mumps, and other infectious diseases spread throughout the North, killing many of those afflicted and weakening the rest. In the Yukon, the First Nations population plummeted from an estimated seven to nine thousand people before contact with Europeans to no more than twenty-six hundred in 1895.[1] Losses in Alaska were on a similar scale. Native people were still numerically dominant in the North, but even that was about to change dramatically.

———

As the shock waves generated by the discovery of gold on Bonanza Creek rolled out across the Yukon and Alaska, no one was more affected than the Tr'ondëk Hwëch'in, a group of Hän-speaking people who lived at the epicentre of the gold rush. Their fishing village, located by the mouth of the Tr'ondëk (or Klondike) River, was where Skookum Jim and his nephews had found George, Kate, and Graphie Carmack in August 1896. Tr'ochëk, as the Tr'ondëk Hwëch'in called this ancient seasonal settlement, was one of the most important places within their territory.

The Tr'ondëk Hwëch'in, with a population of sixty to seventy people at the time of the gold rush, was one of the three groups of Hän that called the western Yukon and eastern Alaska home.[2] Guided by traditional knowledge about the animals and plants that provided them with food, clothing, shelter, tools, and trade goods, each group followed an annual cycle of movement throughout their lands.[3] Families lived independently during the seasons when game was scarce and scattered, but joined forces to pursue caribou and moose in fall and winter, and to catch salmon in summer.

Salmon fishing was the most critical provisioning activity of the year. The first migrating salmon typically reached the mouth of the Klondike around mid-July, but the Tr'ondëk Hwëch'in started gathering at Tr'ochëk in late spring to prepare for their arrival. The Tr'ondëk Hwëch'in set up their summer homes and constructed or repaired canoes, fish traps, dip nets, and drying racks. Their name for the river came from the heavy rocks they used for pounding stakes into the riverbed when they built weirs to direct the fish into basket traps: *tr'o* meaning hammerstone, and *ndëk* meaning river.[4]

As the fishing season wound down in late summer and early fall, the women and children roamed the hills around Tr'ochëk, picking blueberries, highbush cranberries, rosehips, and other fruit. In the fall the village was used as a base for staging moose hunts up the Tr'ondëk valley. Families then moved into the mountains on either side of the Yukon River to hunt caribou and sheep before going their separate ways for the rest of the winter and early spring.

No matter what season they were born in, the lives of Tr'ondëk Hwëch'in children followed the same time-honoured patterns. Delivered into the capable hands of experienced midwives, Hän newborns were washed in warm water, then wrapped in soft rabbit skins. Their parents celebrated the arrival of each new child by inviting nearby kin to a special dinner. From infancy through adolescence, all elders would be their teachers, training and instructing them in the practical skills and traditional beliefs that would prepare them for adult life.[6]

Charlie Isaac was born in 1912, after the gold rush had severely disrupted Tr'ondëk Hwëch'in culture, but he knew of several customs intended to ensure

Two Tr'ondëk Hwëch'in girls pause near the fish-drying racks at Moosehide around 1898.

that boys developed the endurance, agility, speed, and surefootedness critical to hunting success. "A young man should not eat fish skin, especially the skin of the king salmon, because it is slippery, and people thought it would make him slip when chasing caribou," he reported. As well, they "should not sleep with their legs stretched out, but always with their legs bent. If someone in the lodge noticed a boy sleeping with legs straight, they would take a little stick and hit his legs hard, until he curled them up. If he slept stiff-legged, he would be stiff-legged on snowshoes. When you are running on snowshoes, especially in deep snow and uphill, you have to be able to step high and bring your knees up in a good place. Our people were very good runners, famous for it."[7]

A boy's first successful hunt was a significant event that indicated the end of childhood. Fathers generally marked this coming of age with a community feast, especially when the boy was an oldest son. For girls, the transition to womanhood came with their first menstruation, an occasion also honoured with a feast. After the celebration, the girl was taken a mile or two from her home to a specially constructed shelter, where she would live alone for one year. The food her mother brought her during her period of seclusion could not include fresh meat or fish. If her family had to travel in winter, the girl left her shelter and went with them, wearing a special moose-skin hood that prevented her from seeing any man or much else besides the ground at her feet. She would be guided by a suitor who broke a separate trail, with the two of them holding on to opposite ends of a six-foot-long pole—no easy task when snowshoeing.

Marriage partners were often selected by parents and elders when children were still very young, though the betrothed couple was generally given a say in the matter before the union was finalized. Once both sets of parents had agreed to the marriage, typically when a boy was ten to fifteen years old, he left his childhood home and began living with his prospective wife and her parents, becoming a permanent part of this family. A year or more later, once the couple had reached maturity and proven capable of supporting themselves, they moved into their own dwelling.[8]

In August 1896, the Tr'ondëk Hwëch'in were camped as usual at Tr'ochëk. Their hide-covered houses were scattered across the triangle of level ground at the junction of the two rivers, and their wooden drying racks were loaded with strips of salmon, slowly curing over the smoky fires that smouldered below. They may have cordially welcomed the Carmacks and Kate's Tagish relatives, or perhaps they paid them little attention. The Tr'ondëk Hwëch'in were accustomed to visits from members of other First Nations who came to Tr'ochëk every summer to socialize, trade, and fish, and even from the occasional non-Native. But whatever hospitality they may have extended to these particular visitors, it brought them nothing but trouble.

Within weeks of the discovery of gold on Bonanza Creek, the Tr'ondëk Hwëch'in were ousted from Tr'ochëk by an onslaught of prospectors and entrepreneurs who wanted a riverside campsite with good access to the Klondike goldfields. Initially the Tr'ondëk Hwëch'in tried to stay close to their fishing grounds, moving just across the Klondike River to where the city of Dawson was taking shape, but their tenure there was short-lived. Well aware that this swampy floodplain was better suited to moose than humans, they selected the only elevated area of Dawson that was close to the river mouth. Unfortunately, the North-West Mounted Police (NWMP) desired the same piece of ground and had more pull with the authorities in Ottawa.

In the spring of 1897 the Tr'ondëk Hwëch'in relocated again, this time three miles away to a long-established campsite known as Jëjik Ddhä Dënezhu Kek'it or, in English, Moosehide.[9] By then, maintaining access to the salmon was a moot point anyway. Logs rafted down the Klondike by the newcomers to feed the demand for building materials in Dawson and Klondike City had obliterated the Tr'ondëk Hwëch'in fish weirs, and it would have been futile to rebuild them.

Moosehide sat on a high bench overlooking the Yukon River. Even though it couldn't match Tr'ochëk's natural advantages, it did offer access to alternative fishing sites and good hunting country, an abundance of berries on the hills behind the village, a plentiful supply of clean water from Moosehide Creek, and ample firewood. However, it represented only a tiny fraction of the land the Tr'ondëk Hwëch'in needed to continue their traditional lifestyle, and much of that had been overrun by non-Natives who were rapidly tearing up the creeks, cutting down the forests, and killing off the wildlife.

The Tr'ondëk Hwëch'in were baffled by the newcomers' obsession with gold. They were well aware of its presence, but the only ones who attached any value to it were children like Lucy Wood, who was nine years old when her people were forced to leave Tr'ochëk. Before the gold rush, her favourite pastime was searching the creek beds for shiny yellow stones, which she squirrelled away in a moose-skin bag. After August 1896 the creeks and their treasure became the property of foreign adults, who seemed crazed by their desire to possess those yellow stones. According to the daughter of one Hän witness to the gold rush, it was "very strange to my father that all those people come for gold . . . The way my dad used to say, 'They throw the money around; they throw the gold around. There's too much of it.'"[11]

While the gruelling and often fruitless work of placer mining held little appeal for most Tr'ondëk Hwëch'in, they were quick to embrace other economic

The move to Moosehide brought many changes to the lives of the Tr'ondëk Hwëch'in, but parents continued to pass on traditional skills such as making clothing from tanned hides.

opportunities that came with the gold rush. For women, making mittens, moccasins, and other clothing for ill-equipped Southerners was the primary source of earnings. For men, it was selling fresh meat and fish. Tr'ondëk Hwëch'in children were often present when their elders did business with the Klondikers, and these transactions gave them an opportunity to learn more about their new neighbours. While accompanying her father on his fish-selling rounds, one little girl from Moosehide met two of Dawson's more eccentric early residents, Mary Hitchcock and Edith Van Buren.

The two women, both wealthy, upper-crust Americans, had arrived in Dawson on July 27, 1898, bearing more than a thousand pounds of luggage, even though they planned to depart before freeze-up. Their dozens of trunks and crates were filled with fashionable garments, tinned luxury foods, and every domestic item they imagined they might need to live in comfort and style in the forty-by-seventy-foot tent they had brought to dwell in. They had also packed a portable bowling alley, a soda machine, a gramophone and record collection, and a one-hundred-pound mahogany music box, and they were accompanied by a pair of Great Danes, a parrot, two dozen pigeons, and a single canary, its companion having died en route.

In her memoir, Mary described a visit to their tent by a Native fisherman—possibly the highly respected Tr'ondëk Hwëch'in leader Chief Isaac—and his daughter. "The Indian followed us with great dignity, holding the hand of a small child of three years of age. After receiving payment, he stood calmly surveying the decorations. I started the music-box, to which the child listened with awe; then took her hand to show her the parrot. The father objected, however, saying, 'got no time.' But the child had caught sight of the strange bird and was so eager to make its acquaintance that it was some time before he succeeded in leading her away."[12] Mary insisted on taking photographs of the man and his daughter before they left, but it is doubtful the girl got one of these souvenirs of the encounter.

Growing up during the gold rush era, Tr'ondëk Hwëch'in children were exposed to many outside influences that had not been part of their parents' world. They still learned about the traditional ways from the older generation, but church and state had different priorities for their education. Because Bishop William Carpenter Bompas had been instrumental in establishing Moosehide as a permanent refuge for the Tr'ondëk Hwëch'in after Tr'ochëk's appropriation, the Anglicans exerted a strong influence on the community from the beginning. The most prominent

Native children and Klondike stampeders on the Thirty Mile section of the Yukon River, north of Lake Laberge, around 1898.

building in the village was St. Barnabas Church, with its wooden steeple rising high above the villagers' dozen or so log homes. Next to it stood the church-run day school.

The Tr'ondëk Hwëch'in's introduction to classroom education coincided with the chaotic period at the start of the gold rush. In the fall of 1896 Bompas recruited Frederick Flewelling, fresh out of theological college in Toronto, to minister to the residents of Tr'ochëk. Upon arriving on October 17, the twenty-four-year-old New Brunswicker arranged for the construction of a sixteen-by-twenty-foot log cabin to serve as his living quarters, as well as the mission's church and school-house. As soon as it was completed, he began holding classes from ten until noon each morning, as well as afternoon prayer sessions.

"School is very popular," he wrote in his journal in November, "and I have from 20 to 30 pupils of all ages learning the A.B.C.'s." However, he resented "the continual annoyance of the natives who are always wanting something. My parishioners . . . walk in on me at all hours by the squad, never knock at the door nor take off their hats, spit on the floor, poke at the fire, leave grease marks where ever they sit down on bench or floor, never know when to go away."[13]

In the spring Flewelling started to expand the mission, with plans for a separate school building, only to discover that the Tr'ondëk Hwëch'in had been elbowed aside by the NWMP. The move to Moosehide left no time to build a school, and after the strain of sacrificing his privacy the year before, Flewelling decided to give up teaching instead of having his home double as a classroom. Over the following months the young clergyman continued to struggle with loneliness and feelings of repugnance for the very people whose souls he'd come to save, and he finally resigned from his posting in July 1898.

Flewelling's replacement was the Reverend Benjamin Totty, a more experienced missionary who was ably supported by his wife, Selina, the daughter of pioneering American trader Al Mayo and an Alaskan Native woman named Margaret. By September Totty had a one-room schoolhouse up and running. Then, in 1899, the Tottys left for England on a year-long furlough, and Bompas and his wife came from Forty Mile to oversee the mission and the school.

In April, after ill health sent Charlotte Bompas back to Forty Mile, the bishop wrote to the Anglican minister in Dawson, asking him to "see some of the ladies who have tried schooling in Dawson and have failed and propose to them to try teaching at Moosehide."[14] Since no suitable candidate stepped forward, the schoolmaster's job was still open when Totty returned, and from then until his retirement from the ministry in 1926, he was the only teacher at Moosehide.

The school operated seasonally, closing for about four months each year when the Tr'ondëk Hwëch'in families left to go hunting, trapping, or fishing. But even when the school was open, the children didn't always show up. In 1906, Bompas reported that, "At Moosehide we had an average attendance of 20 to 25 [in previous years]. Now I think it may be only 10 to 12 though with 30 children on the Books. They are away from the Mission half the time."[15] In 1908, eighteen children were enrolled in Moosehide day school but the average number present in class was seven.[16]

As visiting school inspectors repeatedly noted, sporadic attendance contributed to the students' slow progress, but that wasn't the only obstacle to learning. The school day was usually limited to a two-hour morning session, there was a woeful lack of textbooks and other teaching materials, and—perhaps the biggest problem—the quality of the instruction was questionable.

Totty, who lived in Moosehide for more than a quarter-century and raised his five children there, was devoted to his Hän parishioners, but he never excelled as a schoolmaster. The diffident Englishman had neither the training nor the natural talent for this part of his job, and his partial deafness further impeded his efforts. Nevertheless, he approached the challenge conscientiously, if unimaginatively, faithfully adhering to the Church Missionary Society's instructional principles.

Built on a foundation of Christian teachings and the cultivation of "civilized" behaviour, the curriculum focused on the fundamentals of reading, writing, and arithmetic. Despite the modest aspirations of schools like Moosehide, one member of the Anglican clergy noted that owing to "the start they received in [day] schools quite a number of Indians in different parts of the Territory are able to write letters and read a letter, and also work out arithmetical problems such as are necessary for trading."[17] It would be decades, however, before the Moosehide children were allowed to attend the public school in Dawson and learn alongside their non-Native peers.[18]

⌒

At the beginning of the gold rush era, Tr'ondëk Hwëch'in children still played traditional games. One of these was described by the American journalist Tappan Adney, who went north with the first wave of stampeders in the fall of 1897 and stayed in the Klondike until the spring of 1898. That winter, he spent more than a month with Chief Isaac and about forty or fifty of his people on a moose-hunting expedition that took them far up the Klondike River valley. The experience allowed Adney to get to know the Tr'ondëk Hwëch'in in ways that few other Klondikers ever did.

"The children, dressed in their warm thick furs, have as happy a time as children anywhere," Adney wrote in *Harper's New Monthly Magazine* in 1900.

Most of their play is out-of-doors, where they make play-houses in imitation of the large ones, and roll about in the snow like little polar bears. Sometimes they take papa's snowshoes and slide down some little bank, but they did not use

Standing in front of a traditional hide-covered house, a Tr'ondëk Hwëch'in woman and group of children pose for the camera of journalist Tappan Adney.

the toboggans for that purpose. A favorite game was "kli-so-kot," or "throwing-the-stick." A row of five or six small stakes is set up in the hard-packed snow of the village street, and another row thirty or forty feet distant. Each contestant provides himself with two clubs and taking turns, they throw these at first one, then the other, of the group of upright stakes, the one who knocks down the greatest number of stakes being the winner.[19]

The other Klondike children—the ones who came from far away or were born to parents who came from far away—might have enjoyed playing the stick-throwing game, but the Tr'ondëk Hwëch'in were never given an opportunity to teach them. Even though the newcomers lived mere miles away from the children of Tr'ochëk and Moosehide, they inhabited a world apart and participated in the gold rush on vastly different terms.

My father's sure to go
and if he goes, I'm going too.

Chapter 3

Klondicitis

In the summer of 1897, A.C. Craig, a Danish immigrant living in Chicago, was one of hundreds of thousands of people around the world who came down with Klondike fever. As his wife, Emily, later recalled, it wasn't long before he'd passed it on to her. "My husband read every word about the goldfields and at night would talk about the reports . . . when he was at work I would read the same pages and thrill at the stories. Once he told me of seeing some nuggets . . . in a jeweller's window . . . and his eyes had a long and faraway look in them. The next day I hunted up the store, and there, sure enough was the gold . . . From then on I could believe any story—we both caught the fever—and that is no childhood disease either."[1] Before the end of August they were on their way north.

Certainly Klondike fever was first and foremost an adult affliction, but children also suffered. Fathers or mothers, and sometimes both, departed for the Northern goldfields and were not heard from for months or sometimes even years. While most returned home or sent for their families after a year or two, others disappeared forever. Only a few parents took their offspring with them when they joined the stampede. Older children were often keen participants, inspired by their own visions of buried treasure or caught up in the novelty and adventure; the youngest had no idea what all the fuss was about.

The Klondike wasn't the first gold-mining region to draw hordes of fortune hunters from around the world—earlier events in California, southeastern Australia, and the Transvaal had already written the script for a long run of gold-driven dramas that played out across four continents during the 1800s and early 1900s—and it didn't even yield the greatest quantities of the precious metal. But it did inspire an unprecedented frenzy of media attention and trigger the largest mass movement of gold seekers in history. That is, once word got out.

For nearly a year after George Carmack emptied Forty Mile by announcing his Rabbit Creek discovery, the Klondike's riches remained a Northern secret. The news spread to other parts of the Yukon and Alaska over the winter, prompting every prospector who heard it to abandon whatever he was doing and make a bee-line to Dawson, but it was many months before rumours about the new El Dorado began to trickle south, and even then they garnered little attention from news-papers or the general public until they were backed up by irrefutable evidence.

Many of those who found rich diggings during their first winter in the Klon-dike headed Outside as soon as the ice left the Yukon River in spring. Weighed down with their earnings, they travelled by riverboat to St. Michael, Alaska, then changed vessels for the month-long ocean voyage back to civilization. The van-guard reached San Francisco on July 14, 1897, on board the steamship *Excelsior*. Between them, the thirty passengers carried at least $500,000 worth of gold dust and nuggets, which they immediately set about spending with wild abandon.

Three days later, at six in the morning, the S.S. *Portland* steamed into Seattle bearing "a ton of gold"—according to the advance reports—and nearly seventy more Klondikers. They were greeted by thousands of excited spectators and a bat-talion of reporters. In the final reckoning, the *Portland*'s golden payload actually exceeded two tons, with a value of more than $1 million, but the most thrilling news was that there was plenty more where it came from. By nightfall, Seattle's citizenry was so overcome by gold fever that the city was barely functioning.

With the telegraph wires buzzing, word of the Klondike strike circled the globe, producing the same electrifying effect everywhere. For years the United States and Canada had been in the grip of a brutal economic depression, which showed no sign of abating, and countries elsewhere were facing similar trials. Now newspapers that had been filled with grim tales of bankruptcy, unemployment, and poverty were overflowing with fabulous accounts of ordinary people who, over the course of one winter, had gone from penury to unimaginable affluence. People like Ethel Berry, who was said to have gathered $10,000 worth of nuggets from her husband's Eldorado Creek claim "as easily as a hen picks up grains of corn in a barnyard."[2] And former Michigan farm boy Frank Phiscator and his two partners, who didn't reach the Klondike until the dead of winter but still managed a spring cleanup that put $50,000 in each man's pocket.

Over the following weeks and months, the press regaled readers with Klon-dike stories, most of them heavily weighted to rumours and hearsay, and people everywhere became obsessed with the idea of joining the stampede north. In the words of one *Seattle Post-Intelligencer* headline, the word "Klondike" had become "the 'Open Sesame' to a Dreamland of Wealth."[3] Thousands of gold seekers were already on their way to Dawson, scrambling to get there before freeze-up shut down river travel and locked them out. Thousands more were making plans to follow.

Meanwhile, the flow of wealth from the Yukon continued as Klondikers who had missed the first outbound boats made their way south. On September 15, 1897, the *Excelsior* returned to San Francisco on its second trip of the season from St. Michael. Once again it was loaded with Klondike gold barons and their treasure, but one passenger stood out from the rest.

"This is the First White Baby Born in Dawson" proclaimed the caption beneath a pen-and-ink drawing of a chubby-cheeked toddler in a frilly cap and long dress, which appeared in the next day's *San Francisco Examiner*.[4] Never mind the minor detail that Dawson didn't actually exist when little Ora Wold was born on November 23, 1895. This was the kind of story that sold newspapers.

Ora had actually come into the world at Forty Mile, making her the first (or possibly the second) white child born in the upper Yukon River basin and the youngest to live in the Klondike during the first year of the gold rush.[5] Her parents, Maren and Bernt Lovold, were recent immigrants to North America who had anglicized their Norwegian names to May and Ben Wold.

On March 1, 1895, the newlywed Ben and five fellow countrymen had set out from Tacoma, Washington, to go prospecting in the North.[6] As soon as they had settled at Forty Mile, Ben Wold and Lars Langlo sent for their wives, May and Ingeborg, and the Langlos' little daughter, Marie. It was early summer when May, Ingeborg, and Marie set out, and they enjoyed calm seas and congenial company on the trip north to St. Michael and up the Yukon River to Forty Mile. By the time they arrived in late July, however, May knew without a doubt she was pregnant and when she saw the tiny log home her husband had built, a wave of self-pity swept over her. How, she wondered, would she cope with a newborn in such cramped quarters in winter?

May's labour pains started on a cold November day, prompting an anxious summons to be sent across the river to the North-West Mounted Police post. The detachment surgeon, Alfred Wills, arrived in due course, as did the baby, and the proud

Ora Wold, born in Forty Mile in November 1895, was one of the few non-Native children in the Klondike during the first year of the gold rush.

parents were soon showing off their new family member to a steady stream of well-wishers who called to see the history-making infant.

Despite the *Examiner*'s confusion about Ora's birthplace, the sentiments attributed to May were probably genuine. "I have spent two years of hardship and privation with my husband on the Yukon," she said during an interview shortly after disembarking in San Francisco. "I know what it is to be deprived of all the luxuries and most of the necessities of life, and I would not advise any woman to go there. One would think that children would be a great care in such a country, but you don't know the pleasure and happiness which the little one brought me."[7]

Like almost every other man in Forty Mile, Ben had joined the charge upriver to the Klondike in August 1896. After staking Number 26 Above Discovery on Bonanza Creek, he returned to collect his wife and daughter and the family's few possessions. Eleven months later, he departed Dawson carrying $35,000 worth of gold—$12,000 being from the sale of his claim and the rest the product of his own sweat and toil. Already he was questioning whether he'd quit too soon, though May was ready to be done with the Yukon.

"Neither my husband nor myself cared to winter on the Klondyke, so I induced him to sell his claim and come out," May explained. "He has made enough to insure our living comfortably for the rest of our lives. After a few days' in this city we will leave and go to the old country direct . . . I am glad that my husband [and] I can return to my old home rich."[8] Wealthy they were, but when Ora died before reaching adulthood, May bitterly attributed her daughter's death to the hardships of her first two years.

Despite those hardships, the Langlo family stayed on in the Klondike after the Wolds left. In April 1898, the *Klondike News* described the Eldorado Creek claim owned by Lars Langlo, now known as Louis Langlow, and his Norwegian partners as "very rich." The article also noted that Louis was "the father of a bright and beautiful daughter, now five years of age, who is the pride of Eldorado. This golden-haired little fairy, not only absolutely bosses No. 12 Eldorado, but the entire Creek from Chief Gulch to the Klondike River. The collection of nuggets owned by little Marie would astonish almost anyone who has never been in the Klondike."[9]

After spring cleanup was finished, Louis and Ingeborg planned to leave the North and embark on a world tour before resettling in their old home in Washington state. During the winter they were to "visit the East [and] Europe, and spend a few months in Norway." Then, after "viewing the wonders of the Paris Exposition in 1900, they [would] return to Tacoma, and take up permanent residence there."[10]

While May Wold suspected that she and her husband had paid a high price for prosperity, Thomas and Salome Lippy knew for sure that they had. Their Klondike triumph was marred by a tragic, unforgettable prelude, which they seldom spoke about publicly.

Randolph Percival Lippy, better known as Percy, was just four years old when his parents bundled him up and set off for Alaska in April 1896. Struggling to make ends meet on the pittance Thomas earned as the general secretary of the Seattle Young Men's Christian Association, they had decided to join the search for Northern gold. They realized it wouldn't be an easy undertaking, but at thirty-five years old Thomas still had the muscular build and athletic abilities that had earned him the title of World Champion Hose Coupler when he was a fireman in Fargo, North Dakota, and a reputation as Seattle's best handball player. And Salome, a small, slender, thirty-three-year-old with delicately pretty features, was hardier than she looked.

That summer, Salome and Percy lived at Forty Mile while Thomas worked nearby as a hired hand on another prospector's claim. On August 25, he returned home to find the town almost deserted. He was soon hot on the heels of the leaders in the race to the new goldfields, but by the time he got to Bonanza Creek,

This Hunker Creek cabin with canvas-covered ceiling and walls, and rooms defined by cloth partitions, was typical of the rough accommodations of the early gold rush years.

its entire length had been staked. So Thomas did as other latecomers had done and settled for a piece of Bonanza's "pup"—a feeder stream originally known as Whipple Creek and soon to become famous as Eldorado Creek.

Later Thomas loved to recount how he secured the property that earned him $1.75 million before he finally sold it in 1903. His first claim on Eldorado Creek was Number 36, but the day after he staked it, he and the owner of Number 16 decided to trade claims, a chance decision that put him in possession of what turned out to be one of the most profitable slices of the Klondike pie. He also enjoyed telling of the dark December night when he first hit pay dirt, just as he was on the verge of giving up after three exhausting and discouraging months of failed efforts. The story he kept to himself was the one from August 28—the day Percy died.

The date of Percy's demise is one of the few documented details of this event. There is no record of what caused his death and no one knows whether he might he have survived had NWMP surgeon Alfred Wills been on hand. Unfortunately, Alfred, like most members of the detachment, had taken a leave of absence and joined the initial charge to the Klondike. It is not even clear whether Thomas was with Salome when their son passed away or if he had already gone upriver. The only certainty is that Percy was buried at Forty Mile in a small grave surrounded by a white picket fence. Some time later his remains were transported to Greene's Mortuary in Dawson and then shipped to Seattle, their final resting place.

On July 14, 1897, the grieving parents were among those who walked down the *Excelsior's* gangplank and set the world on fire. The Lippys' $65,000 share of the gold that was on board was believed to be the largest personal fortune brought out from the Klondike that summer, and reporters clamouring for a word from them besieged their San Francisco hotel. One of those who managed to interview Thomas and Salome before they withdrew from the limelight wrote that "both speak pathetically of the death of their little son . . . and they would gladly exchange their present good fortune if he could but be with them." Almost a year after their loss, the rawness of their pain was still apparent.[11]

Gold fever, Klondicitis, the yellow malady—by any name it was a highly contagious disease. Stories of death and hardship did little to slow its spread, especially among those who felt they had little left to lose. Like many of the early victims of gold fever, thirty-seven-year-old John Mclymont Whyte of Seattle had lost his business, his home, and almost everything else he owned in the financial crash of the 1890s. In 1897 he was unemployed despite his previous business success and a degree from the University of Edinburgh, and his family was subsisting on what his twelve-year-old son, Harry, made from selling newspapers. Desperate to find a way to support his wife and five children, John decided to join the stampede, confident that he'd come home with "a washtub full of gold." That never happened, but he did get a steady job working for his old friend Thomas Lippy and was eventually able to send for his family.[12]

P.B. Anderson had similar reasons for going to the Klondike. He and his wife, both Swedish immigrants, were living in Bellingham, Washington, with three young children and no income. P.B.'s last job, cutting firewood for the railway, had earned him only $1 per fourteen-hour day, but at least it had put food on the table. By the summer of 1897 the Andersons were subsisting on game birds and fish that P.B. brought home from excursions into the countryside, supplemented by occasional donations from compassionate neighbours. All he really wanted was to earn enough money to start up a commercial sawmill, build a house for his family, and buy a horse and buggy, but even those relatively humble ambitions seemed hopelessly out of reach. When he heard about the Klondike there was no holding him back.

Promising his wife that he would come home soon with "every pocket full of nuggets," P.B. kissed his loved ones goodbye and hurried off to Seattle to book his passage north. As his daughter, Ethel, later recalled, "Mama cried because he was leaving for the faraway Klondike, that no one knew anything about. My two little brothers cried and I cried too, mostly because mama cried, I suppose." The next time they saw him, more than a year later, the children hardly recognized their father.[13]

Such tearful scenes were repeated many times all across the continent and in distant countries over the next few years as some one hundred thousand people left their homes and set off for the land of opportunity. Living in rural Quebec, Gédéon Pepin managed to avoid catching Klondike fever when the epidemic was at its peak, but he succumbed in 1901, when one of the village's native sons returned from the Yukon with $50,000. Suddenly, working all week in a butter factory and playing the organ at mass on Sunday to make a little extra money was no longer enough for Gédéon. Although it would mean leaving his twenty-year-old wife and two daughters, one of them a very sick infant, he yearned to join the seven other young local men who had decided to try their luck in the goldfields. Knowing her husband would be miserable if he stayed behind, Merilda Pepin gave him her blessing and bid him adieu. Two years later, she and their daughters joined him in Dawson.[14]

Whether or not the women who stayed behind shared their husbands' feverish dreams and approved of them chasing after Klondike gold, they had to keep the home fires burning. In addition to the responsibility of raising children single-handedly, some, like Mary Kinglsey, also carried an increased financial burden.

When the gold rush began, Jack Kingsley was leading what was for him a very staid life. Born John Edward Knightley on the Isle of Wight, he had crossed the Atlantic by joining the British Marines, then jumped ship and changed his surname once he reached North America. A stint in the American army got him to the West Coast, at which point he deserted, moved to Canada, and found work as a cook on a sealing schooner. But by 1897, Jack's days of roaming appeared to be over. At forty-one years old, he was a husband, the father of two young children, and a homeowner in Victoria, British Columbia. That summer, however, ships filled with gold seekers started steaming out of the city's harbour and his adventurous spirit was reawakened.

Within weeks of hearing about the Klondike, Jack quit his job as a streetcar motorman and joined the stampede with his next-door neighbour. They got as far as Lake Laberge before they were forced to stop for the winter. The next spring they nearly made it to Dawson, but their boat capsized and they lost their outfit. Undeterred, they returned to Victoria to resupply, then headed north again.

Mary Kingsley was twenty-six years old when her husband first left for the Klondike. Their son, Jim, was almost four and their daughter, Ethel, was two. For the next six years they were essentially on their own while Jack tried, unsuccessfully, to make his gamble pay off. During these lean years, Mary went back to

From left to right, Ethel, Mary, and Jim Kingsley in Victoria in 1899. Mary raised the children single-handedly for six years while her husband chased Klondike gold.

waitressing, a job she'd done before her marriage, but she still couldn't make ends meet. Finally, in 1901, she sold her home and all its furnishings and moved to her father's farm, about a hundred miles north of Victoria. On the farm Jim learned to ride and handle a hunting rifle, and by the time the family was reunited in 1903, he had grown from a cherubic, golden-haired tot into a sturdy, capable nine-year-old who faced the world with a resolute expression.[15]

Mothers who left their young ones and joined the stampede, either alone or with their husbands, did so for a variety of reasons. Many desperately hoped for a chance to bring home a nest egg. Others felt their place was by their mate's side, even if that meant entrusting their children to the care of others. And some were simply caught up in the excitement of the event.

As a single parent struggling to make a living, Georgia White answered the Klondike's call for purely financial reasons.[16] Having divided her three offspring between friends in Reno, Nevada, and the Ladies Protective Relief Society in San Francisco, she boarded the *Australia* on February 21, 1898, and sailed north.[17] Once she reached Dyea it took her several months to make arrangements for the next stage of her journey. In the meantime, a job at a hotel allowed her to send $80 to those caring for her children. Then in mid-June she departed for Dawson, travelling with a party of several men and one other woman.

Georgia found her new acquaintances generally agreeable, but the separation from her children weighed heavily on her spirits. "The gentlemen are kindness itself toward us in every way," she wrote in her diary on June 25, "but oh I miss my darlings so that it makes me quiet where I ought to try and be pleasant and cheerful but I can not—my thoughts are always on home." Her entry two days later was even more anguished. "I fear very much that I am a damper on our company . . . I think constantly of my little ones and God knows at times it seems more than I can bear but I must—for Oh deliver me from becoming insane up here."[18]

The group arrived in Dawson on July 8 and Georgia immediately began looking for work. She soon learned that there were few vacancies and a multitude of people vying to fill them. Although she eventually secured a $5 a day job in a laundry, it did little to console her. On August 13, she noted sadly that she was spending her birthday away from her children. Summer was already winding down and she knew she had to decide whether stay through the winter or book her passage south. Not surprisingly, she chose the latter, departing with more relief than regret on September 6.

Chicago socialites Sophy Gage and Martha Purdy had never had to worry about how to feed and clothe their children, but they too found the magnetic pull of the Klondike irresistible. Sophy caught gold fever almost at the source. She and her husband, Eli, were in St. Michael to visit her brother, the president of the North American Transportation and Trading Company, when the first contingent of victorious miners came floating down the Yukon River in June 1897.

Eli Gage was one of the company's directors and so departed at once for Dawson to assess the situation in person, while Sophy joined the southbound Klondikers aboard the *Portland*. After nearly a month of soaking up her fellow passengers' stories and making periodic visits to the ship's safe to feast her eyes on the treasure, she returned home enraptured by the idea of going back north. By spring, Eli and his best friend, Will Purdy, had formed a Klondike expedition company, and Sophy and Martha had convinced their husbands to let them come too.

While Will went west to finalize some of the business arrangements, Martha took their two sons, aged six and nine, to her parents' estate in Kansas. As she said her farewells, knowing that it would be a year before she saw them again, Martha experienced "a few wavering moments, which always come to mothers when parting with their little ones." However, her hunger for adventure and visions of "living in luxury for the rest of our days" propelled her onward.[19]

Sophy may have experienced a few doubts of her own when she and Eli left their fifteen-month-old baby in the care of friends in Chicago. As one journalist commented, "When she sees her darling again the baby lips will have learned the use of speech to welcome her, and the tiny feet will know how to fly to greet her coming."[20] As it turned out, though, the separation was much shorter than expected. After Eli fell ill in the early part of their journey, the Gages gave up their quest and returned home.

During the first few years of the gold rush, mail service between the Klondike and the rest of the world was notoriously slow and erratic. The Northern postal system was ill-equipped for the task of handling the avalanche of letters penned by the stampeders and their anxious families, friends, and financial backers at home, and correspondence typically took many months to reach its destination. Worse yet, some entire mail shipments were lost when boats sank or buildings burned.

Aaron Moulton of Tacoma, Washington, was one of the many gold seekers who wrote faithfully to his distant wife and children, even though he was not particularly literate. He addressed his letters to "Dear Mamma, Grace and Ruth" and always included a few special words to his daughters.

On September 18, 1897, he noted that he did most of the cooking for his party and jokingly added, "I supose whin I get home I will be quite a cook. Tell Grace she had better look out or I will get a head of her." Later in the same letter he addressed each of the girls in turn. "Well Grace you must be a God girl and help mamma and study hard at school this winter and Pappa will bring home something to you. Dont know yet what it will be but it will be something nice." And to Ruth: "I supose you are helping mamma to sweep the floor and lots of other things. How is your Doll or have you got aney now. Mamma will have to get you one for Christmas. Do you go in a class at Sunday School yet. I think you are old enough now to go in a class." The letter ended with his usual, "Kiss the girls for me. Your loving Boy, A. W. M."[21]

A month later, Aaron had not yet received any mail and was feeling rather melancholy. "I often dream of being with you there at home," he wrote on October 22, "but when I wake up I am disapointed but I hope there will be a day when I can be with you all again."

The last of his four surviving letters was written on January 29, 1898. He was in a more cheerful frame of mind because he had finally received a letter his wife had sent in mid-August, and he and his partners were starting to see some returns from their labour. Even so, a wistfulness comes through in his words. After describing a little of his work and home life, he asks, "Do you get lonesom or do you have time . . . How is little Ruth. Does she ever speak [of] Papa."

At the height of the Klondike stampede, Dawson's streets thronged with men, but women and children were rare.

Aaron also posed one other all-important question: "Do you want me to come home next summer of shal I stay here untill I can come out with 10,000.00 dollars." His January letter—signed "From your far off boy"—didn't reach Tacoma until late April. Whether or not he received an answer to his query, it seems he'd already realized what mattered most to him. By August he was back home with his family. The following May, his wife gave birth to their third child.[22]

⁓

Klondike fever took both Schuldenfrei parents away from their children, but all the members of this tight-knit Jewish family were avid correspondents, and their letters were filled with news, descriptions of daily life, endearments, and fervent wishes to be reunited.[23]

Rebecca and Solomon Schuldenfrei were an improbable pair of prospectors, and like so many of those who rushed to the North in 1897, they had only the vaguest notion of what they were getting themselves into. Both were lifelong city dwellers with no experience of frontier life. Sol, a dapper forty-one-year-old with an extravagant moustache, had never even chopped firewood, let alone dug for gold. Thirty-four-year-old Becci, though tougher and more practical than her mild-mannered husband, was more accustomed to strolling the streets of New York City in silk skirts than slogging through mud and clambering over boulders, as she would soon be doing on the Chilkoot Trail.

When news of the tons of gold brought south on the *Excelsior* and the *Portland* reached the East Coast, Sol's necktie and shirtwaist manufacturing business was doing poorly, and he eagerly seized this once-in-a-lifetime chance to reverse his fortunes. Six weeks after the first Klondike headlines appeared in the *New York Times*, he and Becci were on their way. By mid-October they were in Dawson, looking for a cabin where they could spend the winter.

Meanwhile, the Schuldenfrei brood had happily settled into life with Becci's sister and brother-in-law in Coudersport, Pennsylvania. Aunt Gussie and Uncle Deiches, with no children of their own, doted on fifteen-year-old Bert, thirteen-year-old Lu (short for Ludwig), and eleven-year-old Nellie, and all three returned this affection in full. Nevertheless, they missed their parents and frequently told them so in writing.

The children, it seems, were immune to gold fever or perhaps they were quickly cured by the strong dose of realism delivered in their parents' letters. Any hint of acquisitiveness was promptly brushed aside, as in the postscript Nellie added to her letter of March 3, 1898. "I hoped you (Dear Pa) had a claim," she wrote. "But I don't care for the money but I care to see you soon."

Like Nellie, the boys pressed for their parents' return in every letter. They also worried about their well-being, so much so that at Yom Kippur in 1898, when Becci was already on her way back to New York, Lu convinced his brother they should both fast until sundown to ensure her safe arrival.

The family's joy at Becci's homecoming on October 8, 1898, was tempered by their disappointment that Sol had decided to spend a second winter in Dawson. Although none of the business ventures he and Becci had tried during their first year had been particularly lucrative, he wasn't ready to give up. By spring, Sol was suggesting that he make a short trip back to New York and then return to the Klondike, a plan that none of his family supported.

Becci missed him terribly and refused to endure another year apart, but she was equally unwilling to leave Nellie, Bert, and Lu again. "I have had all the parting & separation I care for & so we would certainly have to take them along," she wrote to Sol on March 30, 1899. Yet she knew that neither the children nor their aunt and uncle supported this idea. As she explained in the same letter, "I truly fear that if you cannot possibly make other arrangements, that [Deiches and Gussie] will *never* forgive us and we will hurt them to their very hearts core."

Ultimately, Sol submitted to the combined force of the family's entreaties and came home to stay in the summer of 1899. Within the bundle of letters he brought with him was this plain-speaking missive from his middle child, who might have presented the deciding argument.

April 2 1899

Dearest Papa

Your letters which we lately received states abouts your going back to Dawson. Mama says that she wouldn't be away from you again for no money so that means that she goes with you on your return. Now, do you think that your children are such dumb-founded, thick headed fools as to have you part from them again and spend another such a year as they did the one past. We are told that we may go also. But Bertie [who was by then back in New York City] gets all the honey kuchen and pleasures he can handle so N.Y. is good enough for him.

I am in almost perfect health and enjoy myself so Coudersport satisfies me and Nellie is also contented.

As we don't care for Dawson and are not anxious for you to spend $2500 car-fare on us, you must prepare yourself to return for good.

Your loving son.

Lu.

In contrast to the Schuldenfrei threesome's indifference to the Klondike's attractions, some children were as keen to go north as the adults around them. One such child was Hallie Heacock, whose initial craving for adventure developed into a full-blown case of gold fever after he washed out his first paying pan.[24]

In the fall of 1897, Hallie was sixteen years old, a gangly adolescent with straight brown hair, big ears, and an aptitude for art. His parents and younger siblings had recently moved to British Columbia, where his father had taken a job as a coal mine superintendent, while Hallie had remained in Spokane, Washington, to attend school. He boarded with a family with two sons about his age. Every evening after dinner, the three boys raced up to their bedroom to read, immersing themselves in a world of daring heroes and bold exploits. As Hallie recalled years later, "This put me in the mood for real adventure. Then It happened."

The "It" that changed his life was a letter delivered to Hallie at school by two men who had just returned from the Klondike. The letter was intended for his father, but hearing he was out of town, the pair tracked down Hallie instead. They explained that the missive was from John Wallace, a prospector whom H.P. Heacock had grubstaked and sent to Alaska three years before the Klondike gold rush began. After a long silence, Wallace was reporting back to his sponsor and the news was excellent.

Hallie could barely contain himself. "If they've struck gold, my father's sure to go," he told the two emissaries, "and if he goes, I'm going too. He always takes me with him when he goes to look at mining property." The Klondikers shook their heads doubtfully. "I'm afraid that's a mighty rough country for a boy your age," one of them said, but Hallie knew his father better than they did.

Early in the new year, Hallie, H.P., and several acquaintances who had been won over by H.P.'s optimism departed for Alaska and on February 25, 1898, they joined the crowds of stampeders on the White Pass Trail. When they arrived in Dawson in early June, Hallie needed every hour of the long days to fit in all he wanted to do. He couldn't wait to look around the town or to cast his line in the Klondike River or to visit the mining operations on the creeks. Above all, he wanted to pan for gold. His interest in panning evaporated, however, after a few unsuccessful attempts. Fishing proved far more rewarding, so he turned all his attention to that pursuit, silently scoffing at the continual parade of new arrivals who eagerly dipped their pans into the Klondike's waters and came up as empty-handed as he had.

Once H.P. finished his business in Dawson, the Heacocks set out for Wallace's claim on Eldorado Creek. During one rest stop, a friendly miner offered to give Hallie a first-hand experience of the spring cleanup that was in full swing all around them. Pointing to the pile of gravel by one of his mine shafts, he told H.P. he'd dug up "some very good dirt" that winter. "Why not let the boy try a couple of pans?" he asked.

Following the miner's instructions, Hallie scooped gravel and water into his pan and began swirling it around. When he was done he was amazed to see an appreciable amount of gold in the bottom of the pan. He repeated the process twice more, and by the time he was finished he had a poke of gold dust worth $4.50—a fortune in his sixteen-year-old eyes. "So this is what brought all these people to the Klondike," he thought as they continued down the trail.

Hallie's wealth increased substantially after they reached Number 22 Eldorado, where Wallace had just completed a highly profitable cleanup and was happily surprised to see the Heacocks. As a welcoming gift, he presented a hefty $18 nugget to H.P. and another worth $14 to his son. Then he told the boy to open his pocketbook and proceeded to fill it with nuggets worth $3 to $5 apiece. Hallie "felt like a millionaire."

The rest of the summer passed just as pleasantly for Hallie. His father got a logging contract and they travelled far up the Klondike River with a crew of five Swedes to cut timber. As they made their way upriver, Hallie took advantage of every stop to indulge his newfound passion for panning, but minimal yields gradually cooled his gold fever and his love of fishing once more took over.

Before the Heacocks left to go logging, Wallace had stunned Hallie by buying him $16 worth of fly hooks, the entire stock of the store where he purchased them. Although such extravagance was common in Dawson in those heady days, Hallie hardly knew what to make of it. Once on the river, however, he put the hooks to good use. Each day after supper he fished until midnight in the long summer twilight, catching more than enough grayling to feed himself, his father, and the Swedes. When he had extra fish, he sold them.

Two young gold seekers, Nellie and Jimmie Park, on Bonanza Creek around 1901.

Once H.P. and his crew had cut enough trees to fulfill their contract, they floated them downriver to Dawson. Then the Heacocks returned to Skagway, planning to shop for new clothes and have hot baths before continuing to Seattle. Unfortunately, they ran short of time and had to board their boat looking as scruffy and smelling as bad as the rest of the miners who were going south. But Hallie didn't care if they were shunned by the cleaner, better-dressed passengers. He had his poke of gold dust and nuggets in his pocket, where he had carried it all summer, as well as his memories of a grand adventure that surpassed anything he'd ever read about in any novel. Instead of being one of the multitudes who burned with gold fever but would never get to the Klondike, he'd been there and was returning home much richer than when he left.

Coming days will be filled
with mournful thoughts
of a lonely, little grave buried
beneath the winter's snow.

Chapter 4

A Steep, Steep Place

Early in the afternoon of March 2, 1898, nine-year-old Emilie Craig of Denver, Colorado, arrived at the Chilkoot Pass, the highest point along the Chilkoot Trail and the place where it crossed from US into Canadian territory. Her parents, Morte and Nelle, and her father's unmarried sister, Lulu, were elated to reach the summit and know the worst of the trek was over. What most impressed Emilie, however, was the sight of the Union Jack flapping above the North-West Mounted Police camp on the inland side of the border. It was the first time she'd seen a British flag flying or set foot in a foreign country.

Hordes of men milled about at the pass, and as usual, the female members of the Craig party stood out from their fellow stampeders. Nelle and Lulu wore tight-waisted, ankle-length coats with mutton-chop sleeves over their long dresses and sported small-brimmed felt hats. Emilie, conspicuously smaller than everyone around her, was dressed in heavy leggings, a plain, knee-length coat, and a wool hood with a long collar that wrapped around her neck.

When the attending Mounties realized two women and a child had just arrived, they politely invited them to wait inside while Morte paid the duty on the goods their packers had delivered. "Congratulations," one of the officers said to Emilie as they entered. "You're the second little boy to come over the pass."

"I'm not a boy. I'm a girl," she protested, tugging off her hood to reveal a tumble of long brown curls.

"Well, in that case," he replied, "you're the first little girl to climb the Chilkoot."[1]

⸺

The Chilkoot Pass was one of the great milestones for Klondike-bound stampeders, and the precipitous ascent that led to it was legendary. Although it covered only

At nine years old in the spring of 1898, Emilie Craig was one of the youngest stampeders on the Chilkoot Trail.

about half a mile of ground, no other section of the thirty-three-mile-long Chilkoot Trail filled Klondike-bound travellers with such trepidation or was remembered afterwards with such awe. In summer, the steep, forty-five-degree incline was a jumble of boulders in a stark, treeless landscape. For most of the rest of the year, a deep covering of snow smoothed the alpine terrain's rough surfaces.

Travellers going over the Chilkoot Pass typically started at Sheep Camp, the last comfortably habitable spot before the summit. They began their day with a three-mile grind up the aptly named Long Hill. If necessary, they paused at the Scales, a small but bustling way station that offered basic services and a place to cache goods in transit. Then they took their place in the line of climbers ascending toward the heavens.

In the winter of 1897–98, the chain of humans slogging up to the pass was almost endless, broken only by nighttime darkness or when snowstorms or avalanches made travel impossible. The constant traffic packed the snow, but made for slippery footing, so several enterprising men chopped fifteen hundred steps into the slope, rigged up a rope handrail, and started charging a fee to all climbers. The Golden Stairs, as this improved stretch of trail was often called, traced a relentlessly straight line up the mountain wall that closed the north end of the valley. From a distance it was intimidating. Up close it was no better.

Stampeders who packed all their own gear and supplies over the pass had to repeat the climb dozens of times and rarely managed more than one or two trips a day. It could take twenty minutes or more to gain a place in the procession, and progress up the mountainside was slow. Even unencumbered travellers had no choice but to move at the plodding pace of their heavily burdened companions, with each person taking a step upward as the stair ahead was vacated.

Beyond the topmost stair, the grade moderated and the trail threaded through a narrow chute before opening up to the much-anticipated pass, a cold, windy, desolate place where few wished to linger. Before moving on, all parties had to report to the Canadian customs shed, manned by members of the NWMP. After that it was four miles to Happy Camp, a bleak subalpine refuge for those who could go no farther, or nine and a half miles to the more desirable destination of Lindeman City on the shores of Lake Lindeman.

After being stuck at Sheep Camp for two weeks because of blizzards, the Craigs were blessed with warm, sunny weather for their summit crossing. Emilie had walked most of the way from Dyea to Sheep Camp, but the group made allowances for her short legs on this longest, toughest day of the journey. She began by riding up Long Hill on a sled pulled by the family dog, a St. Bernard cross called Belle. Then, at the foot of the stairs, a family friend swung her up onto his shoulders and started climbing. Halfway up, her father took over. Although she couldn't claim to have mounted the Golden Stairs under her own power, she did walk the final stretch to the pass, where she made history by being the first girl to reach that spot—or so she thought.

In reality, Emilie was not as much of a trailblazer as she was led to believe. The recently arrived NWMP didn't know that the first white children to cross the Chilkoot Pass had preceded her by four years and several others had accomplished the same feat in the meantime. But they were all latecomers compared to the countless generations of Native children who had stood at the summit before them and for whom travelling the Chilkoot route was not a glamorous exploit, but merely a routine though arduous journey.[2]

Long before the Chilkoot Trail was adopted as the road to riches by non-Native prospectors and other gold hunters, it had been an important trade route linking the coastal Tlingit peoples and the inland-dwelling Athapaskans, including the Tagish and the Tutchone. In the late nineteenth century, the coast-interior trade network included at least half a dozen trails. The Chilkoot Tlingits owned both the Chilkoot route and a less-favoured alternative, which the gold rush made famous as the White Pass Trail.

Originally the Chilkoots protected their lucrative fur trade interests by prohibiting their inland trading partners from using these trails. They also excluded all Europeans. But by the 1880s their position had weakened and it became difficult to control access. However, all was not lost. The growing numbers of gold seekers coming and going from the upper Yukon River basin brought a new business opportunity—transporting the prospectors' supplies.

As interest in the Yukon goldfields increased over the next decade, packing became a regular source of seasonal employment for men of the Tlingit and the Tagish communities on both sides of the Chilkoot Pass. During the busiest times, women and children worked alongside them. All of them bore their loads on their backs, supported by a tumpline across the forehead and, if needed, another strap across the upper chest. Children were prepared for this work from an early age, packing small bundles every day for an hour or so, with a gradual increase in weight.

Tlingit and Tagish packers were renowned for their strength and the children were no exception. On his first trip into the Yukon interior in 1887, Ben Moore, who later settled in the Skagway area and married a Tlingit woman, saw "Native women and their young daughters and sons from ten years of age up . . . packing from fifty to seventy-five and one hundred pounds on their backs for miners, earning from ten to twenty dollars per day."[3] According to another observer, one boy who weighed no more than eighty pounds carried a hundred-pound pack over the Chilkoot Trail.

Even before they could carry full loads, children could make an important contribution. In 1893, Frederick Funston and his companions hired five Tlingit men and two women to convey their goods over the Chilkoot route. Assisting them were "Several children [who] carried on their backs light loads, consisting of food and cooking utensils for the use of the Indians . . ."[4]

As the Klondike stampeders started pouring north in 1897, the Tlingit and Tagish packers found themselves barely able to keep up with the demand for their services. For a brief time, a portion of the region's gold flowed their way, but in the end the gold rush was the ruin of their profession. Once such a large volume of people and goods started moving over the Coast Mountains, outside entrepreneurs began setting up their own transportation ventures and the original inhabitants were powerless to stop them. The First Nations packers managed to hold their own against horse pack trains and aerial tramways, but the opening of the White Pass and Yukon Railway (WP&YR) in July 1899 effectively put them out of business. Not only had their gains been fleeting, they didn't even come close to compensating for the cataclysmic effects of tens of thousands of strangers tearing through their homelands.

The first non-Native children to travel the Chilkoot Trail were the Snow siblings, Montgomery Adolph (more commonly known as Monte) and Crystal Brilliant,[5] both of whom were born in Sonora, California. Monte was five years old and Crystal almost three in 1887, when they moved to Juneau with their parents, George and Anna.

The Snows were, in Anna's words, "the first Legitimate Dramatic people in Alaska."[6] George had worked sporadically in California mines and was lured north partly by stories he'd heard about Alaska gold, but show business was what he knew best and he saw an opportunity to introduce theatre to the fledgling mining town. The Snow Family troupe, which included George's brother, Joe, came prepared with scripts, costumes, stage makeup, and hand-painted scenery. What they lacked was actors, so Monte and Crystal were recruited to help swell the company's meagre ranks. While the senior Snows and a few hastily trained amateurs handled the major speaking roles, the children sang and danced, much to the miners' delight.

A year after their arrival, George headed off for the Yukon interior, enticed by news of a big gold strike on the Stewart River. During the sixteen months he was gone, Anna received only one letter from him. She supported herself and the children on a line of credit, supplemented by her modest earnings from sewing, nursing, and putting on small family shows. Despite having nothing to show for his efforts, George couldn't resist going to the Yukon again in 1892. When he proposed a third trip in 1894, Anna decided she and the children would not be left behind this time.

It was April when the Snows and George's two prospecting partners set out to cross the Coast Mountains via the Chilkoot route. The first night on the trail, Crystal hardly slept. She had never camped before and every noise outside the canvas walls sounded to her ears like a bear. Although she was almost ten, she might have liked a doll to hug, but there had been no room to bring the only one she owned.

Both Crystal and Monte were small in stature, so the men had to carry them across the many places where the river cut the trail, the water flowing fast and deep. Nevertheless, the children did their part whenever possible, dragging a sled loaded with a portable organ and other theatrical accoutrements. It took the group five days to reach Sheep Camp. Then, for the next two weeks, Anna and the children bided their time in camp while the men lugged load after load over the Chilkoot Pass. Once they had all their supplies cached just north of the summit they could resume travelling, but that was easier said than done. The first time they tried to cross the pass they were driven back by a blizzard. The second time, they almost lost their lives.

They began their almost-fatal attempt in the company of some gold-seeking Montana cowboys. Everyone had reached the summit when it became apparent that another major storm was moving in fast. Agreeing that it would be madness to stay up there, they all started back toward the safety of Sheep Camp, but by the time they reached the Scales, Anna and the children were exhausted. As the wind rose, the Montanans helped the Snow party pull out a tent and drape it over a small hole in a snowbank. Then they fled down the trail. George and one of his partners also hurried off, heading for the timberline, half a mile away, to get firewood and a pole to support their makeshift shelter. The other partner found the party's grub box and cookstove and brought them inside.

For three days the blizzard raged outside while the stranded travellers huddled inside their cramped refuge. The snow piling up overhead was a growing worry for the four adults, but somehow they hid their fears well enough that Crystal

Crystal and Monte Snow at Forty Mile in 1894, the year they made history as the first non-Native children to cross the Chilkoot Pass.

and Monte remained "happily ignorant of the fact that had the blizzard lasted a half day longer rescue would have come too late." Unperturbed, the two children "played eskimo" to pass the time.[7]

By the morning of the fourth day, the sapling that braced the middle of the canvas was bent nearly double and even the children were reduced to crawling on their hands and knees. Fortunately, when the storm abated and the cowboys returned to see whether their friends had survived, a wisp of smoke rising from the infinity of whiteness told them where to dig.

As soon as they were liberated, the Snows started once more for the summit, but the weather turned again and they were forced to retreat to Sheep Camp. The next day, after a paltry breakfast, they departed at 3 a.m. The men broke trail, wading through the eighteen inches of fresh snow that blanketed the ground and pulling the heavy sleds. Anna, Monte, and Crystal struggled along in their wake. When at length they reached the pass and could take a break from their exertions, they were left feeling more chilled than rested.

Watching her daughter shiver as they waited for the men to haul up the last sled, Anna wished she could give her some food to warm her. On the way up, the children had shared the party's last provisions—a single biscuit and a leftover leg of grouse. Their next meal would have to wait until they reached camp and could unpack their stove and supplies. But Crystal's mind was not on her discomfort. To Anna's surprise, she suddenly broke into song, and as the last note faded away, she turned to her mother and said, "Mamma, I guess no other little girl ever sang on top of the summit."[8]

Crystal would need all her spunk to get her through the rest of the day, but this time they did make it to their destination. Although it was already dark when they reached Lake Lindeman, there to greet them were the Montana cowboys, who immediately began doling out hot coffee and pancakes and refused to take any for themselves until Anna and the children were served.

Three months after they'd left Dyea, the Snows arrived at Forty Mile. They spent the winter there, performing plays from their standard repertoire, such as *Rip Van Winkle, Camille*, and *Kathleen Mavourneen*. In the summer of 1896, Circle City, Alaska, supplanted Forty Mile as the largest mining centre in the Yukon basin and the family relocated there, following both the gold and the audience. When news of the Klondike discovery reached Circle that winter, George was uncharacteristically reluctant to join the latest stampede, perhaps because he had just finished building a two-storey log opera house. By late winter, however, he could hold back no longer and headed up the still-frozen river to Dawson. Once boat travel resumed in spring, Anna and the children followed.

After Monte and Crystal's perilous crossing of the Chilkoot Pass, the next non-Native child to make the journey seems to have been Vera Barnes. Born in Juneau in 1889, Vera was that town's first white baby. By the time she was seven, her family had moved to Seattle, but her father still had his sights set on the North. In March 1896 he concocted a plan to take some horses over the Chilkoot Trail and down the Yukon River to sell to the miners of Circle City. He wanted his wife to accompany him and they decided that Vera should come too.

On the day the Barnes party went over the pass, the men were preoccupied with trying to drag the horses up to the summit, so Vera and Mrs. Barnes were mostly left to fend for themselves. Eighteen months later, when she was interviewed by Helen Dare, the *San Francisco Examiner*'s Klondike correspondent, Vera still vividly recollected the ordeal.

> *I would get cold—ooh, so cold! . . . that I would have to stamp my feet and slap my hands together to get them warm. I did walk fifteen miles [that] day, though—without any dinner, too. The summit is a steep, steep place, with steps cut in, and I slipped once and nearly fell, but one of the men caught me and straightened me up again. It was so high and steep that nobody wanted to look*

back. An Indian was walking up in front of mamma with a big pack of canned tomatoes on his back, and mamma was afraid he might slip, so she made him walk behind us. When we got to the top there was a sliding place about as wide as a sack of flour down the other side, and we sat down in that and slid instead of walking.[9]

Somewhere on the far side of the pass, a man passing by with a dogsled noticed that Vera was almost ready to drop in her tracks and offered her a ride, but it was too cold for her to sit still for long, so Mrs. Barnes hoisted her daughter onto her back. She struggled along for a mile, then had to put her down. At that point, "Vera in her childish way guessed that it was a question of going on or dying in the snow, and pluckily trudged along with her mother to camp."

From then on things were easier. The family travelled at night to take advantage of the hard snow crust and slept during the day. "We had pie and cake and bread—not biscuit, you know—all the time we were on the trail," Vera recalled. "Mamma . . . used to put the bread dough to rise in her feather bed to keep it warm." At Tagish Lake the ice was breaking up, and the party stopped so the men could build boats to take them the rest of the way. During the long spring days, after they had taken care of their domestic duties, mother and daughter wandered the hills gathering wildflowers and filling buckets with pitch for waterproofing the boat hulls.[10]

After they arrived at Circle in late June, Vera and Mrs. Barnes returned to Seattle by way of St. Michael. When Dare met them in September 1897, they were on their way back north to join Mr. Barnes in the Klondike, but this time they were making the trip the easy way, by steamer.

———

Once news of the Klondike discovery reached the outside world, traffic on the Chilkoot route increased tremendously. Children, however, were still a rarity, especially in the early days of the stampede when there were almost no services or amenities along the way.

One of the first families to get on the trail was that of an irrepressible, fifty-one-year-old Irishman named Martin Barrett.[11] When he was only eight years old, Martin had stowed away on a ship with his five-year-old brother in tow and sailed from Ireland to find their grandmother in America. Having succeeded in that quest, he had followed up with many other escapades, including buying a schooner and sailing to Alaska with his family to go prospecting.

That adventure ended with the Barretts being marooned on a storm-racked island in the Gulf of Alaska for ten months, but that didn't cure Martin's gold fever. In June 1897, shortly after their rescue, he heard about the Klondike strike and immediately began organizing to go to the goldfields, accompanied by his long-suffering wife, Florence, a dainty little woman twenty years his junior, and their three children, thirteen-year-old Lawrence, five-year-old Freddy, and an eleven-year-old daughter who was named for her mother and had the same petite stature. Completing the entourage was a black pup named Shaddy.

With Martin packing all their supplies in relay, the family progressed only a few miles each day. The trail was a muddy quagmire and there were no bridges yet, so he often had to carry the younger children across the river and over the most difficult sections of trail, including the Golden Stairs. By the time they reached Sheep Camp in July, the route to the pass was bare—a near-vertical boulder field that was a true test of Martin's strength and determination. He must have made the climb to the summit appear easy, because young Florence later remembered it as "a glorious game, riding aloft astride Dad's neck, watching the snow gather on the bowed backs of the men struggling up ahead of us."[12]

Like the Barretts, Juneau residents Fred and Ella Card were well positioned to get ahead of the mass of stampeders. With a hastily assembled outfit and their first-born child in their arms, they joined the rush up the coast to Dyea and over the mountains in the late winter or early spring of 1897. Excitement and anticipation turned to grief, however, on May 23, when their seven-month-old daughter died while they were camped at the head of Lake Lindeman. The unhealthy conditions that developed in the crowded trailside camps were likely to blame.

"Kind hearts sympathized with them and willing hands did all that could be done," wrote a fellow stampeder in a dispatch to the Juneau newspaper, "but nothing but time can heal the wound and coming days will be filled with mournful thoughts of a lonely, little grave buried beneath the winter's snow, beside the frozen lake."[13]

Among those who assisted the Cards were Mr. and Mrs. J. D. McKay, who helped build a small wooden box lined with a soft blanket and white cloth, and covered on the outside with black cloth. After laying the baby in the casket, Mrs. McKay took a bunch of artificial violets from her hat and placed them in the tiny, lifeless hands. A small tent served as a temporary funeral parlour for the viewing, and the next day, amid tears and prayers, the Cards lowered the coffin into the ground and set a wooden marker in place.[14]

The McKays could well appreciate the Cards' sorrow, as they too were new parents. They had no way of knowing that their own child would soon become the stampede's second young casualty. The seasoned Alaska trader and his wife were still camped at Lake Lindeman when their infant daughter also became ill and died. Perhaps they found some small comfort in being able to bury her beside the Card baby, with a picket fence surrounding the two little plots.[15]

Ella Card carries her infant daughter as she and her husband Fred (probably on far right) and unidentified companions head up the Chilkoot Trail near Dyea in the spring of 1897. The young Native boy second from left was probably a hired packer.

Both bereaved couples carried on to the Klondike. The McKays stayed and mined there for three years, then moved to Fairbanks.[16] The Cards remained in the area for at least six years. On July 2, 1898, about a year after they reached Dawson, they were blessed with a son, whom they named after his father.[17]

Most prospectors venturing into the Yukon interior before 1897 used the Chilkoot Trail to cross the Coast Mountains. Once the Klondike stampede got under way, however, the White Pass Trail, which began outside Skagway and ended at Bennett, gained popularity. The attraction of the latter lay in its more moderate grades. Its disadvantages were its length—it was nearly nine miles longer than the Chilkoot route—and Skagway's reputation as a hotbed of criminal activity led by the notorious Soapy Smith. Sixteen-year-old Hallie Heacock, who travelled the White Pass Trail with his father in February 1898, never saw the Skagway crime boss during their brief stay in town before they started for Bennett, but the violence came rather too close for comfort.

On the Heacocks' first night on the trail, a congenial young man from Iowa pitched his tent beside theirs and confessed that he was afraid to be alone. Over the following week, as they all laboured to move their outfits along the route and

A group of stampeders on the White Pass Trail, around 1898.

shared meals at night, the Heacocks and their companions began to think of him as a full-fledged member of their party, so they were surprised when he failed to show up in camp one evening. The next morning they discovered why. Half a mile back down the trail, the Iowan's worst fears had been realized. He had been shot just below his heart and was dead by the time he was found.

The goal of everyone who crossed the mountains was to reach the head-waters of the Yukon River system so they could travel the final five hundred miles to Dawson by water. At the start of the gold rush, before paddlewheelers began operating on the upper Yukon River and the series of lakes that fed the river, the stampeders had to build their own transportation for this part of the journey. The main boat-construction centres were Bennett, a sprawling boom town at the south end of Bennett Lake, and Lindeman City, on Lake Lindeman. But as more gold seekers poured off the twin trails, they spread out all along the shores of those lakes, as well as along Tagish Lake to the east.

The Heacocks were among those who trekked to Tagish Lake, where there was less competition for lumber. While his father and the other men worked on the boats, Hallie's duties were limited to cutting firewood and washing dishes and laundry, so he spent much of his free time ice-fishing. When that became monotonous, he made himself an iceboat by lashing together a couple of dogsleds, rigging up a canvas sail, and creating a rudder with his skates.[18]

The Barrett family made their boat-building stop at Lake Lindeman. Like most of the stampeders, Martin Barrett was not an experienced shipwright, but within a few weeks he and his newly acquired partner had managed to cobble together "a large rowboat, clumsy and strange as to line, and daubed with black tar."[19] The *Buga-boo* was roomy enough to hold the Barretts and their new partner, as well as all their gear, with space left over, so Martin took pity on a couple of penniless vaudevillians and invited them to squeeze in too. One of the performers willingly took the oars whenever the other men needed a break, but his companion shunned all manual labour, preferring to earn his passage by singing and playing his banjo as they floated northward.

There was no musical accompaniment, however, for the passage through Miles Canyon and down the Whitehorse Rapids. In June 1898, after 150 boats had been smashed on the rocks in this turbulent stretch of water and ten men had died, NWMP Superintendent Sam Steele decreed that all women and children would have to disembark and walk around these navigational hazards. This precaution was already common practice when the Barretts passed by and there was a well-worn track along the top of the cliffs above the rapids.

Eager to find a good vantage point from which to watch the *Buga-boo* challenge the white water, the younger Barretts ran down the path, followed by their less-enthusiastic mother. They lost some of their bravado, however, when they realized what the men were up against. As Florence later described the scene, halfway through the gorge "the walls suddenly widened, forming a round basin in which the river leaped and churned and whirled into giant whirlpools. Even though we children believed our father to be as invincible as the blessed St. Michael himself, we gazed breathless and frightened into the seething cauldron. We began to wish our father didn't have to run the boat through, and we looked for him anxiously."[20]

Chastened by this dose of reality, they continued to the end of the rapids and settled down to wait. As the minutes ticked by and "the roar of the gorge beat upon [their] ears," the tension mounted and Freddy began to whimper. Before long, even his older brother and sister were in tears. However, their crying stopped abruptly when the boat appeared with Shaddy in the bow, Martin leaning hard on the steering oar at the stern, and the other three men rowing and bracing with all their might.

"Tiny, helpless-looking, incredibly swift it came, one minute buried in foam and flying spray, the next leaping like a fish to the crests of the breaking waves." Thrilled at the sight of their father "catapulting by," the children "sprang to [their] feet and cheered him at the top of [their] voices. Then, yelling like Indians, [they] raced down to the lower bank, where he was already swinging the 'Buga-boo' into quiet water."[21]

Despite the risk, a few children did go by boat through Miles Canyon and down the Whitehorse Rapids before Steele's decree took effect. One baby made the run in his mother's arms. According to stampeder Mont Hawthorne, who witnessed their passage, it was a wild ride and resulted in the death of one of the three men with whom they were travelling.

Their troubles began when their scow hit a rock as they entered the canyon, which stopped them briefly and "scared them bad." Then they got into a whirlpool and spun around for some time before managing to extract themselves, only to hit another rock. "It wasn't a sharp one," reported Hawthorne, "so all it done was to throw them over and they bounced agin another one on the other side. That got them back on balance again and they made it just fine down around the point."

The next rock they struck was a big one known as "the boat buster" and it lived up to its name by punching a hole in their bow. Although the scow was still afloat, one of the men panicked and leapt overboard. There was nothing his companions could do to save him and he drowned as they sped on down the rapids. After finally running aground on a sandbar, the mother and child and the two surviving men disembarked "without even getting their feet wet."[22]

⌐⌐

The Chilkoot Trail provided many of the most compelling images of the Klondike gold rush, yet its heyday was quite brief. In May 1898 a business syndicate began building a railway that would link Skagway and Bennett and eliminate the need to slog across the mountains on foot by way of either the Chilkoot or White Pass trails. Trains began running that summer on the White Pass and Yukon Railway line, even though only seven miles of track had been laid. The Chilkoot's appeal waned quickly as the work progressed, especially after the tracks reached the White Pass summit on February 20, 1899. The following July, completion of the railway to Bennett marked the end of the short but dramatic period when some thirty thousand to fifty thousand fortune seekers crossed the Coast Mountains the hard way.

Among the last stampeders to toil up the Golden Stairs were Matthew and Martha Watson and their four children.[23] In 1897, Matthew and his namesake eldest son, then eleven years old, joined the leading edge of the stampede to Dawson. By February 1898 they were back in Dyea, where Martha and the other three children joined them from Tacoma. Maybe the Klondike had been a disappointment for Matthew Senior, or perhaps he didn't want to risk taking his little ones on a long wilderness expedition. In any case, the family remained in Dyea for the next year.

It took a newer and nearer gold strike, this one in Atlin, British Columbia, to entice them onward. In the spring of 1899, the Watsons packed their belongings and headed up the Chilkoot Trail. At thirteen years old, Matthew Junior was expected to do a man's work on the trail, while eleven-year-old Bruce and six-year-old Bill would be required to pitch in as needed. Only two-year-old Grace, the baby of the family, had no responsibilities.

When the Watsons arrived at Sheep Camp in early March, they likely found it eerily quiet. In its glory days, this stampede boom town had offered abundant amenities, including sixteen hotels, fourteen restaurants, two laundries, a hospital, and a post office, and had boasted a transient population of six thousand to eight thousand people. In February 1899, the month before the Watsons passed through, another traveller had counted only eighteen residents.[24] Unlike earlier stampeders, who were sometimes hard pressed to get a bunk for the night, the family spent a comfortable week in "a nice log cabin" while their goods were conveyed over the pass by the Chilkoot Railroad and Transport Company's aerial tramway.

On the day they crossed the pass, they started out with the family's two dogs towing a sled that carried the two youngest children. While Grace slept peacefully, Bill could not be convinced to stay in the sled, even though he would need all his strength for later. At the Scales, the Watsons unhitched the dogs and put their horse in their place. Only Grace could ride from there for it was clear that getting a horse and sled up the steep ascent to the summit would be a challenge. Martha's subsequent diary entry documents how much of an ordeal it was:

M. [Matthew] Sr. led the horse. He just went by spurts about twenty yards at a time and every time he stopped it took three of us to put on the brake to keep the sled from coming down again. We had not reached half way when the horse fell and began to roll down. I thought for a minute he was to go to the bottom. M. Sr. had the hardest work to hold him. If the rope had broken we would have been minus our horse. Whenever he fell, Matthew cut the sled loose, while Bruce and I held it. Then I hastened and took Grace off and got to one side. We were all in a flurry. M. Sr. holding onto the horse for dear life, Matthew the sled and me with Grace, when lo and behold, help came in sight. Two men who happened to come along helped to get the horse on his feet and then they led him up the rest of the way and tied him to something at the top. M. Sr. then carried Grace up and here I had to get behind Bill and give him a boost every little while. Bruce carried some of the stuff the horse was taking and we left Matthew holding the sled. Now one more little hill. Here we hitched the dogs again. M. Sr. taking the horse. But when we got up the tables turned for before we knew it we were going down again. M. Sr. here gave the horse to Matthew and it took M. Sr. and me to hold back the sled. Bruce held the dogs back. Bill had a stick under the runner

Few children passed through Sheep Camp during the Klondike stampede and even fewer lived there. This girl's parents, Mr. and Mrs. Courtney, ran a combination store, post office, and laundry.

doing very effective work. I was just in the act of saying I would like our picture when I lost my footing. I still held onto the rope attached to the sled but I was quite a little while before I got my feet again. However, we got safely down.[25]

After collecting their goods from the tramway terminus half a mile beyond the summit, the Watsons began moving everything in stages, with the senior Matthew in charge of the horse and the junior running the dogsled. The first week, young Matthew hauled four hundred to five hundred pounds a day, using two borrowed dogs in addition to the family's pair. Once they got the entire outfit to Lake Lindeman, they replaced the borrowed team with a third dog of their own and continued on to Bennett and the chain of frozen lakes that served as the winter road to Atlin.

The team effort required to move a family of six and all their supplies along the trail was highlighted the following week when Martha was struck by an incapacitating headache, which forced an unplanned stop. "It took M. Sr. to throw up the tent and me to throw down the bed and get in," she wrote a few days later. "I was so sick. I asked Bruce to find me a basin and when he brought me a pie plate, sick as I was, I had to laugh and he said so solemn like 'Well, Mother, it's the best I can do,' so we had to let it go. After that the baby crawled in beside me with her coat and hood on and she fell asleep. I had my jacket and cap on also. I kicked off my boots and took off baby's and there we slept as we were till morning."[26]

Bruce prepared supper that night while his father attended to the horse, a job that was normally his older brother's. Matthew Junior, the family hostler, wasn't on hand because he'd had to return to Lindeman City to retrieve something they'd forgotten, a round trip of sixty-eight miles. When night began to close in, the teen was still on the trail and the dogs were showing signs of fatigue. Understandably nervous about travelling alone in the dark, young Matthew stashed his load and covered the final ten miles as quickly as possible. Even so, it was nearly 11 p.m. when he reached camp.

On April 10, the Watsons reached the junction where their trail turned off from the Dawson route. Five days later they were in Atlin. Only the two Matthews had the distinction of being true Klondikers, but the entire family shared the memory of braving the Chilkoot Trail together before it faded into history.

Much of the time I sat
on the stern "like a good girl."

Chapter 5

Bring Me a Stocking Full of Gold

If children were rare on the Chilkoot and White Pass trails, they were practically unheard of on the tangle of overland routes to the Klondike that started from Edmonton in the District of Alberta. These ill-defined trails, which ranged in length from about fifteen hundred miles to nearly twenty-six hundred miles, meandered across the wilds of northern Canada, following various treacherous rivers and cutting across vast swaths of boreal forest and muskeg.[1]

Some sixteen hundred people attempted to reach the Klondike by way of what Edmonton promoters liked to call the "back door" to the Yukon. More than half never made it and those that did succeed typically took two years or more to attain their goal. This approach to the goldfields was the only one on which a baby was both conceived and born en route.

The parents of that baby were Mr. and Mrs. Braund of Michigan, known to some as Mr. and Mrs. Sam Brown.[2] The Braunds left their Detroit home in mid-March 1898, with half a dozen other citizens of the city. By May they were cruising down the Athabasca River on a fifty-foot, steel-hulled boat called the *Enterprise*. Nearly nineteen hundred miles later, on July 14, the *Enterprise* steamed into Fort McPherson, a long-established trading post north of the Arctic Circle.

Among the many stampeders gathered in Fort McPherson at the time were Emily and A.C. Craig, the Chicago couple whose gold hunger had been fed by the sight of Klondike nuggets in a jeweller's store window. Hearing of the new female arrival, Emily hastened to meet her and compare experiences. Her immediate conclusion was that Mrs. Braund would have been better off at home. "She did not like the natives and the handshaking, and the dirt in general," Emily observed.[3] Worst of all, the men that she and her husband started out with were so unappreciative of her cooking efforts that they threw dishes at her.

The Craigs agreed to let the Braunds join their party for the next leg of the journey, though Emily was apprehensive about their compatibility, fears that were soon realized. Both the Braunds were "quick-tempered," in Emily's opinion, "fussing at each other to such an extent that it was unpleasant for us all."[4] What she didn't know was that Mrs. Braund was four months pregnant and probably terrified of giving birth in the wilderness. Apparently she convinced her husband that this would be folly, for less than three weeks after leaving Fort McPherson, the Braunds returned there.

The Craigs and their other travelling companions pushed on until winter's approach forced them to stop at Destruction City on the Rat River. Since Fort McPherson was two days away by dogsled, residents of the temporary stampede community occasionally visited the trading post during the winter and carried mail between the two settlements. In October, the Craigs received a letter from the Braunds saying they were "expecting a little miner in the not far distant future."[5]

It was the beginning of January before the Craigs made it to Fort McPherson, aiming to celebrate New Year's Eve there but arriving on New Year's Day. They immediately called on the Braunds and found that the baby had not yet arrived. Mrs. Braund must have been grateful for their presence when she went into labour on January 6. While A.C. went in search of the doctor, Emily attended to her friend, who delivered a healthy, nine-pound baby boy before the doctor arrived. Emily spent the next few days helping Mrs. Braund then returned to Destruction City in answer to an urgent appeal for her to come back and nurse a number of men who had fallen sick.

The Craigs and the Braunds didn't see each other again until the following June, when they happened to meet at Fort Yukon on the Yukon River. Mother and son were both doing well, but the Braunds had decided to abandon their Klondike plans. They headed downriver on a steamer bound for St. Michael, while the Craigs continued upriver to Dawson.

———

Only two other children are known to have been part of the stampede through Edmonton. Their stories are incomplete, but it seems neither had a happy ending.

In the spring of 1898, a group of German immigrants living in Sandon, British Columbia, a thriving silver-mining town, decided to try for some Klondike gold. Whether or not Frank Hoffman and his wife of two years realized she was pregnant before they left home isn't known. But even with the concealing women's clothing typical of the time, her condition was obvious to other stampeders who met them around the end of April at Athabasca Landing, ninety miles north of Edmonton. Carrying on was a risk, but Frank had survived some terrible battles during his days as a German soldier and felt capable of dealing with any challenges that came their way.

By the time the Germans reached Great Slave Lake that summer, Mrs. Hoffman was in an advanced state of pregnancy. Behind them were hundreds of miles of fierce rapids and long, tedious portages, but the worst was yet to come. When Emily Craig met Mrs. Hoffman in Destruction City that October and heard her story, it affected her so profoundly that she was sick for two days.

It was, as usual, windy when the Sandon party began their run down the west arm of the vast lake. As they pulled away from the shore, the boat began to roll and soon the waves were soaking them with spray and threatening to swamp their heavily loaded vessel. Standing at the sweep, the long oar used for steering, Frank tried to hold their course while the other men rowed and Mrs. Hoffman bailed frantically. As she later described it to Emily, one moment her husband was there in the stern and when she looked again, he was gone. "Where is Frank?" she asked and in the stunned silence that followed, she caught one last glimpse of him in the water before he disappeared forever.

According to a second-hand account of the incident, the surviving members of the group split up after the drowning. Some returned home, while Mrs. Hoffman and a man named Joe Schneider joined another party. There were rumours of a romantic triangle involving the Hoffmans and Schneider, but Emily made no mention of these.

Although Mrs. Hoffman's English was poor, she was able to talk easily with Emily, who had studied German as a girl in Denmark. They visited and baked bread together when they first became acquainted in Destruction City and hiked up a mountain when they met again in May, yet Mrs. Hoffman apparently never spoke of her pregnancy or losing her baby. Whenever and however that happened, it was a heartbreak she kept to herself.[6]

The route the Hoffmans took mostly followed the Athabasca, Mackenzie, and other rivers, heading north from Edmonton, then veering west at Great Slave Lake. The other routes out of Edmonton all angled northwest toward the Peace River country and alternated between overland and river travel. These variations offered the shortest distance from Edmonton to Dawson. They also turned out to be the toughest. Thousands of horses perished on the atrocious trails, which pushed mercilessly through scrubby forest and across boggy muskeg, prompting many of the overlanders to give up and go home or to divert toward the rivers route.

Mr. and Mrs. G. W. Larrabee and their three-month-old baby were part of a group of seven Montanans who arrived in Edmonton in January 1898. Outfitted with twenty-five horses, they planned to ride to the Klondike on one of the mostly overland routes. There is no record of how the party fared after it left Edmonton or if they ever reached the Klondike, but a small, fenced grave beside the trail near Fort Assiniboine, ninety miles from Edmonton, suggests they met with misfortune. The grave is anonymous, identified only by a wooden marker bearing a poignant epitaph: "In memory of a little girl buried here by her father in the days of the Klondike Gold Rush 1898." Since the Larrabees are the only stampeders known to have left Edmonton with a child, there is a strong possibility that the child was theirs.[7]

———

Like the Edmonton routes, the Stikine Trail was touted as an all-Canadian approach to the Klondike. Many of the patriots who chose it for that reason regretted their decision. The Stikine route began in Wrangell, Alaska, but an 1871 treaty gave Canada the right of free navigation on the Stikine River, exempting Canadians from reporting to US customs.

For all Klondikers, regardless of nationality, the Stikine route purportedly offered an undemanding alternative to the Chilkoot Trail. In fact, its particular challenges tested travellers at least as severely as the ones they were trying to avoid. The sternwheeler trip up the Stikine River was harrowing enough, but the 150-mile trail that linked the Stikine to the Yukon River system was even worse. One optimistic guidebook author called this trail "the best highway to the goldfields from the coast" and explained that it would "traverse a newly-discovered pass and then [proceed] straight across the smooth table land to Lake Teslin."[8] Those who actually travelled the crude track spent weeks slogging through mosquito-infested swamps, clambering over wind-thrown trees, and picking their way across stretches of sharp, ankle-twisting rocks.

Few stampeders could have had a harder time on this trail than nineteen-year-old Lucille Hunter. Born and raised in the southern United States, Lucille had started working on a plantation at thirteen. Now she and her husband, Charles, both the descendents of slaves, were on their way north to find a better life for themselves and the child who swelled her belly. The baby arrived while they were camped at Teslin Lake and was greeted with considerable curiosity by the local First Nations residents, who had never before seen a non-Native infant, let alone one who was black.

The Hunters named their daughter Teslin, in honour of her birthplace, but they didn't linger there for long. By February 1898 they had reached the Klondike and staked a claim on Bonanza Creek, which they would call home for many years. Growing up in the goldfields as an only child, Teslin knew few other black children, but she and her parents were well accepted by their white neighbours. Charles and Lucille spent the rest of their lives in the Yukon, while Teslin left when she reached adulthood and married a Danish fisherman from Seattle.[9]

———

Compared to all the other routes to the Klondike, the all-water route was the safest and least strenuous, but also the most expensive. The two-part journey began on an ocean-going steamship, which travelled up the Pacific Coast to St. Michael, Alaska, at the mouth of the Yukon River. Passengers then transferred to a smaller sternwheeler for the seventeen-hundred-mile trip upriver to Dawson. There were no mountains to climb or rapids to run and there was no need to lug any heavy loads, but this option was not always trouble-free, especially at the start of the stampede.

The window of opportunity for travelling from St. Michael to Dawson by boat was small. Paddlewheelers couldn't launch in spring until the ice cleared, and the season ended just two or three months later when low water levels made the river impassable. As the summer progressed, steamers were increasingly apt to run aground on gravel bars. In the fall of 1897, freeze-up trapped a number of boats, leaving twenty-five hundred passengers stranded along the river until spring. But for Ellen Gibson and her teenage sons, Tom and Elmer, the problem with the all-water route wasn't the weather or the captain's competency: it was an unscrupulous manoeuvre by the Alaska-Yukon Transportation Company.

Originally from Ontario, the Gibson family was living in San Francisco when the *Excelsior* arrived with its golden cargo in July 1897, immediately infecting both Ellen and her husband, Joe, with Klondike fever. Three weeks later, Joe and two partners left for Dyea. Ellen and the boys were to join him in the spring, travelling via St. Michael.

After encountering and surviving the usual hazards and hardships as he travelled over the Chilkoot Trail and down the Yukon River, Joe made it to Dawson before the end of the year and staked a claim on Dominion Creek. The following June, Ellen, sixteen-year-old Tom, and fourteen-year-old Elmer followed, taking the all-water route at Joe's insistence. Their fares and the freight charges for their nearly four thousand pounds of provisions and supplies came to $389, a considerable outlay of money. But when the *National City* reached St. Michael, they and the rest of the steamer's passengers discovered that the ticket agent had lied when he said their tickets would take them all the way to Dawson. They would have to shell out extra for the trip upriver, and only cash payment would be accepted, a condition that few of the stampeders could meet.

Under the threat of violence, the company eventually agreed to provide free passage back to San Francisco on the *National City* for anyone who decided to return, but the Gibsons were determined to get to the goldfields. They found a place to stay in St. Michael and all three took whatever jobs they could find until they had earned enough money to carry on later that summer.[10] It was a blunt introduction to the reality of the Klondike, where—as in the South—children's labour was often essential to families trying to make ends meet.

Whether they were headed for St. Michael or for the Chilkoot and White Pass trail-head towns of Dyea and Skagway, steamships travelling up the West Coast during the gold rush carried few adolescents and even fewer young children, so the sight of Emma Feero ushering her brood of four onto the S.S. *Al-ki* in August 1897 must have astonished the spectators and well-wishers swarming the Tacoma docks.

The *Al-ki* was the first ship to carry stampeders north that summer, leaving just five days after the *Excelsior* arrived in San Francisco. For its Klondike debut, the *Al-ki* was loaded well beyond any reasonable limits, with 110 passengers, 900 sheep, 65 cows, 30 horses, and 350 tons of supplies.[11] When it made its next trip to Skag-way about three weeks later, it was again filled to capacity and the only children on board were the Feeros: fourteen-year-old Willie, eight-year-old Frank, and the ten-year-old twins, Edith and Ethel.

The scene at the dock on the day they left was chaotic, just as it was every time a boatload of Klondikers departed. Looking down at the crowds from their place at the railings, it was difficult for the Feeros to spot Emma's sister and the numerous friends who had come to see them off and impossible to separate their shouted farewells from the general uproar. All Edith could hear was a multitude of voices yelling, "Bring me a stocking full of gold!"

John Feero had gone north ahead of the family, jumping at the chance to rebuild the prosperity they'd known before the financial crash of 1893 wiped out his transportation business. Within hours of landing at Skagway, a horse-packer offered him work at a good wage. He took the job and wrote to Emma, telling her to come with the children.

Because of the fierce competition to book passage on any Alaska-bound steamer, Emma only managed to secure three single berths, though the tight sleeping arrangements mattered little to the children. Their fellow passengers gave them special attention and some were also a source of entertainment. Their rather proper mother may have cringed, however, when she heard her offspring singing "Hot Time in the Old Town" and other songs they learned from the dancehall entertainers who lounged on the deck at night, rehearsing their repertoire.

In the lean years since John's business had failed, the Feeros had often gone hungry, so the children were awed by all the fruit, nuts, and candy they got to eat during the voyage. Then, as the *Al-ki* neared its destination, the captain brought Frank, Willie, and the twins up to the bridge and gave them a generous stock of these treats for after they disembarked.

At Skagway, the passengers clambered into lifeboats, which ferried them to the shallows just offshore. The men had to wade the rest of the way. The women and children were carried to dry land. Amidst all the commotion on the beach, it soon became evident that John was not there to greet his family. Emma, with only twenty-five cents in her pocket, wondered where they'd sleep that night, but before day's end her husband, who was confused about their arrival date, was located.[12]

A year after the Feeros travelled to Skagway, another Emma undertook the same journey with young children, but hers were all under six years of age. Emma Anderson was the wife of P.B. Anderson, the Swede from Bellingham, Washington, who had joined the stampede at the start and promised to come home with pockets full of nuggets. In late August 1898, tired of waiting for his return, she boarded the *Utopia* with one-year-old Clay in her arms and Dewey and Ethel, age four and five respectively, clinging to her skirts. Like the Feeros, they were the only children on their boat.

The seas were rough all the way to Skagway and almost everyone was seasick throughout the nearly week-long voyage. The children were completely unaffected by the ship's rolling and pitching, but their mother was incapacitated. One evening Emma was so weak from retching that she collapsed on their cabin floor and lay there until the steward came to see why the baby wouldn't stop crying. He gathered her up and gently laid her in her berth, then tried to calm Clay's wailing.

"He won't go to sleep unless he gets a sugar tit," Ethel informed the steward from her place on the upper bunk. So the young man dutifully went off to the kitchen and returned a short while later with a mixture of milk, bread, and sugar tied in a cloth as a pacifier for the baby, as well as apples for the two older children. After he left, Ethel and Dewey devoured the fruit, consuming even the cores and seeds. Then to amuse themselves they started a contest to see who could make the biggest ball of wool by rubbing the nap off the blankets. As Ethel later admitted, "No [other] boat ever had such energetic moths!"[13]

In addition to those children who sailed north with their parents, more than one youngster went up the coast to the Klondike unaccompanied and without parental consent. In the summer of 1899, eight-year-old Tommy McMillan of Seattle hid in the coal bunkers of a steamer just before it sailed for Skagway. His father had departed for Dawson a year earlier, leaving the motherless boy in the care of his aunt and grandmother, and had not been heard from since. With their main breadwinner gone, the family was facing destitution, so Tommy decided to go find his father.

Having reached Skagway undetected, the young stowaway slipped off the ship and headed down the White Pass Trail on foot. He slept outside wherever night found him and survived on handouts from sympathetic strangers. But when he got to Bennett, the North-West Mounted Police "kindly but firmly" turned him back.

Tommy's free trip home on the *City of Seattle* was very different from his northward journey. No longer forced to conceal himself, he could enjoy the scenery along the way, as well as the attention his plucky endeavour had earned him. Moved by his plight, passengers on the boat started a collection in his name and raised enough money to pay his fare all the way to Dawson, provided his story was verified once they got back to Seattle.[14] Whether he ever made it to the Klondike or found his father is not known.

One runaway who did reach the goldfields was twelve-year-old Martin Egan. Martin absconded from his home in San Francisco in the spring of 1901 and arrived in Dawson soon afterwards. He came to the attention of the Dawson authorities in mid-July, when he and a newfound friend, Mark Stein, appropriated a canoe from the waterfront and disappeared downriver.

Mark's parents didn't report him as missing until the next morning, but by then the canoe's owner had already notified the NWMP of his loss and the police had wired other detachments along the river, telling them to look out for the presumably stolen property. A few days later, a message came back from Forty Mile saying that "the canoe had been captured in midstream . . . together with two hungry and badly frightened boys." They confessed to having taken the craft without permission but said they'd only intended to paddle around near shore. When they got caught by the current, their fear of being punished for stealing the canoe had stopped them from calling for help.

After cooling their heels in Forty Mile for nearly a week while they waited for the next passing steamer, the pair were returned to Dawson, where they "were given a good lecture and some good advice regarding their future conduct." Mark was then handed over to his parents while the police decided what to do with Martin. Prior to the escapade he had been "under the care of a man connected with the Standard theatre," a guardianship that was unlikely to be sanctioned by the police, and it was expected that he would be shipped back to San Francisco.[15]

Everyone with an interest in the Klondike was pleased when the White Pass and Yukon Railway company started laying track in May 1898, but the promise of effortless travel over the Coast Mountains was not fulfilled immediately because the line didn't reach Bennett until July 1899. In the interim, travel beyond Bennett improved significantly with the introduction of steamers to the upper half of the Yukon River system. Over the spring and summer of 1898, several transportation companies started running paddlewheelers between Bennett and Dawson, providing a safer, more refined alternative to travelling by scow or rowboat. The only complication was that the steamers couldn't navigate the twin hazards of

Floating down the Yukon to Dawson June 19th 1899

By 1899, steamers plied the waters between Bennett and Dawson, but some stampeders still travelled down the Yukon River by scow.

Miles Canyon and the Whitehorse Rapids. This was addressed by having one fleet of boats plying the headwater lakes between Bennett and Miles Canyon, and another operating downstream of Whitehorse Rapids. A three-mile footpath ran alongside this turbulent stretch of river and steamer passengers who weren't up to walking the distance could ride with their baggage on a tramline that ran on log rails and was powered by horses.

Arriving in Skagway in the fall of 1898, the Anderson family had no time to lose if they were to make it to Dawson before freeze-up. The only thing Ethel later remembered of their hurried journey from Skagway to Whitehorse was a bitterly cold ride in an open tramcar. Her wool coat and little red hood were scant protection against the icy wind that was blowing that day, and when her teeth began chattering, a sympathetic man lifted her down and showed her how to get her blood circulating. "We danced and jigged and swung our arms until I was warm again, then walked hand in hand behind the slow tram car for some distance."[16]

In Whitehorse, Emma booked passage on the *Eldorado*, one of the last riverboats heading for Dawson that season. She was still recovering from the effects of the seasickness she suffered on the ocean voyage, but by then Ethel and Dewey had become quite self-sufficient. "Much of the time I sat in the stern 'like a good little girl,' and watched the paddle wheels thrash the river into white spray arched through with fairyland rainbows," Ethel later wrote. "The shore slipped by so close at times we could almost pick the yellow aspen and willow leaves."[17] During the regular refuelling stops, she and her brother burned off some of their pent-up energy by running around onshore while the crew replenished the supply of firewood to feed the insatiable steam boiler. But the captain kept the breaks short, for he was racing against winter.

Ethel was mesmerized by the slabs of ice that swirled in the current and nudged up against the steamer's hull. However, as the ice pans proliferated and the boat's progress slowed, her mother grew increasingly anxious. Finally they reached Dawson, only to find that the ice had built up so thickly along the shore that they couldn't push through to the pier. For three days the captain held the boat in place, waiting for the river to freeze solid. When at last it did, the three excited children and their travel-weary mother climbed off the boat with the rest of the passengers and gingerly made their way across the ice to their new home.

The first passenger trains started running on the WP&YR as soon as the first seven miles of track was completed in July 1898, and the terminus shifted north as the line progressed. By the time the Miller family landed in Skagway in the early summer of 1899, there was no longer any need to traverse the White Pass Trail on foot or horseback if you had the money for the train fare—and Louis Miller certainly did. A mining engineer from Nova Scotia with a gentle face and a bushy black moustache, Louis had joined the Klondike stampede in 1897, while his California-born wife, Mary Catherine, and one-year-old daughter, Dorothy, stayed in Seattle. After spending the winter in Dawson, he returned south just in time for the birth of his second child, Addie Elizabeth, soon dubbed Bessie, on June 11, 1898.

Louis had done well during his short time in the Klondike, so well, in fact, that he was able to move his family down to San Francisco, rent a suite at the Palace Hotel, and hire a nursemaid to help care for the children. It was the happiest year of Mary Catherine's life and perhaps of her husband's, but as the months passed, Louis grew increasingly anxious to return to the goldfields, taking his family with him this time.

When the Millers left San Francisco in the spring of 1899, Bessie was barely a year old, a fair-haired child with porcelain-doll features, just like her older sister. Accompanied by the nursemaid, the family retraced Louis's original path up the Pacific coast and over the White Pass, riding in comfort on the train from Skagway to Bennett, in marked contrast to his arduous trek of just two years

Louis and Mary Catherine Miller with their daughters Dorothy (left) and Bessie (right) on the eve of their departure for the Klondike.

earlier. The tram trip over the Miles Canyon–Whitehorse Rapids bypass was much less deluxe.

A cold drizzle fell as the two women clambered gamely onto the flat, open bed of the tramcar and perched themselves on a couple of wooden crates. While the nursemaid pulled her heavy wool coat tight against the chill, turned up her collar, and pulled her fedora lower, Mary Catherine arranged her own wraps for maximum coverage and raised an umbrella over her large, ornate hat. She fastened a second umbrella over Bessie and Dorothy, who rode in style in a big-wheeled wicker pram wedged in amongst the freight. It was a handsome vehicle, which had undoubtedly drawn admiring glances as she wheeled it along the streets of San Francisco. As she would soon discover, though, it was quite unsuitable for Dawson's high, wooden sidewalks and muddy roads, let alone the home on the creeks to which they were headed.[18]

Steamer transport on the upper Yukon River did much to ease the journey to the Klondike, but it took the completion of the WP&YR line all the way to Whitehorse and the subsequent elimination of the tramline to truly civilize it. Once the last spike was driven at the end of July 1900, travellers could enjoy seamless connections from ship to train in Skagway and from train to riverboat in Whitehorse. And then, if the river was running high and fast, they could be in Dawson as few as three days later. It was with such speed that the Murphy family travelled to the Klondike in September 1903.

William Murphy was one of the Klondike's late recruits. In the fall of 1900, he quit his job as village blacksmith in Middle Musquodoboit, Nova Scotia, and set off for Dawson, leaving behind his pregnant wife and three young children. He soon learned that there were no claims left to stake in the Klondike, but with a blacksmith's physique and stamina it wasn't hard for him to find employment. William settled down to a life of toil on Bonanza Creek and in three years' time had saved enough to send for his family.

Thirty-year-old Mary Murphy had never travelled more than sixty miles from her birthplace before the late August day in 1903 when she boarded the train in Truro, Nova Scotia, with her four young children. Walter and Henry barely remembered their father and two-and-a-half-year-old Hilda had yet to meet him. Even the eldest, seven-year-old Edith, didn't fully understand what kind of a trip they were embarking upon. When she saw the well-stocked food hamper her aunt had packed for them, she thought they were going for a picnic.

After a week of train travel, the family arrived in Vancouver and transferred directly to the steamship *Amur*. As they sailed north, Edith was happy to find another girl her age to play with, though puzzled when her new friend told her that she and her parents were on a holiday. Coming from a place where people stayed put for life, Edith couldn't fathom why anyone would leave home and travel to distant lands if they didn't have to.

At Skagway the Murphys boarded another train for a ride that turned out to be quite different from anything they'd experienced on their transcontinental journey. The narrow-gauge railway that climbed to the White Pass summit was infamous for its steep grades and tight turns and the way it alternately clung to the cliffs, plunged into pitch-black tunnels, and soared above the valley while crossing the dizzying spans of its numerous bridges. Edith was so terrified as she looked down into the dark abyss of the canyon from one of the highest trestles that she scarcely noticed anything else on the six-hour, 110-mile run to Whitehorse.

She found the three-day boat trip from Whitehorse to Dawson much more agreeable, especially when the steamer stopped at the wood yards and she and her siblings were allowed to go ashore. While the crew wheeled cartloads of logs on board, the children explored and picked flowers, a welcome change of pace after so many days of forced inactivity. Then, suddenly, the travelling was over. On September 7, just thirteen days after leaving the Atlantic coast, the Murphys arrived in Dawson.[19]

Another advance in travel to the Klondike was introduced in 1902, when the Yukon government built a winter road between Whitehorse and Dawson. When the 330-mile Overland Trail was completed that November, the WP&YR inaugurated the White Pass Stage Line. For the next twelve years, the company used horse-drawn sleighs to transport freight, mail, and passengers between the two communities throughout the winter, switching to wheeled coaches in spring and fall, and suspending service during the few months in summer when the Yukon River was open to navigation. Roadhouses, spaced twenty to twenty-five miles apart all along the route, provided meals, overnight accommodation, and fresh teams of horses.

Most parents with small children preferred to travel to or from Whitehorse by riverboat since the overland journey took anywhere from three to ten days, with only three or four scheduled stops a day—a long time for a restless child to sit still. Furthermore, the uncovered sleighs and coaches were completely exposed to the elements.

To help fight the winter cold, the company placed a metal box filled with hot bricks or burning coals on the floor of each sleigh and provided buffalo robes for the travellers to tuck around their legs. Most passengers wore well-insulated felt

In 1902 the White Pass and Yukon Railway introduced stage service between Whitehorse and Dawson, a long, hard journey for passengers of all ages.

shoes or moccasins and bundled up in fur coats and hats, with nose covers and mitts to protect their extremities, but not four-year-old Master Wells, who made the trip from Whitehorse to Dawson with his mother at the beginning of February 1904. According to two men who rode on the same sleigh as Mrs. G. P. Wells and her son, "the little lad steadfastly refused to wear mittens or keep his face covered at any stage of the trip [yet] appeared to suffer from the cold less than any of them."[20]

Perhaps the most unusual White Pass Stage Line trip was made by a passenger who saw none of the scenery along the way. In the early winter of 1903, Captain Hulme, a prominent Dawson lawyer, was offered a new position in London, England. Since the paddlewheelers had all been pulled from the river for the season, the Overland Trail was the only way for Captain and Mrs. Hulme and their two young children to travel to Whitehorse.

The week before the family left Dawson, the temperature had been hovering around minus fifty degrees Fahrenheit. The weather had moderated somewhat by the time of their departure, but the Hulmes were still worried about how to keep their seven-month-old baby from getting chilled. Their innovative solution was to pack the infant in a trunk "fitted up warmly and snugly, so that the young traveler experienced no inconvenience from the cold. At every stopping place the baby was taken out of the trunk and packed away when the trip recommenced." Although it took a full week to cover the distance, this novel approach worked remarkably well and both of the Hulme children "stood the journey in excellent shape."[21]

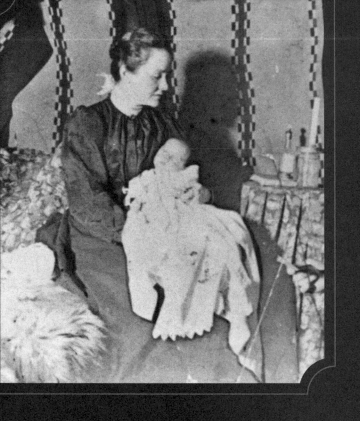

they are born in the empire
of golden promise.

Chapter 6

The Arctic Brotherhood
of Babydom

It was barely dawn on the July morning in 1898 when the S.S. *Hamilton* pulled up to the Alaska Commercial Company dock at Andreaofsky, Alaska, and woke little Lucia, the company agent's daughter. She knew at once that something was amiss. Despite the early hour—not yet even 3 a.m.—and the fact that the *Hamilton* belonged to a rival firm, the boat's captain and purser came straight to the house to speak with her father. When they emerged from their discussion, his expression was as grim as theirs.

As the sky lightened, Lucia watched several deckhands come ashore with spades and climb the slope to the village cemetery, then return to the ship a while later. Shortly after that, a procession of passengers and crew members carrying a long, white box came down the gangplank and followed the same route. By then Lucia's father had told her why the sternwheeler had made an unscheduled stop. Just after midnight, one of the passengers, a young woman of only twenty-four or twenty-five years, had passed away. After a brief service, a freshly painted marker was placed at the head of the grave, identifying the deceased as Augusta Schultz. Then the sombre parade retraced its steps and the *Hamilton* continued down the Yukon River bearing a motherless baby who was not yet a year old.

When Augusta and Charles Schultz had left Seattle in April 1897 on board the steamer *Al-ki*, the future must have seemed bright. Having caught wind of the gold rush rumours that were drifting down from the North, they wanted some of the fabled wealth for themselves. Whether or not they knew Augusta was four months pregnant when they left, there could have been no doubt about her condition by the time their journey to the Klondike via the Chilkoot Trail was completed.

More than a thousand stampeders, including the Schultzes, poured into Dawson that summer, most of them without sufficient provisions to see them through the winter. The transportation companies had done their best to fill

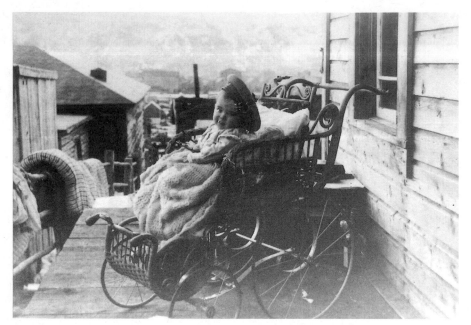

By 1900, many Dawson babies led pampered lives compared to those born in the earliest days of the gold rush.

their warehouses before the close of the navigation season, but by September it appeared there wouldn't be enough food to sustain the Klondike's abruptly inflated population until spring. Everywhere in town there was talk of starvation warnings and speculation as to whether it would be best to leave before freeze-up.

On September 8, while everyone else was preoccupied with these concerns, Augusta gave birth to the first white child born in Dawson.[1] Bursting with pride, the Schultzes named their daughter Dawson Klondike and welcomed the many well-wishers who came to greet her, including eleven-year-old Florence Barrett, who visited the famous baby on September 12. Florence and her family had just arrived in town after their long journey down the Yukon River in the *Buga-boo* and were living in a tent on the waterfront. Finding no children her own age to play with, she had struck up a friendship with Mrs. Howard, the wife of the Lousetown toll-bridge operator, and tagged along on one of her regular visits to the Schultz cabin.

The pregnancy and birth had taken a heavy toll on Augusta and her health only became worse as the winter wore on. When she rallied a little in late May, Charles urged her to go south while she had some strength. The sale of their cabin netted them $1,000, of which $300 went for a boat ticket to Seattle. The rest of the proceeds were to cover Augusta and Dawsie's living expenses until Charles could send additional funds or join them.

On June 24 Charles escorted his wife and nine-month-old daughter down to the docks and onto the waiting steamer.[2] He stayed with them until the last moment then hurried off the boat as the crew loosened its moorings. As soon as he left, one of the other passengers went to Augusta and, after introducing herself, took Dawsie in her arms. Mrs. George Guy had her own young son and a gravely ill husband to care for during the journey, but her kind nature and great fondness for babies made it impossible for her to ignore the obviously ailing young mother.

After that the two women were seldom apart, spending long hours talking or sitting together and watching the scenery slip by. One afternoon, Augusta handed Dawsie to Mrs. Guy and said she was going to her state room to rest, as she was not feeling well. Over the following hours Mrs. Guy checked frequently on her friend but left her to sleep undisturbed until she began to worry that she'd been lying too long in the same position. She quickly fetched one of the boat's officers and they entered the cabin together, where her worst fears were confirmed. Augusta was dead.

With a heavy heart, Mrs. Guy prepared Augusta's body for burial. Later, when they reached Andreaofsky, she watched as the casket was lowered into the ground and said a silent farewell to a woman she barely knew but would always remember with affection. It was to be a month of sorrow for her. Her husband died at St. Michael a short time later.

When the *Hamilton* reached St. Michael, Dawsie was handed over to the US commissioner, who put the baby in the care of a Yup'ik woman and sent news of Augusta's death to Charles. On August 6, the *Klondike Nugget* reported that "Schultz has just received word and is crazy to go down and mark the grave and take possession of the child. He has asked the manager of the N.A.T.T. Co. to refund him part of the fare, seeing that the company had only carried his wife a part of the distance to Seattle, but it was refused on the grounds that 'they didn't want to take her in the first place.'"[3]

Even if Charles had had the means to head downriver, he wouldn't have found his daughter at St. Michael. On July 4, the US authorities had taken her from the Yup'ik woman and entrusted her to the wife of the first mate of the sailing vessel *Hayden Brown*. A few days later, in a prearranged rendezvous in Kotzebue Sound, Dawsie was delivered to a Coast Guard cutter that was on its way to Seattle.

For the next few years, Dawsie lived in Seattle with a woman named Mrs. Hume, who had little good to say about her charge's father. In January 1901 Dawsie's guardian wrote to the *Klondike Nugget*, saying that she would be forced to place the three-year-old in an orphan's home if Charles didn't start providing for her. She claimed he had given her no financial support and "never so much as written to explain his conduct." When tracked down and questioned about the matter, Charles declared that "he had never heard from Mrs. Hume concerning his child or its welfare" and "promised to write at once and send some money."[4]

A month later Mrs. Hume wrote to the *Yukon Sun* with further allegations about Charles's negligence. After Augusta's untimely death, she said, the people of Dawson had raised several hundred dollars to help with Dawsie's care and the money had been deposited in a Seattle bank. In 1899, Charles had "made a trip to the outside and secured the money and used it for his own pleasure." He had then returned to the Klondike and had not been heard from since.[5]

Dawsie's early years may have been, as the *Nugget* reporter put it, "one long, drawn out note of pitiful misfortune," but her luck was about to turn. At the end of April, "the poor little waif who no one seems to want or care for" was turned over to the Washington Children's Home Society. A few weeks later, she got a permanent home with Dr. and Mrs. C. L. Erwin, a Seattle dentist and his wife. Charles came to see Dawsie soon after she moved in with her new foster parents and visited a few more times over the following years. Then, when she was twelve, he disappeared without a trace, leaving her with more questions than answers about her part in the Klondike story.

Klondike Timothy Crowley missed being Dawson's first gold rush baby by less than a month, but he could claim the distinction of being the first white boy born in the town. His father, Timothy, was a frontier-loving Irishman who had spent time in Australia and Montana before seeking his fortune in the Yukon in 1895. When news of the Klondike strike hit Forty Mile in August 1896, Timothy headed straight to Bonanza, but it was not until the following summer that he staked Number 5 Below Discovery on Sulphur Creek, one of the richest claims on that drainage.[6]

Mary Crowley, who also hailed from Ireland, joined her husband in 1896 and gave birth to their first child on November 2, 1897.[7] Five days later, the Crowleys went to Father William Judge to have their son christened. To Dawson's gold-frenzied residents, Klondike Timothy seemed a fine moniker for the baby, but most expected the Catholic priest to reject the unusual choice as too worldly. Surprisingly, when he heard the proposed name he merely nodded and carried on with the baptism. Only decades later did Klondike Timothy discover that Judge had "satisfied father, mother and his own conscience by silence." Having not uttered the offending name himself during the ceremony, Judge had no qualms about entering the name he deemed appropriate—a simple "Tim Crowley"—in his records.[8]

In the summer of 1899, Klondike Timothy and his mother went to visit her family in Butte, Montana, stopping in Seattle along the way. After interviewing the junior celebrity and his mother in their hotel suite, the *Seattle Post-Intelligencer* reported that "the pet and pride of the mines" was "a bright, blue-eyed little fellow" who was "spry of limb as well as glib of tongue" and "just now on the threshold of that interesting period of babyhood, the 'chattering' age."[9] The Crowleys' second child, Stephen, was born in the United States, and Mary returned to Sulphur Creek with the two boys in 1901.[10]

Dawsie Schultz and Klondike Timothy Crowley were charter members of an exclusive club, hailed in 1901 by the *Dawson Weekly News* as "the Arctic brotherhood of babydom . . . the most interesting and flourishing fraternity of all the Northland."[11] The only other gold rush baby on record as being born in the Klondike in 1897 was Robert Frederick Schoenbeck, son of stampeders Robert and Mathilda Schoenbeck, who made his debut in Dawson on November 29.[12]

In 1898, tens of thousands of stampeders, including a few thousand women, converged on the goldfields and the Klondike baby boom started to gather momentum. It would be some time before Klondike births ceased to be a novelty. Before the turn of the century, many were reported with great fanfare in the local papers, for they were truly newsworthy.

"Babies are not born every day in the Klondike," began one front-page story in the *Klondike Nugget* on May 20, 1899. "So, when Mr. and Mrs. James Harrison became the parents of a bouncing handsome fellow of twelve pounds avoirdupois

Mary Crowley on Sulphur Creek with sons Stephen (in front) and Klondike Timothy, around 1901. Klondike Timothy, born November 2, 1897, was Dawson's second gold rush baby.

on Wednesday last, they stepped into immediate and enviable distinction . . . The NUGGET staff tender their felicitations."[13]

No baby could have been kept secret for long in the Klondike, but some women either concealed or terminated their pregnancies, often for reasons known only to themselves. One such case came to light a few weeks before the Harrisons' happy event, when a Dawson man discovered a pasteboard box partly hidden under a large rock on the hillside east of St. Mary's Hospital. Imagining that he'd stumbled upon some treasure trove, he eagerly opened the box and took out the newspaper-wrapped bundle that was inside. When he removed the final layer of paper, he found "the body of a little baby in the foetus stage." Although decomposition hadn't begun, the doctor who subsequently examined the body was unable to estimate how long it had been there. Not surprisingly, the mother was never located and the circumstances that led her to place her unborn baby there remain unknown.[14]

In general, the rarity of children, especially babies, in the Klondike made them as precious as gold itself, and many newborns had more riches bestowed on them in their first days than their parents earned in a year. When Marie Eldorado Lennon was born in 1898, she was Eldorado Creek's first gold rush baby and "was so joy-ously welcomed by the hardy miners that they flocked to the Lennon cabin with gifts of pure gold, and gave to the wee newcomer $1,000 in choicest nuggets."[15]

A year later, Pettie Gray, the first white boy born on Bonanza Creek, was given a similar reception. According to a newspaper account written in September 1900, as the Gray family passed through Skagway on their way south, "Pettie was not born with a silver spoon in his mouth, but when he was four hours old the miners of Victoria gulch on upper Bonanza assembled around him and laid at his feet the biggest nuggets they had." As a result of this generosity, the one-year-old allegedly owned "the largest poke of nuggets there was on the train," which his parents planned to use for his future education in California. The Grays declined to say how much gold they had reaped from their Bonanza claim, but agreed that their son was "the nugget of greatest price they ever got out of it."[16]

Ella Lung, who became Dominion Creek's first Klondike baby on January 5, 1901, was honoured with poetry as well as gold. At Christmas, just before Ella's birth, the Lungs' neighbours presented them with a small leather poke filled with gold dust, bearing a tag that read, "For a new little cheechako and future Sourdough."[17] Later, one of the more literary miners took pen to paper and captured sentiments that seemed to be shared by so many of the lonely men on the creeks.

The poem's author, the Reverend Olson, was an ordained minister who had traded the pulpit for a pickaxe. According to Velma Lung, he was her daughter's "willing slave" from the moment he first held her when she was just a few days old.

Prospector Fred Crewe takes a break from the drudgery of work to delight in the company of Marie Eldorado Lennon, the first non-Native child born on Eldorado Creek.

From then on, Olson often came to the cabin "just to see Ella and to hold her and softly croon lullabies." It was, perhaps, his way of blocking out the dehumanizing drudgery of work in the mine shafts. As he wrote in the third verse of his ode:

> Sweet Ella has come to bless us
>   In this frozen land of treasure;
> The radiance of her smile has cheered us,
>   Brought joy and happiness beyond measure.[18]

For former Chicago socialite Martha Purdy, the company of some of the "strange uncouth men who called to pay their respects"[19] when her son Lyman was born in Dawson on January 31, 1899, might have been disconcerting, but by then she had been forced to abandon many of her prejudices and revise her standards. Besides, their adoration touched her heart and helped her forget the unhappy circumstances of Lyman's birth.

After leaving her two young sons at her parents' estate in Kansas in the spring of 1898, Martha had travelled west to meet her husband, Will, for their planned Klondike expedition. She was in Seattle with her brother and other members of their party when Will sent her a letter from San Francisco calling off their trip. Martha was outraged that he would so casually dismiss her Klondike dreams. So, instead of acquiescing, she wrote to tell him she was going to the Klondike with the rest of their party regardless of his change of heart. She also announced that she "would never go back to him, so undependable had he proven," and that she "never wanted to hear from him or see him again."[20] With those heated words, the Purdys' ten-year marriage ended and the two never did meet again.

Martha didn't know she was two months pregnant when she struggled over the Chilkoot Pass in July, hauled along by her brother, George Munger. In fact, it was fall before she admitted to herself, and then to George, that she was carrying Will's child. There was still time before freeze-up for Martha to go south via St. Michael with her cousin Harry, but she didn't feel well enough to face the long journey. Harry left without her and when he got home he bluntly told his mother that Martha was most certainly dead by then. "She was going to have a baby," he said, "and she couldn't possibly live, she looked so ill."[21] He underestimated her, though. Subsisting on a diet completely lacking in fresh fruit and vegetables, as well in as milk, butter, and sugar, Martha somehow managed to remain healthy and to deliver a vigorous, nine-pound baby in the dead of winter.

Dressed in little gowns that Martha had sewn by hand from tablecloths and napkins—the only fabric available—baby Lyman received an enthusiastic welcome from friends and strangers alike. Besides gold, they brought gifts of freshly baked bread and cakes, chocolates, olive oil, and fresh game, and vied for the chance to hold the infant, some speaking longingly of their own faraway children. Lyman's daily bath hour was particularly popular, with grubby miners who hardly ever bothered to bathe themselves crowding into the overheated cabin to supervise the baby's ablutions.

Far from being disturbed by all this attention, Lyman thrived on it. From the day he was born, Martha found him to be the happiest and most contented baby she ever knew. Once he became mobile, he "would go to the roughest-looking of them all, gurgling and laughing and pulling their beards."[22]

In later years Martha told two different stories about Lyman's birth. According to one version, her birth attendants were an old sea captain and "a one-armed man [with] a big hook for a hand, wrapped around with cotton." In the other, she said she went into labour unexpectedly while home alone and that her unassisted delivery was quick and "incredibly easy."[23] Whatever the truth of the matter, she definitely didn't have the kind of expert medical care she'd had when she gave birth to her first two children in Chicago.

The shortage of midwives, nurses, and doctors to help deliver babies was a universal concern for pregnant women in the early Klondike years and the few that were available were unaffordable for many women. Martha had considered going to St. Mary's Hospital for her confinement until she heard how much it would cost. The hospital's standard rates were $50 for an annual ticket, which entitled the bearer to unlimited care as required for one year, or $5 a day for nursing, board, and washing, with an additional $5 charge for each visit by a doctor. These fees were beyond Martha's means at the time, and although Father Judge had offered to defer payment until she could get the money from home, her abhorrence of debt was greater than her fear of giving birth on her own.[24]

Martha probably wouldn't have received such a sympathetic reception from the Presbyterian-run Good Samaritan Hospital, which was never as inclined to accept impecunious patients as its Catholic counterpart. In 1901, the Reverend Andrew S. Grant made his hospital even less welcoming to expectant mothers, regardless of their financial position. Faced with a $7,000 debt, Grant argued against the Good Samaritan being used as a maternity hospital and began refusing to accept indigent pregnant women at the rate paid by the government for patients who were unable to pay their own way. His justification for raising the maternity fees

Martha Purdy holds her new baby, Lyman, in the Dawson cabin where he was born. On the wall behind her brother George are photographs of the two sons she left behind in Kansas.

to $15 a day, with several days' payment required in advance, was that post-natal treatment was more time-consuming than other types of medical care.[25]

Besides St. Mary's and the Good Samaritan, women who wanted a hospital birth at the peak of the gold rush had the choice of several private infirmaries, but most of these smaller hospitals had closed by the end of 1899. One that was still operating in 1903 had the distinction of being the birthplace of Dawson's first set of twins. The two babies, a boy and a girl, were born to Mrs. Carl Lueders on March 23, in a private hospital run by nurse Jennie Muir. The next day, Mrs. Lueders and "the crowing little Klondikers" were said to be "doing splendidly" while "Papa Lueders . . . the most important man in Dawson today . . . [was] busy hustling a second installment of clothing, inspecting double-end buggies, duplicating orders for nursing bottles and at the same time making explanations and receiving congratulations."[26]

Many of the Klondike's first doctors were Americans, but in 1898 the newly formed Yukon Medical College prohibited foreign-trained doctors from practising medicine unless they met certain stringent requirements. This move was controversial from the start and attracted even more condemnation after a woman died from complications following childbirth—a death some critics blamed on the persecution of US doctors.

Belle Conder and her husband had met Dr. Luella Day while all three were on their way to the goldfields, the Conders from Australia and Day from the United States. On August 4, 1898, Belle went into premature labour and the frightened couple summoned their physician friend to their home in Klondike City. Although Day's medical practice had been shut down because of the new rules, she went at once. But as soon as she had delivered the baby and made Belle comfortable, she hastened back across the bridge to Dawson and went directly to the North-West Mounted Police to confess what she'd done.

Day told Captain Cortlandt Starnes that Belle's condition was critical and would likely remain so for several days. She also pointed out that the Conders were destitute and that she hadn't charged them for her services. If the police would not allow her to continue caring for Belle as a charitable act, she considered that "the government itself was in duty bound to see to it that the sufferer received the proper medical attention."[27] Starnes agreed and said he would send a government doctor to the Conder home.

Despite being run off his feet with cases demanding his attention, the appointed physician, Dr. Thompson, responded promptly, but he didn't stay long and the medicine he left had no effect on the childbed fever that had struck

Belle. Mr. Conder sent repeated unanswered pleas for Thompson to return. Finally, in desperation, he called for Day.

Torn between trying to help and abiding by the law, Day went first to the police headquarters, where she was given permission to attend Belle as long as she didn't charge a fee. Then she hurried to her erstwhile patient's bedside. But when she found Belle delirious and running a temperature of 106.5 degrees Fahrenheit, she lost her nerve. Instead of administering any kind of medical care, she turned and fled back to the NWMP headquarters and "notified the authorities . . . that the woman was practically dead—killed through neglect—and that she (Dr. Day) absolutely refused to have anything to do with the case." Thompson was then "dispatched hastily to the scene of the tragedy" but was unable to save Belle, who died on August 12.[28] There is no further record of the baby or Mr. Conder.

After the Yukon Medical College imposed its restrictions, most US physicians left the Yukon, though some stayed and worked as nurses. At times the distinction may have been largely semantic, but it did reduce their fees, which, for struggling stampeders like the Grumanns, was more important than any concerns about their qualifications.

Edward Grumann had joined the stampede in 1898 and returned to Wisconsin the following summer to marry his sweetheart, Theresa Benzinger. Ten days after their wedding, the newlyweds headed north with nine relatives. The youngest member of the party was six-week-old Harold Grumann, the son of Edward's brother and sister-in-law, John and Lena. For the next year, Edward and Theresa shared a small cabin at Number 15 Below on Hunker Creek with John, Lena, and Harold, with only a curtain separating the two families' respective quarters. A whiskey crate mounted on wooden wheels served as Harold's playpen.

John, Lena, and Harold went back south in August 1900, but the playpen would not remain unused for long. Edward and Theresa's first child, Raymond, was born in the cabin that December, delivered by Dr. Beauche, a US physician who was working nearby as a miner. The Grumanns knew he wasn't licensed to practise but considered themselves lucky to get his services for only $100. They also paid a nurse $50 to come in for an hour each morning for the first few days after Raymond was born.[29]

⌒

While some women left the Klondike to have their babies, others rejected that option as either too expensive or disruptive. When Velma Lung realized she was pregnant in the late summer of 1900, she kept her condition secret from her husband until after freeze-up so he wouldn't "give up the claim and make a dash for the Outside."[30] Ed Lung was upset when Velma finally broke the news, but she

Harry and Ella Campbell (centre) and friends outside the Gold Run Creek cabin where their children were born: Viola Mae (seated in cart) in June 1901 and Arthur (in his father's arms) in November 1902.

allayed some of his fears by telling him that she'd already secured the services of Mrs. Webster, a practical nurse who lived three miles away in Caribou City.

In addition to counting on Mrs. Webster's presence at the crucial time, Velma had decided to "trust in God and Nature to carry [her] through the ordeal ahead."[31] But Nature, in the form of extreme winter weather, was nearly her undoing. Although the Lungs had thought the baby might arrive at Christmas, they were still waiting a week later. On New Year's Day, a severe storm blew in and the temperature plummeted. Velma tried to convince Ed that he could deliver the baby if necessary, but he was terrified at the prospect and insisted that he would go fetch Mrs. Webster no matter what the weather.

In the middle of the night on January 4, Velma's first labour pains jolted her from sleep. As soon as she woke Ed, he leapt from their bed, throwing on clothes as he hurried to alert their neighbour, Joe, by ringing a signal bell they'd rigged up outside the cabin. Joe arrived within minutes and took charge of the Lungs' six-year-old son, Clemy, while Ed ran to a nearby roadhouse to get Selma, a young woman who worked there and who had agreed to help with the birth if necessary. Then he hitched up his dog team and raced off to collect the nurse.

By this time, the storm had abated, but it had left a deep blanket of snow across the hills and the temperature had hit a new low of seventy-two degrees

Fahrenheit below zero. Halfway to Caribou, the oil in Ed's lantern congealed and the flame flickered out, plunging him into darkness without a single star or sliver of moonlight to light his way. Almost immediately he lost the trail and began to panic, until his lead dog relocated the route and got the sled back on track.

Upon arriving in the little town, Ed went straight to Mrs. Webster's residence, or so he thought, and banged on the door, shouting out his urgent message. To his surprise, he was answered by an irate woman who said she had no intention of opening for business in such weather and that she was fed up with miners trying to con their way into her premises. He had to repeat his appeal several times before she would believe that he wasn't a prospective customer, and even then she only grudgingly directed him across the road. Once he found the correct house, it didn't take long for Mrs. Webster to wrap herself in furs and climb into the sled for the return journey.

Meanwhile, Velma's contractions were coming faster and harder, and she was wondering whether her husband and the nurse could possibly get there in time. Nineteen-year-old Selma, who had no previous experience with childbirth, was even more frightened than Velma, though she had made herself useful by putting large quantities of water to boil on the stove and setting out the clean sheets and cotton that Velma had prepared earlier.

When Ed finally returned he was breathless from running behind the sled for most of the return trip, but Mrs. Webster was calm and composed. She sent the anxious father to Joe's cabin, and shortly before 5 a.m. baby Ella arrived. It had been a far more harrowing episode than Velma had anticipated, but not so traumatic that she wasn't willing to risk a repeat. In the summer of 1902, she found herself pregnant again and made the same decision about where to have the baby. Almost two years after Ella's birth, with the outside temperature once more hovering near minus seventy-two, Mrs. Webster returned to the Dominion Creek cabin and delivered the Lungs' third child, Paul.

In the chaos and confusion of the early gold rush period, no one really knew how many babies were being born in the Klondike or how many children had come north with their parents. The first rough head count conducted by the NWMP in 1898 did not differentiate between adults and children. Their second count, conducted in the late summer of 1899, found 4,445 people living in Dawson, 163 of them being children under the age of fourteen.[32]

The following spring, a census by the NWMP of the Yukon's non-Native residents put Dawson's population at 5,404, including 4,516 men, 646 women, and 242 "infants." In the Yukon Territory as a whole there were 13,147 men, 1,195 women, and 505 "infants." Aside from 1,260 people counted in the Tagish

Joseph and Ellen Acklen on the front porch of their Dawson home around 1901 with their California-born daughter, Charlotte, and Klondike baby, Joseph.

district, most of the non-Native population was in the Klondike area, concentrated in Dawson and along Bonanza, Hunker, and Dominion creeks.[33]

The 1901 federal census, which was more rigorous and comprehensive than the previous counts, tallied 6,695 people residing in Dawson City proper on March 31. Of those, 411 were children aged fourteen and under. Another 808 people, including 51 children, were resident in the adjacent communities of Klondike City, South Dawson, West Dawson, and Moosehide.[34] In the same year, the NWMP recorded 27 births in Dawson.[35]

Although the police were responsible for keeping track of all births in the territory, some new parents didn't know they were required to report family additions. On July 7, 1902, Anton Vogee, a Dawson sign painter and wallpaper dealer, found himself in the embarrassing position of being hauled into court because he and his wife, Inga, had failed to register their son's birth. There was no question of the couple having tried to hide the event, for when little Arthur Edward was born on May 3, Anton "had not hesitated to herald the news of the arrival of his heir from the housetop." They simply weren't aware of their legal obligation. Seeing how mortified and apologetic Anton was, the judge let him off without a fine but admonished him "to be more thoughtful next time, at which a gentle titter tip-toed around the court room."[36]

Officially logged or not, the ranks of the Arctic brotherhood of babydom continued to swell with each passing year as the same kind of "infantile wails and 'ootsie tootsie' talk" that were heard in the Vogee home came to other clapboard houses and log cabins in town and out on the creeks.

In the opinion of the *Dawson Weekly News*, "these prided and fast multiplying youthful Yukoners" were privileged simply by virtue of their birthplace. "Native sons and daughters of the golden North—sons and daughters born in the blaze of the midnight sun or under the living streamers of the radiant aurora borealis have doubly enchanted lives, and the soothsayers say they are doubly fortunate . . . they are born in the empire of golden promise and in a realm that has for the future all that hope and prospect of wealth in development can afford."[37]

Their ruddy cheeks and sturdy fingers prove their physical appreciation of the climate.

Chapter 7

A Particularly Healthy
Place for Children

At the beginning of the gold rush, the idea of children accompanying their parents to the goldfields was considered imprudent, if not downright reckless. Most married men balked at letting their wives come with them and flat-out refused to bring dependents of more tender years. Generally, however, neither the Klondikers nor the relatives they left behind were happy about being separated. Some men and women quickly abandoned their golden dreams and returned home to their spouses and children, but others were not willing to quit so soon. As transportation to Dawson improved, families started moving north to join those who had led the way and Klondike life thus became more of a family affair with each passing year.

A population made up mostly of single men meant good business for dance-halls, brothels, and bars, but government officials believed that the Klondike's future prosperity depended on building a more domesticated society. In an 1899 report, Dawson medical health officer J. W. Good recommended that "men should bring in their wives and their children to prepare for the comforts of home." The climate was agreeable for both women and children, he maintained, and their presence would benefit family men by encouraging better eating habits. "If they try the experiment this way," Good said, "they will, at least, enjoy life, and in any case preserve their health."[1]

In September 1900, a special edition of the *Yukon Sun* devoted to "The Dawson of Today" presented similar arguments. In the lead article, Faith Fenton Brown observed that "more people, especially women and children" had arrived over the previous summer. "[There] are more homes today in Dawson than ever before," she continued, "and in consequence, social and religious interests, those chief factors in civilization, are advancing by leaps and bounds."[2]

Yet, while the number of women and children arriving to join husbands and fathers in the Klondike had noticeably increased by 1900, families had been trailing north after their menfolk—or, less frequently, after female relatives—since the early days of the gold rush.

One of the first families to be reunited in the Klondike was that of P.B. Anderson, who had joined the stampede in August 1897. About fourteen months later, he watched from the shore as his wife and their three children disembarked from the paddlewheeler *Eldorado* and tramped across the newly frozen Yukon River. There was some awkwardness in the first few moments of their meeting. To Ethel and Dewey, P.B. seemed familiar yet foreign—"a strange papa with whiskers all over his face"[3]—but they were so happy to see him that his exotic appearance and the moustache that tickled when he kissed them didn't really matter. One-year-old Clay, on the other hand, hid behind his mother's skirts and refused to have anything to do with the stranger.

Even when the separation between parents and children was relatively short, reunions could be uneasy, as the Hartshorn family of Ellensburg, Washington, discovered. In the spring of 1898, Hazel Hartshorn said goodbye first to her father, Albert, who departed for the goldfields in April, and then to her mother, Florence, who left in mid-June, just before Hazel's fifth birthday. Florence had been longing to join her husband and experience the Klondike excitement first-hand, and her parents were willing to care for Hazel, but she still found it "hard to break away" and leave her only child.[4]

Instead of going all the way to Dawson, the Hartshorns stopped at Log Cabin, a thriving stampede settlement on the White Pass Trail about a day's walk south of Bennett. Albert took up his former trade as a blacksmith, while Florence, a trained photographer, cooked in a friend's restaurant and, when she had time, used her camera to document the gold rush. "How I enjoyed those four months in the North," she later wrote. "Only for the little golden-haired girlie at home, we would have stayed longer."[5]

The couple began their journey home on October 5, and a few weeks later they reached Florence's parents' home in Olympia, Washington. To Florence's dismay, Hazel was painfully shy with them when they first arrived back, unlike the family cat "who did all kinds of tricks to show us how pleased he was to see us."[6] Unwilling to risk further estrangement, Florence vowed not to leave her daughter again. When Albert headed north once more in the spring of 1899, she and Hazel stayed behind. In October, after he found employment with one of the companies that operated the lake steamers, they joined him in Bennett.

Northern living held great appeal for the Hartshorns, and over the next eight years they made their home in various communities in the southern Yukon and northern British Columbia before finally moving to the Klondike in 1907. The only drawback was that separation became a regular feature of their family life. Starting in 1903, Hazel spent her summers with Florence and Albert, and her winters at school in Washington state. Her love of the North stayed strong, though, and in her early twenties, Hazel made a number of extended trips to the Klondike to see her parents, meeting her future husband during one of these visits.

Long separations were standard fare for many Klondike families, even those who originally came north together. Especially during the early years, children were often sent south for some or all of their education and returned to the Yukon only during the summer vacation. Trips out of the territory to deal with health concerns, visit relatives, or attend to business matters also often divided families for months at a time.

On August 23, 1902, the *Klondike Nugget* published two stories highlighting the fact that it was the season of farewells for many locals. One noted that Dawson would be well represented in Toronto schools—"the best in the Dominion"—that winter. Eliza McLennan, the daughter of Mr. and Mrs. J. P. McLennan, was one of twelve children from five families who would be going to school there. The others were the unnamed offspring of "Clerk Chas. E. MacDonald, Dr. Thompson, Crown Prosecutor Congdon [and] a son of Postmaster Hartman." Eliza had started her journey the previous evening, travelling in the company of a Dawson lawyer, C. C. McCaul, and his wife.[7]

The second story, titled "Another Lonely Man," commiserated with Charles E. Taylor, whose wife and daughter also departed on August 22. Lucille Taylor was on her way to attend school in Tacoma, the family's former home, while her mother planned to "spend the winter in southern California for the benefit of her health," which had deteriorated since her arrival in Dawson a year earlier. Charles's job as an assistant cashier for the White Pass Company was evidently too good for him to give it up and move back south with them.[8]

The Anderson family experienced their second Klondike separation less than a year after getting back together, when Emma had to go to Seattle for medical care in the summer of 1899. She took Clay with her, while five-year-old Dewey and six-year-old Ethel remained with their father on Eldorado Creek. Emma might not have agreed to this arrangement if she'd realized how nonchalant her husband would be about childcare.

Early every morning, while the children were still sleeping, P.B. filled a bowl with hard-boiled eggs and left it on the table, then departed for the distant hills where he was cutting timber. Ethel and Dewey got up when they pleased, ate some eggs, and wandered out to play. Sometimes they picked wildflowers or crushed coloured rocks from the tailings piles and poured the multihued dust into glass bottles.

When they tired of these pastimes, the two youngsters would investigate the openings of abandoned mine shafts, crawling cautiously to their rims and dropping stones into the holes so they could watch their reflections become "all wobbly in

Tailings piles and mine shafts, like these at Number 22 Below on Hunker Creek, were enticing but dangerous places to play.

the water some twenty, thirty, forty feet below" and listen to the varying tones made by stones of different sizes. "Surely there is a God who watches over children," Ethel later said, "or we would never have survived [mama's] absence."[9]

When Emma and Clay returned, Ethel and Dewey were surprised by the change in their little brother. In just a couple of months he had lost his baby fat and shot up several inches. He wore a new outfit, too: a frilly white shirt, knee-length pants and matching jacket, and shiny black boots, and a jaunty sailor's hat perched on his head above his cropped blond hair. His siblings had already become so accustomed to the rough frontier styles of the gold creeks that they "hardly knew him in his city clothes."[10]

Families that overcame the challenges of going to the Klondike together or reuniting there would have expected to live together, but sometimes that wasn't possible. When the Barretts reached Dawson in the fall of 1897, they initially camped on the Dawson waterfront, then moved to more secure quarters after a dog broke into their tent and stole two precious slabs of bacon. Once Florence and the three children were settled into the one-room log cabin they'd rented, Martin headed up to the creeks and staked a claim. That winter, and for much of the next few years, he lived on Victoria Gulch while the rest of the family remained town-based.[11]

For the Barrett children, the phrase "up on the claim" was laden with enticing possibilities and they were thrilled whenever they got to spend time there with their father. In winter they made the thirty-mile journey by dogsled, snuggled down under fur robes on the sled, while their mother "bright-eyed and glowing in her little reindeer parka 'mush[ed]' the dogs."[12] At lunchtime they would stop at some friendly stranger's cabin so they could thaw out their frozen bread and beans.

One of the most exciting parts of the winter visits to the claim was Martin's nightly ritual of testing samples from the day's digging in the "panning hole," a watertight wooden box he kept in the cabin. "We children gathered eagerly about him while he squatted down with a gold pan full of gravel, and began shaking and twirling it in the water of the 'hole.' Little by little the dirt washed out over the lip of the pan, until only fine black sand was left crawling in the water. Then even the sand was worked out, until there in the bottom lay a tiny heap of gold, glittering in the dim light."[13] More mundanely, when not being used for its primary purpose, the panning hole served as a bathtub for the children.

When the first school opened in Dawson in November 1899, the Barretts enrolled seven-year-old Freddy, but not Lawrence and Florence Junior, who were sent south to Catholic boarding schools to complete their education.[14] At her school, Florence shocked the teachers with her "infelicity of language"—a result, she claimed, of all the time she'd spent around the miners on Victoria Gulch.[15] When the senior Barretts and Freddy moved from Dawson to Catalla, Alaska, in 1903, Florence had just graduated, so she happily joined them there. Her childhood experiences in Alaska and the Klondike had left her with a passion for the North, which she would later share with the world through her popular romantic novels, written under the pen name Barrett Willoughby.

The Carroll family also maintained two residences almost from the time they arrived in the Klondike from San Francisco in 1898. Jim Carroll, a former world-champion lightweight boxer, gave sparring lessons in Dawson and worked at the North American Transportation and Trading Company store. His wife ran a highly successful roadhouse on Bonanza Creek, where she lived with their son. Every Saturday Jim brought provisions from town; every Sunday he returned to Dawson. Eventually, however, the family may have split permanently, for a profile of Mrs. Carroll published in the *Dawson Daily News* in 1902 makes no mention of either her husband or her son.[16]

However, the vagaries of Klondike life brought some families closer together than ever. After a year in Dawson with her brother and sister-in-law and their

Taking a break from his mining labours on Sulphur Creek, A. Baird cuddles his young son.

nine-year-old daughter, Lulu Craig was convinced that "the great sympathy extended to children, whose parents took them so far from the homes of their births, was not needed . . . One advantage they had was the companionship of their parents, of which they had much more, than a number of them were accustomed to have in their homes; especially was this so with the fathers whose business cares in a city gave them little time to walk and talk with their children."[17]

Lulu's perspective was informed by her years of experience as a schoolteacher, as well as observations of her niece, Emilie, and other Klondike children. One encounter that impressed her was with a father and his three sons, the youngest about four years old. When she met them, they were crossing the frozen Yukon River on their way to cut firewood in the forest. "They were all laughing and chatting together and seemed to be in fine health and their appearance was picturesque in their parkas and mucklucks . . . The little one was somewhat in advance of the others and he was merrily singing 'Old King Cole was a merry old soul,' and his bright eyes and rosy cheeks and happy face betokened a heart e'en as merry as the jolly old king . . ."[18]

Although sharing the Klondike adventure strengthened the bonds between Emilie and her parents, their family idyll was short-lived. On June 12, 1899, about sixteen months after they had started up the Chilkoot Trail, Lulu, Emilie, and Nelle boarded a steamer bound for St. Michael, leaving Morte to pursue his mining interests. Nelle would be back with her husband before the end of summer, but she would be alone. Lulu was returning to her teaching job in Saint Joseph, Missouri, and Emilie, who had just turned eleven, was on her way to a nearby boarding school in Kansas City.

For the rest of her school years, Emilie made the long trek between Kansas City and the Klondike each spring and fall. Until she was in her late teens, Dawson was her summer home only, and her relationship with her parents depended heavily on the postal service. After graduation she moved back with them for a while and spent at least one more winter in Dawson. Then she went south again to attend finishing school in Seattle, where Nelle and Morte joined her in 1909.[19]

⁓

Being parted during the school year was hard on parents and children alike, but few had as much reason to regret such a separation as Mrs. D. A. McKenzie. A single mother who ran the Monte Cristo roadhouse on Bonanza Creek, Mrs. McKenzie had decided to send her academically inclined daughter to a parochial school in Tacoma, Washington, where the girl's grandmother lived, instead of settling for what the local education system could offer.

In the spring of 1903 Mrs. McKenzie learned that ten-year-old Nesta had been struck by spinal meningitis. Her first instinct was undoubtedly to rush to her child's side, but the cost of getting there and the difficulty of finding someone else to manage the roadhouse in her absence probably deterred her. The trip south may also have seemed unwarranted, for it appeared that Nesta was recuperating, even if she wasn't well enough to travel. She seemed as bright as ever when she wrote to her "dear mamma" from her sickbed. The letter was "a model in substance, adherence to grammatical rules, neatness and handwriting," though it pained Mrs. McKenzie to read of Nesta's disappointment at not being able to see her during the holidays.[20]

That correspondence turned out to be their last, for on June 2 a telegram arrived, saying that Nesta had suffered an unexpected relapse and passed away. Grief-stricken, Mrs. McKenzie sent instructions to have the body embalmed and placed in a vault until she could travel to Tacoma later in the summer. There was no need to hurry now, but having not seen her daughter since the previous August, she was determined to say her final farewell in person.

Distance undoubtedly accentuated Mrs. McKenzie's anguish, but death could come for children anywhere and the Klondike had its share of illness and accidents. During the first two years of the gold rush, one of the greatest health threats was typhoid. Poor drainage, dismal sanitation efforts, and crowded living conditions made Dawson a fertile breeding ground for the disease, which reached epidemic levels in the summer of 1898 and returned annually until the early 1900s, when a proper municipal water system was established.

During the early gold rush days, typhoid was the second most common cause of death in the Yukon, surpassed only by accidents. However, uncharacteristically, typhoid mortality was almost exclusively restricted to adults. Although no one realized it at the time, the Klondikers who were at the greatest risk of contracting typhoid were habitués of Dawson's saloons and dancehalls, where tainted water often ended up in the drinks. The exclusion of minors from these establishments may have been why they largely escaped this scourge, even when it was at its peak.[21] According to the territorial death register, none of the one hundred people who died from typhoid between 1898 and 1904 was younger than twenty years old.[22] But Herman Thomas Knabel's death was missed from this list.

Herman, a "very healthy, large and vigorous" baby, was the pride and joy of German bakers Mr. and Mrs. H. Knabel, who also had three older children, all living Outside. When two-month-old Herman fell ill in December 1900, there seemed little cause for alarm at first. On the third day, however, his condition suddenly deteriorated, and within a few hours he was dead, the cause unofficially described as typhoid pneumonia. His funeral was held a few days later in the Knabel home.[23]

⌒

Perhaps because so few children fell sick with typhoid, many people considered the Klondike to be a remarkably salubrious environment for youngsters. "There was little sickness among [the children] and I personally knew of several, who grew stronger and healthier during their stay in Dawson," recalled Lulu Craig in her gold rush memoir.[24]

Writing in the *Yukon Sun* in September 1900, journalist Faith Fenton Brown concurred. "Dawson appears to be a particularly healthy place for children. Numbers of these little people have come in during the past year or two, and their ruddy cheeks and sturdy figures prove their physical appreciation of the climate. They endure the cold remarkably well . . . A sick child in Dawson is rare, and even the babies born in winter thrive and flourish."[25]

Whether or not children were truly healthier in the Klondike than in similar-sized Outside communities isn't clear, but they seem to have fared at least as well as their contemporaries elsewhere and possibly even better. The main difference was in some of the maladies that afflicted them.

Initially food was scarce and expensive in the Klondike, and although fears of mass starvation were never realized, many stampeders suffered from malnutrition and associated afflictions such as scurvy and anemia. Three-year-old Dean Hyde, who "wast[ed] away through lack of nourishment" and died on October 31, 1897,

Winter weather rarely kept Klondike youngsters indoors. Some observers thought the Northern climate improved their health.

may have been the first child to perish due to an inadequate diet.[26] She wasn't the last, though, for even after the general food shortage eased, fresh produce, meat, and milk remained difficult to obtain or were simply beyond the means of some people.

Aside from those who were malnourished because of poverty, the Klondikers who were most apt to eat badly were men who had little experience of cooking for themselves and whose single-minded devotion to getting rich left them with little time or energy for preparing meals. Thanks to the domestic efforts of women, often assisted by their children, the average family ate better than most of their bachelor neighbours.

Emma Anderson, for example, planted lettuce, radishes, and onions on the dirt-covered roof of the family's cabin in springtime and took Ethel, Dewey, and Clay berry-picking in the hills around Eldorado Creek in summer and fall. The barrels they filled with cranberries and blueberries were placed in a deep hole dug into the permafrost outside the cabin door. When the Andersons managed to lay in a stock of fresh apples in 1899, Emma stored them in this makeshift icebox and doled them out over the winter, one to each child every night before bedtime. According to Ethel, they "prolonged the eating, and the going to bed, by thawing the apple a little at a time against the stove."[27]

Arriving in Dawson in 1897, the Barretts experienced the worst of the food shortages, but the children's fall berry-picking efforts ensured that the family avoided scurvy over the winter. When the first boats arrived the following spring, the more vitamin-deprived stampeders were desperate for fresh produce and Florence Junior was amazed to see men on the streets eating raw potatoes like apples. Her own family spent a precious $18 on a dozen eggs, only to find when they cracked them open that eight were rotten.[28]

For nursing mothers and growing children, one of the most serious limitations of the Klondike diet was the scarcity of fresh milk. Dawson's first dairy cow arrived on a barge in 1898, and by the following year the city boasted five dairies. Yet fresh milk remained a luxury for many years, especially out on the creeks. In 1903, when a quart of milk was selling for $20 to $30 in Dawson, the only people on Dominion Creek who owned a cow were a Mr. and Mrs. Thompson. Velma Lung credited their generous sharing of their milk supply with saving her life and possibly that of her youngest son, Paul.[29]

Velma was already in poor health when she gave birth to Paul in January 1903, partly because the family's food cache had been robbed and they had no money to replenish their supplies. In the months following Paul's birth, the strain of caring for a newborn and two young children, as well as cooking for her husband's crew, took its toll on Velma and she grew progressively weaker, until one day she collapsed. Hearing of Velma's plight, Mrs. Thompson immediately sent her a quart of milk, wrapped in straw to keep it from freezing. Early each morning for the next six weeks, a young man arrived at the Lung cabin with another quart and only when Velma's recovery was assured did the deliveries stop.

Two-year-old Ella and eight-year-old Clemy didn't get any of the Thompsons' milk, but they stayed healthy enough on the tinned milk that was their regular fare, as it was for most gold rush children. Like others born in the Klondike, Ella considered sweetened condensed or evaporated milk to be its normal form, though those who remembered life Outside knew otherwise.

Edith Murphy, who crossed Canada by train with her mother and younger siblings to join her father in Grand Forks in 1903, made the astonishing discovery that milk could come from somewhere other than the family cow a few days after leaving Nova Scotia. The revelation was delivered by a fellow passenger—a small, elderly lady who gave Edith's mother part of a can of Borden's condensed milk. Mary mixed the thick, creamy liquid with water and offered it to the children. It was an instant success. Although surprised by its sweetness, seven-year-old Edith decided she liked the new drink, a fortunate verdict since it would be years before she tasted fresh milk again.[30]

Dorothy Whyte was six when she moved to Dawson from Seattle in 1900, and for the next four years the only milk she drank came from a tin. Although she had come from a big city, her father had always kept a dairy cow and she had been used to drinking fresh milk. At the age of ten, her taste for the real thing was revived when she and her mother took a year-long trip to England to visit relatives. Returning to Dawson meant forgoing that pleasure, except on one occasion during her early teens, when she was extremely sick with the flu and "just aching for some milk."[31] Since it was the only nourishment she desired, one of her parents crossed the river and bought a beer bottle full of milk from a West Dawson man who owned one of the area's few cows.

Like Ethel Anderson, Dorothy also ate frozen apples one winter, though not thawed against the stove. Originally destined for a Dawson grocery store, a shipment of apples had become trapped in the middle of the Yukon River when the scow it was on failed to make it to the wharf before freeze-up. Once the river solidified, the unmarketable fruit was offered free for the taking to anyone who wished to harvest it. Dorothy's father collected several boxes of frozen bounty, and her mother baked with the apples all winter long.

Fresh produce of any kind was a rarity in early Dawson, and the first cherries to reach town were sold in "little striped candy bags," a sign of how prized they were. Both the novel fruit and the presentation made a strong impression on Dorothy, who had never seen cherries before.[32]

At the beginning of the gold rush, malnutrition increased the susceptibility of children and adults to disease. By 1900, grocery stores like Avery's were well stocked with a wide variety of foods.

While the effects of a nutritionally deficient diet were not always obvious, the wide range of diseases that made the rounds of the goldfields—and were often exacerbated by malnutrition—could not be ignored. These included cholera, dysentery, tuberculosis, meningitis, scarlet fever, bronchitis, and pneumonia, each of which claimed one or more young lives during the gold rush years. The most incongruous Klondike illness was malaria, though it affected only those who had contracted it before coming north. One of the few children to succumb to malaria was four-year-old Ernest J. Younkins, who died on June 1, 1905.[33]

There were several outbreaks of smallpox during the early 1900s, and although there were no fatalities, the potential for a major epidemic was a worry.[34] In October 1901, alarmed by a spate of smallpox cases in the Klondike, Mary Catherine Miller took her three children—five-year-old Dorothy, three-year-old Bessie, and six-week-old Norman—to spend the winter in Seattle. It turned out to be an unnecessary precaution, however, as a vigorous vaccination campaign in Dawson and on the creeks kept the virus in check. Ironically, Norman caught whooping cough while in Seattle, though by spring he was well enough to make the return trip.[35]

Measles arrived in the Klondike for the first time 1902 and struck again in 1904 and 1908, but claimed no lives. The third outbreak was the worst, afflicting seventy Dawson children and prompting the authorities to close the town's schools for three weeks while they disinfected the classrooms and the sufferers' homes with sulphur fumes.[36]

Some mothers also used sulphur as a preventative measure against contagions of all types. At the least hint of a rampant illness in the neighbourhood, Emma Anderson would call her brood into the cabin two or three times a day to be fumigated. Far from objecting to the regime, the children found it entertaining.

"It became a game," Ethel said. "She would sprinkle sulphur over the top of the hot stove and we, entranced, would watch the writhing, pretty colors. As the blues, yellows, reds and purples twisted in the heat, we breathed in the germ-killing sulphur fumes." The routine was deemed effective, since neither Ethel nor Dewey missed a day of school from the time they began attending in 1899 until the Andersons left the Klondike in 1902. Clay, who was too young to go to school, stayed similarly healthy.[37]

As feared as infectious diseases were in the early years of the gold rush, the leading cause of death was accidents, and children were not spared in this regard. In fact, an accident was responsible for the first recorded child fatality in the Klondike.

On July 8, 1897, Edward Chase of Wisconsin, just one month shy of his four-teenth birthday, died in a mishap that was described as the "accidental sliding of a rock & striking his head & knocking him into the river Yukon."[38] The circumstances of Edward's demise were unusual, but death by drowning was not. With Yukon communities and transportation routes centred on the territory's waterways, it was an all too common end for Klondikers of all ages.

Fourteen-year-old Ada Stewart, who died on July 21, 1900, was another drowning victim. Ada and her mother had left their home in Victoria three weeks earlier and were on their way to Dawson on board the *Florence S* when the sternwheeler flipped over while negotiating a tricky corner on the Thirty Mile section of the Yukon River, north of Lake Laberge. Everyone was tossed into the water, but most managed to swim to shore or cling to pieces of freight until they were rescued. Ada, her mother, and ship steward Walter Monastes were the only casualties.[39]

Seventeen-year-old Monastes, reportedly a strong swimmer, went under while trying to assist some of the passengers. Mrs. Stewart floated downriver for almost a mile before slipping from the grasp of a would-be rescuer, and Ada floundered in full sight of one of the survivors, but beyond his reach. "Miss Stewart . . . was in the river a short distance away," G. L. Alleger recounted, when she "suddenly threw up her arms, and after giving one or two screams, sank and was seen no more."[40] Ada's body was the last to be recovered and was badly decomposed by the time it was found near the mouth of the Big Salmon River in late August. In the meantime, the captain of the *Florence S* was charged with manslaughter for his careless handling of the vessel, a charge later dropped due to lack of evidence.

The Klondike River also claimed several lives, including at least one child's. On October 14, 1900, six-year-old Whyner Hill slipped away from his family's cabin to follow his father to work and drowned when he broke through thin ice as he crossed the Klondike. But swiftly flowing water wasn't the only hazard. On May 2, 1905, three-year-old Herman von Feunier Anderson drowned in a ditch on the corner of Fourth Avenue and Albert Street in Dawson, and on July 8, 1901, eight-year-old Elton McLaren drowned in the slough behind St. Andrew's Presbyterian Church.[41]

On the afternoon of Elton's demise, he and several other boys had been at a children's party given by their Sunday school teacher, Mrs. McRae. After the party, paying no heed to her warnings, they went to the slough and commandeered a rowboat that was tied up there. When it was time for Elton to go home, his friends set him ashore, but instead of climbing the bank and walking across the bridge, he headed for a log that straddled the slough at the opposite end. That was the last anyone saw of him until his body was found four days later near an overturned canoe on the slough.

Another eight-year-old drowning victim was Beatrice Putnam, who died on April 22, 1904, at Number 5 Below on Bonanza Creek. Her father was Levi Putnam, a Nova Scotia seaman who had come to the Klondike several years earlier and had sent for Beatrice and her mother, Bertha, once he was established. Sadly, the goldfields were a place of calamity for Levi and Bertha. A year and a half after they lost Beatrice, their second child was born prematurely at the Good Samaritan Hospital in Dawson and died at birth.[42]

Fire never took as great a toll on Klondikers as water did, but it was an ever-present danger throughout the winter, when wood stoves were often pushed to their limits, and candles and kerosene lamps burned through the long, dark evenings. On at least two occasions, children were whisked out of burning homes just before the cabins were consumed by flames.[43] The Bernsie siblings—eleven-year-old Beatrice and four-year-old George—were not so lucky. The fire that destroyed Aurora Roadhouse No. 3 and killed five people on March 4, 1903, was a ghastly event that shook the Klondike community. It would have been distressing had all the victims been adults. That two of them were children made it heartbreaking.

Charles Bernsie had been in the Klondike for five years when the tragedy occurred. He had arrived from Portland, Oregon, in April 1898, and worked as a cook at various roadhouses. In July 1902 he returned to Oregon to fetch his wife, Florence, and their two children.[44] For a while they lived in a cabin in Dawson. Then, when Charles bought the Aurora No. 3 on Hunker Creek, they moved to the roadhouse.

On the night of the fire, the Bernsies had one guest, a government roadworks foreman named Thomas Baird. At least one miner dropped in to visit, but it was a quiet evening and neither Charles nor Thomas partook of any barroom beverages. At nine o'clock Florence sent Beatrice and George to bed and an hour later she followed them, leaving her husband in charge of a batch of bread that was still in the oven. When it was done, he too retired. A few hours later, an oil tank stove in the barroom exploded.

Around two in the morning one of the neighbours noticed that the roadhouse was on fire. He dashed over and tried to enter the one-storey building by the main door, then through a window in the sleeping quarters that he smashed open. Both times he was forced back by smoke and flames. Thwarted, he ran for help, though with the creek still frozen there was no hope of dousing the fire.

Word of the blaze spread up and down the creek, and scores of men and women converged on the scene, led by the bright glow of the inferno, which lit up the night sky. As the *Yukon Sun* reported the next day, "all the horror-stricken spectators could do was to stand by and witness the awful conflagration. They knew human beings were in the burning building on account of the odor of burning flesh but were absolutely powerless to do anything to help them."[45]

By dawn the fire's fury was spent, and by late afternoon the smouldering ruins had cooled enough that the police could perform their grim duty and remove the badly charred bodies. The two men, who apparently had been overcome by smoke while trying to put out the fire, were found lying on the barroom floor. Florence and the children were in a bedroom, all huddled together in one bed. The investigators were baffled as to why they hadn't escaped out the window, but praised Florence for her heroic attempt "to protect her baby boy from his terrible fate" by hugging him close and sheltering his head with her body. Amazingly, although everyone else was burned beyond recognition, George's face had "escaped the flame and appeared natural even in death."[46]

There was talk of burying all five victims on the claim where the roadhouse had stood, and four graves were dug—one each for the adults and one to be shared by the children—but Florence's close friend Ida A. Butler was determined to give them a "decent Christian burial" on consecrated ground.[47] She undertook a vigorous fundraising effort and soon collected enough donations to purchase coffins and cover other funeral expenses.

At 10 a.m. on Thursday, March 12, the mortal remains of the four Bernsies were transported from the premises of Dawson undertaker George Brimston to St. Mary's Catholic Church, with a large contingent of mourners following behind. Three girls and five boys acted as pallbearers for the children's caskets. At the church, Father Emile Bunoz celebrated a solemn requiem mass for the souls of the deceased. Then the bodies were returned to the funeral parlour to await a letter from distant family members, saying whether they should be laid to rest in Dawson or sent south for burial.[48] Thomas, a Protestant, was buried in the Hillside Public Cemetery.

The question of where to inter those who died in the Klondike was not a simple one. There were several options in Dawson, including St. Mary's Catholic Cemetery and the Hillside Public Cemetery, as well as burial grounds in many of the communities along the creeks. But families that didn't plan to stay in the North indefinitely often preferred to ship the departed back to the place they called home, if they could afford to do so.

When Marie Eldorado Lennon, the first white child born on Eldorado Creek, died from spinal meningitis in October 1906, her parents chose the latter option. Eight years had passed since the creek's residents had celebrated Marie's birth with generous gifts of gold. "Now," the Dawson Daily News reported, "those who remain to hear the sad news are sorrowfully preparing to lay on the bier of the little one their choicest flowers in tender tribute to the memory of one they had learned to love."[49]

At the time of her death, Marie was a student at St. Mary's Catholic School in Dawson. Her classmates—the girls all attired in white—were among the many who attended the funeral at St. Mary's Church. After the service, Marie's embalmed remains were held at Greene's Mortuary while her parents finished making arrangements to leave the Klondike. They had recently sold their claim with the intention of taking their sick daughter Outside for medical treatment. Instead, they would take her to be buried in a place where they could visit her grave as often as they wished. The Lennons were "fixed financially to spend the remainder of [their lives] without hard work," but the hard memories would be with them always.

Mr. and Mrs. Guy Goheen of Hunker Creek also decided against burying their daughter in the Klondike, though it meant a long delay before her interment. After eleven-month-old Guyneata died in May 1902, her parents entrusted her tiny body to Greene's Mortuary for safekeeping and departed for the Tanana goldfields. In the fall of 1903, the Goheens returned to Dawson on one of the last steamers of the season and collected their baby's remains, then continued south to Seattle.[50]

Perhaps the most poignant incident was the inadvertent poisoning of one child as a direct result of his family's quest for riches. On November 12, 1900, Ed Welbon of 27 Below on Sulphur Creek fired up his quicksilver retort. It was standard practice to employ mercury in the final stages of cleaning placer gold. A retort was then used to vaporize the mercury and remove it from the gold. It was a task Ed had probably performed many times before, but this time something went wrong. As he worked, his wife, sister, and ten-month-old son, Willis, who were with him in the cabin, began to feel ill. By the time they realized why, it was too late. All three were terribly sickened by the toxic fumes, baby Willis worst of all. Despite their desperate attempts to save him, he died the next day.

According to the *Klondike Nugget*, "the sad occurrence . . . cast a mantle of gloom over that portion of Sulphur where the Welbon family is very popular. The death of their little boy is a great bereavement not only to his parents but to their many friends."[51] On December 22, some of those friends joined the family at Dawson's Methodist Church for Willis's funeral, which his father paid for with gold dust.[52]

Children's deaths in the Klondike brought deep sorrow to their families, as they did anywhere. The deaths of parents, however, were a double setback and sometimes resulted in greater hardship than they would have if they had happened Outside, where support from nearby relatives and long-time friends was more commonly available. Although Klondikers prided themselves on assisting one another in times of trouble, those who faced misfortune must have longed for the comfort of familiar confidants and helpers.

In late winter in 1898, twenty-three-year-old Jesse L. Edgren and twenty-two-year-old Mae Bennett got married in Wisconsin and set off for the Klondike by way of the Chilkoot Trail. The newlyweds made numerous friends en route and petite Mae, whose "bright, girlish ways would have enabled her to pass for 15 years of age," was especially popular.[53] While they were in Bennett, she participated in several entertainments put on by Captain Jack Crawford, a celebrated journalist, adventurer, and showman, widely known as the Poet Scout.

The Edgrens arrived in Dawson at the peak of the stampede chaos, and in late December, Mae gave birth to a baby girl whom they named Mae Eldorado. Two weeks later, on January 3, 1899, Mae died from typhoid fever, leaving her young husband wondering how to care for his newborn daughter. As the *Klondike Nugget* noted, this was no trifling matter. "The care of an infant in this inhospitable latitude is a most serious undertaking and besides being at least five times the expense of a similar charge in California, will require the unremitting care night and day of at least one individual. What this means in a land where each person's time, whether it be a man or a woman, is worth $10 per day is readily seen."

Nevertheless, "[as] soon as it became known that the little cherub was motherless there were no less than fifteen pairs of open arms extended and fifteen motherly hearts yearned toward the helpless stranger . . . fifteen ladies eager to take and cherish the mite as if it were their own—to adopt it, and mother it."[54]

From these volunteers, Jesse chose Mary Mosher, a homeopathic doctor from Boston, to care for Mae Eldorado. He was not pleased, however, with the *Nugget's* insinuation that he had permanently relinquished his daughter. After he visited the newspaper's office, the editor published a correction, stating that "the generous foster-mother will be required to yield up her charge in the spring and the wee mite will be taken outside to the family."[55]

Touched by Mae Eldorado's plight, the community rallied to help defray the costs of caring for the motherless infant and paying for her passage back to Wisconsin. In mid-April, a benefit billed as "Baby's Night" was held at the Family Theatre. Governor William Ogilvie presided and the acts included the Yukon Male Quartet, a violin soloist, and Captain Jack Crawford reciting "his choice numbers."[56] The latter almost certainly included the memorial poem he wrote after Mae's death. Dedicated to her bereaved father, Captain James Bennett, it began:

> Sweet May is dead, your soldier girl,
>   Your sunny household pet;
> Transplanted from a world of peril,
>   A rose in Eden set.[57]

When the rivers reopened, the baby was delivered to her maternal grandparents, while Jesse stayed in the Klondike. By 1910, Jesse had returned to

A sombre procession conveys Mae Edgren's coffin to the cemetery on January 6, 1899. Mae left a two-week-old daughter behind.

Wisconsin and remarried, and Mae Eldorado was living with him, but her time with her father was short, for he died in 1915.[58]

The Edgrens had both family and community resources to help them through their crisis, but others were less fortunate. The week after the "Baby's Night" benefit, typhoid claimed another young mother, twenty-two-year-old Cyntha Daniels. After considering his options in the weeks following her passing, her husband decided he would have to give up his little son. Mr. and Mrs. John Manning offered to adopt him, and the boy was soon ensconced as "the household idol" in the home of his doting new parents.[59]

Harold Phillip Taylor, the son of Rose and A.J. Taylor, was less fortunate. On February 23, 1904, when he was seven months old, his mother succumbed to blood poisoning after an operation to treat internal injuries caused by a fall. A little over a month later, Harold suffered convulsions and died as well. Whether or not a lack of maternal care after Rose's passing played any role in his death, it was a possibility that must have haunted A.J.[60]

Even when children were safely past babyhood, the consequences of losing a parent during the gold rush were often magnified by the family's separation from kith and kin who normally could have been counted on for emotional and financial support. The Feeros, whose gold-seeking took them no farther than the headwaters of the Yukon River, and the Kingsleys, who settled in the Klondike community of Grand Forks, both experienced this kind of adversity.

Edith Feero was eleven when her father died on the White Pass Trail in December 1898, a year and a half after she and her mother and siblings had come north on the S.S. *Al-ki* to join him. Eighty years later, the harsh way the news was delivered to her family in Skagway in 1898 still upset her. "Mother and us children were in the cabin," she recalled. "And this man walked in and he just walked right up in front of my mother and he said, 'John is dead.' That's all the chance we had. You know how that would take you. And that's the way we got the notice that father was dead. He just walked in and stood in front of mother, and said, 'John is dead.' . . . I can see her in her rockin' chair, and that man come in."[61]

John's death was particularly tragic for his wife, Emma, and their four children because it occurred just as he was preparing to take them back south. Since coming north in the summer of 1897, the Feeros had lived mostly in Skagway, with a summer stay in White Pass City, while John ran a pack train on the White Pass Trail. It was a lucrative business, and for the first time in years, he was able to satisfactorily provide for his family.

During the second winter, competition from the new railway and his need for a hernia operation convinced John it was time to sell up and return to Washington state. All he had to do was make one last trip over the pass to Bennett to settle his business affairs. On his way back, however, he got caught in a snowstorm, and the exertion of battling against it caused his hernia condition to suddenly worsen. When he couldn't go on because of the pain, his companion left him and went for help, but it arrived too late.

It was bad enough that John's death was reported to his family in such a callous manner, but their subsequent discovery that he had been robbed just before or after he expired was an added blow. They learned of the theft through an acquaintance, who was certain that John had been carrying "a lot of money" when he left Bennett. The men who first reached his still-warm body found no sign of this wealth, however, leaving the Feeros deeply suspicious that the man who broke the news to them had pocketed the cash and probably had it in his possession when he came to their cabin.

With their main breadwinner gone and no funds to pay for their passage south, the Feeros' survival depended on a collective effort by every family member. Fifteen-year-old Willie found a position as a hotel bellhop, while Edith and her twin sister, Ethel, did odd jobs for other families before and after school. Their tasks included dishwashing, cooking, baby care, and milk delivery and earned each of them twenty-five cents a week. Emma considered nine-year-old Frank too young to work at first, but before long, he had a job weeding a farmer's garden.

At sixteen, Edith left school and began working in a laundry. With her starting wage of ten cents an hour, she felt rich enough to sometimes splurge on tea and a pastry from a restaurant, a treat that cost her fifteen cents. She worked hard for her money, though, spending her days hefting the heavy bins in which the clothes came to the laundry and shaking out the contents. A promotion to working on the mangle raised her pay to twenty cents an hour, and by the time she was eighteen, she was sorting the clothes for twenty-five cents an hour. Her father's death had dashed all hopes of ever possessing "a stocking full of gold," but his quest had changed the course of her life, bringing her to Skagway, which remained her home until she was in her sixties.[62]

Jack Kingsley's Klondike aspirations separated him from his family for six years and, in son Jim's mind, were ultimately responsible for Mary Kingsley's early death. Nevertheless, the four-year interlude when the whole family lived together in Grand Forks left Jim with more happy memories than sad ones.

In the spring of 1903, Mary, nine-year-old Jim, and eight-year-old Ethel boarded the S.S. *May* in Victoria, bound for Skagway. A couple of weeks later, Jack met them in Dawson. Jim's greatest surprise about the gold rush town was that pennies, nickels, and dimes were useless currency; a quarter was the smallest coin any shopkeeper would accept. He had little time to make other observations, however, for the next day the family carried on to Bonanza Creek, where his father had a road-maintenance contract. The family spent the summer living in a tent at 70 Above on Bonanza Creek, then moved to Grand Forks in the fall after Jack bought a store there.

Jim and Ethel attended school with a couple of dozen other children and quickly made new friends who introduced them to the pleasures and adventures of Northern life. And two years after their arrival, they got a new little brother. Charles Joseph was born in Grand Forks on June 5, 1905. On the day of Charlie's birth, Jim asked his father for time off from work at the store. Permission granted, the excited eleven-year-old raced off to tell the Kingsleys' close friend, a restaurateur named Cockney Joe, that the baby's middle name had been chosen in his honour. That evening, Joe summoned Jim back to his restaurant and presented him with a cake and a pie to take home to the jubilant family.

Unfortunately, sadder times were ahead. Mary's health deteriorated after Charlie's birth and on January 9, 1907, she died of peritonitis at the age of thirty-six. Looking back as an adult, Jim blamed the hardships of living in the North. "The Yukon," he maintained, "was no place for a woman with a baby, especially in the winter." One of the chief difficulties was that water deliveries ceased when the temperature dropped below minus fifty-five Fahrenheit. "We had to dig up the snow and melt it—there was a layer of snow and a layer of soot. We strained the water. You can imagine having to cook for a family, as well as bathing a baby under those conditions."[63]

Some months after Mary was laid to rest in Dawson's Hillside Cemetery, Jack took his two younger children south, leaving Jim to run the store. As planned, he placed twelve-year-old Ethel in a convent in Vancouver, but when it came time to leave eighteen-month-old Charlie in an orphanage, he found himself unable to part with the toddler. Instead, he brought him back to Grand Forks.

When they returned, Jack sent Jim to Victoria, where he had arranged for him to stay with family friends and continue his education. Jim had been a half-hearted scholar in Grand Forks, never passing beyond grade three, and he was no more enthusiastic about classroom learning in his new school. Convinced that it was time to become self-supporting, the fourteen-year-old moved to his grandfather's farm, where he had lived before going to the Klondike, and found

When Mary Kingsley died in Grand Forks in 1907, Jack Kingsley brought his two younger children south but couldn't bear to part with his Klondike-born son, Charlie.

a full-time job nearby. Seeing his beloved mother die and feeling he had been "turned loose" by his father—a man who'd been absent half his life—had made Jim grow up quickly. Happily, his employer's wife, an old friend of Mary's, understood that he was still a child in some ways, and she gave him plenty of maternal care and attention in the following years.

Every child who desires attend *school should be given an* *opportunity to do so without ch*

Chapter 8

The Nice Refinements
of Civilization

Whereas most people who joined the stampede to the Yukon goldfields in the summer of 1897 had only one objective—to make a fortune—a few had loftier goals. Harvard University graduate Mrs. L. C. Howland, who left Seattle on August 17, 1897, was one of the latter. "Indeed I am going to the Klondike," she told a reporter from the *Seattle Daily Times*, "to open a school, in fact, and teach the forty children unfortunate enough to live in Dawson City something besides the way to cook beans with a quantity of fat pork or to pan gravel."

Neatly dressed in a plaid travelling gown and a dark derby, the aspiring schoolmistress spoke to the reporter in her cabin aboard the steamship *Humboldt* on the morning of her departure. "I believe the opening for a school is very good," she said, citing reports of at least forty school-aged children living in Dawson. She had made arrangements already for building a log schoolhouse "with benches and . . . that necessity—a blackboard" and had packed an extensive library of standard textbooks, plus some more advanced volumes, which she hoped would interest "the educated miner."

Although Mrs. Howland was eager to shed the light of learning on young minds, she didn't intend to offer her services for free. "I will charge just as much for tuition as I can get, but that will depend on the condition of affairs at Dawson. If my school plan[s] don't work I have others. One never can tell how one's ideas will materialize."[1]

As it turned out, Mrs. Howland's educational vision didn't materialize at all, and it would be another two years before any school was successfully established in Dawson or on the creeks. In the meantime, the two schooling options for Klondike children were to leave the territory or to study at home.

Being tutored by their mother was nothing new for Monte and Crystal Snow, who arrived in Dawson in the summer of 1897. Having spent most of their lives in

Northern gold rush communities, the only proper classroom they'd ever known had been in Circle City, where a US government school had operated for eight months during the previous winter.[2] The year before that, they had attended classes at the Anglican mission in Forty Mile. The lessons in that school had mainly consisted of singing and praying in Hän, though the girls were also taught to sew and knit. Later, Crystal could "hardly remember learning much besides knitting."[3]

Once the Snow family had settled on their Bonanza Creek claim, Anna continued to teach the children as well as she could, but thirteen-year-old Crystal was beginning to chafe at the limitations of this kind of education. It would be a while before she could satisfy her hunger for learning, since the Snows left the Klondike after one year and didn't put down roots again until 1900, when they moved back to Juneau. There Crystal overcame the embarrassment of starting grade five as a sixteen-year-old and graduated from high school five years later.[4] She lived in Alaska for the rest of her life and, in her fifties, was elected to the territorial House of Representatives.

Emilie Craig had the advantage of having her schoolteacher aunt on hand to help her with her lessons during her year in the Klondike, though Lulu would have liked to have done more than tutor just her niece. Within a month of arriving in Dawson in the summer of 1898, she had made arrangements to operate a private school in the Anglican church. "Miss Craig comes highly recommended and her school will doubtless prove a success," observed the *Klondike Nugget* shortly before the scheduled opening on Monday, August 29,[5] but that confident prediction was not borne out. By late November the school had closed, presumably because there weren't enough paying pupils to keep it going.[6] In her gold rush memoir, Lulu made only one veiled reference to this attempt, saying that it "was greatly to be deplored that there was no school in Dawson, at least no public school and as far as I knew no successful private one."[7]

While the *Nugget*'s editors supported Lulu Craig's efforts and believed "private schools . . . should be encouraged by every possible means," they also maintained "that the community at large owes it to itself to see that every child who desires attending school should be given an opportunity to do so without charge."[8] In November 1898 the newspaper estimated that there were "not more than 75 children of school age in the city who would attend," but insisted that "these should be taken care of as though their numbers were ten times as large."[9] Due to various political obstacles and a disagreement between Dawson's Catholic and Protestant clergymen as to whether the town's educational system should be divided along religious lines, it would be another year before the Klondike got its first public school.

On November 6, 1899, Father P. E. Gendreau launched St. Mary's School, which he vowed was "public in every sense of the word,"[10] despite being located

CLOSING DAY. ST MARY'S SCHOOL JUNE 28TH 1905 DAWSON Y.T. PHOTO BY PEPIN

St. Mary's School, opened in November 1899, was the Klondike's first public school. In 1904 it relocated to this new, two-storey building in the centre of town.

next to the Catholic church and staffed by a nun. There would be no tuition fees, he noted, and no religious instruction. Sister Mary Joseph Calasanctius, whom Gendreau had chosen as the first teacher, was surprised when he told her she mustn't lead the students in prayer or even make the Sign of the Cross, but she accepted these restrictions when he explained that he wanted the school to be open to all children, regardless of their faith—and that government funding depended on the school being strictly secular. She was also reassured to know that he would come in daily after classes and teach catechism to the Catholic children.[11]

On opening day St. Mary's drew eighteen "neat little scholars," ten boys and eight girls from eleven families, not all of them Catholic, and within weeks all thirty classroom desks were filled. With little in the way of supplies—four or five readers, a few arithmetic books, and some pencils and paper, but no chalk for the blackboard—and students ranging in age from six to fourteen, Sister Mary Joseph had her work cut out for her. However, she found the children "bright" and "full of good will" and may have welcomed the change from labouring in the overcrowded wards of St. Mary's Hospital. In February a young Catholic woman named Mamie Connor was hired as a much-needed assistant. By the end of the school year the two were teaching fifty-three students.[12]

In addition to St. Mary's, at least one small private school operated in Dawson in 1899.[13] Still, the majority of the town's children continued to study at home or not at all, a situation that few parents found satisfactory. In March 1900 the territorial government finally yielded to persistent pressure from the community and announced that it would open a public school the following fall, provided a suitable building could be found.

In late August, still not certain how many students would have to be accommodated, the territorial commissioner asked the North-West Mounted Police to conduct a census of Dawson children aged seven and up. The results showed that there were 175 children in town, of whom 137 were Protestant, 34 were Roman Catholic, and 4 were Jewish. The gender split was also far from equal, with the 106 boys greatly outnumbering the 69 girls.[14]

When Dawson Public School opened in mid-September under the direction of teacher George McKenzie, it had fifty-seven intermediate-level pupils. The introduction of a kindergarten and primary classes in October added another fifty-four, and twenty-six advanced students joined the student body in January. By the end of the school year, total enrolment had reached 175, exactly the number of children the NWMP had counted in August.[15] There had been no drop in enrolment at St. Mary's, however, suggesting that the last boats to reach Dawson before freeze-up and the first spring arrivals of 1901 had brought in a significant number of children.

Like Sister Mary Joseph, George and his fellow teachers were hampered by a dearth of textbooks and supplies. They were also challenged by the lack of consistency in the standards of the many provinces and states where their pupils had begun their education. This made it difficult to decide at what grade level to place each incoming student, other than the absolute beginners.[16]

Dawson Public School initially operated out of two rooms in a hall leased from the Odd Fellows and the Masons, but when more space was required, additional rooms were rented in the Salvation Army hall and the Methodist church. The completion of a permanent school building in the fall of 1901 was cause for celebration by students and teachers alike, despite being six weeks behind schedule. A handsome, two-storey frame building with large windows and a gracefully arched entranceway, it had four classrooms on each floor. The new school opened on October 14, with an enrolment of 197 pupils, distributed between kindergarten and grade nine and under the tutelage of 5 teachers.[17]

Meanwhile, there was also a growing demand for schools out in the goldfields. Grand Forks, the largest community on the creeks, was the first to get government support, after its residents sent the territorial commissioner a petition stating that there were twenty-five children between the ages of six and sixteen living within a two-mile radius of the town. Grand Forks School, also known as Bonanza School,

Built in 1901, Dawson Public School was one of the town's most prominent landmarks for many years.

opened on November 12, 1900, with the Presbyterian church as a schoolhouse and Adah Lind in charge of twenty-two pupils in grades one to four.[18]

Adah, who held an Ontario teaching certificate, had come to the Klondike in 1899 to visit her sister and brother-in-law on Eldorado Creek and decided to stay after her summer vacation ended. That fall, much to the delight of Ethel and Dewey Anderson and about fifteen other local children—or at least their parents—she began holding classes in a makeshift "tent schoolhouse warmed by a big pot-bellied stove."[19] A popular teacher, she easily won the job when she applied to become Grand Forks' first official schoolmistress the following year.

By December 1902 the government had opened public schools at five additional locations: Caribou City on Dominion Creek, Gold Bottom at the junction of Gold Bottom and Hunker creeks, 30 Below on Bonanza Creek, and the communities of Gold Run and Bear Creek. The six creek schools, including the one in Grand Forks, had a total enrolment of 92 pupils, while Dawson Public School had 260 and St. Mary's had 58.[20] Not only was the number of students growing annually, but unlike in more established communities elsewhere, there were many new faces every year. Of the 178 children who showed up on August 25, 1902,

The teacher and students of Gold Bottom School in 1903. The only one identified is Meta Miller (second from right).

to register for Dawson Public School, 71 were fresh recruits, presenting teachers with the familiar conundrum of trying to determine what grades they belonged in.[21]

The government considered at least five requests for public schools at other locations on the creeks in 1903 but rejected most of them on the grounds that there weren't enough potential students to justify the expense. One of the requests came from Sulphur Creek, where the residents had started their own school in 1902. Although only ten school-aged children were identified, the government, for reasons that have gone unrecorded, agreed to their request. In November 1903 Sulphur Creek Public School began operating in rented premises at Number 23 Above Discovery. By the next year it boasted twenty-one pupils. Unfortunately, the household noises of the family that lived in an adjacent room carried easily through the walls and the building was so close to the road that passing vehicles constantly distracted the students. Nevertheless, the school inspector commended the teacher, Miss McNeil, for her "earnest and faithful work" and the children for their "good attitude toward their studies."[22]

Like Miss McNeil, most of the teachers who were hired to work on the creeks did earnest and faithful work despite their schools' shortcomings and were well liked by their pupils, but their classes grew smaller as the new century unfolded. Since the peak of the gold rush, the population of the creek communities had been declining steadily as the early Klondikers moved on to new goldfields in Alaska or returned home. Newcomers continued to arrive, but not at the same rate as those departing.

When William Murphy brought his family out from Nova Scotia to join him in 1903, they initially lived in Grand Forks. Their home was close to the school but seven-year-old Edith was the only one of the four Murphy children old enough to attend. Then, in early April 1905, the family relocated to Nugget Hill, overlooking Hunker Creek, where William and a couple of partners had begun working a new claim.

On moving day a sleigh drawn by a team of two horses came to the Murphys' cabin and all their household possessions were piled onto it. Once the older children were settled on top of the load, Mary Murphy took a seat beside the teamster, holding the latest addition to the family, eight-month-old Charles, on her lap. It took a day and half to reach their new home, and Edith was fascinated by their overnight stop at Hubrick's Roadhouse, where their bedroom had a blanket for a door and they listened to miners fraternizing down the hall until the bar closed at midnight.

The school nearest to the claim, located at Gold Bottom on Hunker Creek, was too far away for the children to walk to, so the Murphys' stay on Nugget Hill was only temporary. That fall they moved to Dawson and the four older children were enrolled in the public school.[23] Since Dawson Public School was the only one in the Yukon with a kindergarten, the move had the added advantage of letting five-year-old Hilda start school a year earlier than she could have if they'd remained on the creeks.[24]

Miss Edwards and the students of Dawson Public School's first kindergarten class in 1901.

Hilda's teacher, Miss Wilson, was highly regarded by the Yukon schools superintendent, who praised her ability to "win the affection of the children and inspire them with the idea that all the games and work that they do are suggested by themselves." Under Miss Wilson's "tactful, energetic" guidance, Hilda and her thirty-four classmates learned to "sing the kindergarten songs, march to the music, . . . observe the conditions of weather and nature," count, sew, and weave. They were also taught "self-control and their duty and conduct to the other children in their class."[25]

Concern about falling enrolment was common to all the creek communities and emerged almost as soon as the schools were opened. In May 1903 the *Yukon Sun*'s Bear Creek correspondent reported that "parents on the creek are feeling a little worried at the departure of so many children off the creek. Within the last few weeks six have gone away and it means that the public school here looks like being closed, as at present only three children are attending, and I hear one of them in two weeks will be leaving for another creek. Although there are many families here with little ones . . . they are not old enough for school just yet."[26]

Sure enough, in 1904 Bear Creek's little log schoolhouse ceased to be a place of learning. By then, Sulphur Creek School's enrolment was down to nine students, and in 1905 it closed as well. In 1906 those creek schools still operating were given a new status as "assisted" schools and their funding was reduced, with the expectation that parents would share their running costs. The introduction of the assisted option allowed some previously neglected communities, such as Quartz Creek, to have schools for the first time, but there was little certainty about their long-term prospects. Teachers at assisted schools were hired on a month-to-month basis and their salaries varied according to enrolment. If attendance dropped below six pupils, they didn't get paid at all.[27]

Although Dawson's population was also dwindling during this period, its schools were thriving. More and more families were moving to town, either from the creeks or from Outside, and babies born locally in the early years of the gold rush were starting to reach kindergarten age. Both of the town's schools were forced to turn away prospective students, much to the frustration of parents like Mrs. Sharts.

One afternoon in late May 1902, six-year-old Robert Lee Sharts and several friends were playing on some scows that were tied up along the bank of the Yukon River. With a single misstep, Robert suddenly toppled into the river's icy waters, but before the current could sweep him away, he managed to grab a rope, which he held onto tenaciously until a rescuer arrived and pulled him out, "none the worse for his adventure save a good ducking and possibly the worst scare he [had] had during his short lifetime."[28]

Once she recovered from the shock of almost losing her son, Mrs. Sharts, owner of the Atlin Laundry, was quick to deflect any blame for letting him play in such a hazardous place. She'd repeatedly warned her children not to go to the river, she said, but it was an irresistible draw and her business was so demanding that she couldn't keep an eye on them all the time. The real problem, in her opinion, was that her application to get them into Dawson Public School, where they would be kept out of mischief during the day, had been refused.

Ella Card had better luck placing her son in the public school, but only after the US consul intervened on her behalf. After burying their firstborn child beside Lake Lindeman in the spring of 1897, Ella and Fred Card had continued on to the Klondike and welcomed their second child in July 1898. Over the years, they owned various businesses, including a restaurant in Dawson and a roadhouse on Upper Dominion Creek.[29] By the time Fred Junior reached school age, in 1903, Ella was the proprietor of Dawson's Hotel Cecil.[30] Like Mrs. Sharts, she was eager to enrol her son in the public school, but was told there was no room for him.

Unwilling to take no for an answer, Ella somehow got the ear of the consul, who in turn spoke to the territorial commissioner and soon received a letter back from him. "Mrs. Card's little boy . . . will be admitted to the kindergarten at the commencement of the Easter Term about two weeks hence," the commissioner wrote. "The room is crowded to its full extent at present and we have had to turn several applicants away, but in view of the fact that Mrs. Card applied some time ago we will give her preference over others who have only lately come in with their children."[31]

Excited students pour out of Dawson Public School on their way to the Victoria Day parade, May 24, 1904.

A couple of months after his academic debut, five-year-old Fred embarked on a much bigger adventure, heading off to Paris in the care of Dawson ladies' wear importer Mrs. Robert Hutcheon on one of her annual buying trips. As to why he was going to Europe with Mrs. Hutcheon but without his parents, the *Yukon Sun* offered no explanation.[32]

The demand on Dawson Public School's facilities wasn't limited to the lower grades, however. In 1903, high school classes were offered for the first time, with five students enrolled in the inaugural standard VI class, and in 1904, one of the school's classrooms was converted to a chemistry and physics laboratory. For many years after their introduction, the senior grades were the domain of male teachers. According to one former student, Dawson's high school teachers "had to be men of physical vigor to cope with the student body which came from an extremely mixed population and was inclined to be unruly."[33]

In 1904, facing the same enrolment pressures as the public school, St. Mary's relocated to a new two-storey building in the centre of town. This was a more convenient location for most of the sixty pupils, though not for the teaching sisters, who had lived practically next door to the original school. The upper floor of the new building was a parish chapel, while the school occupied the ground floor, offering two classrooms, a recreation room, and a music room.[34]

Those in charge of running the Klondike's schools tried to adhere to Southern standards as much as possible, but Northern geography and lifestyles required them to be more flexible in their scheduling. In December 1901 Dawson's schools "very sensibly delayed the hour of opening in the morning until semi-daylight arrives." The later morning start—9:30 at St. Mary's and 10:00 at the public school—meant it was no longer necessary for "the little tots . . . to carry lanterns to light them to school."[35] Dark classrooms lit only by oil lamps were also a problem, forcing classes to end at 2:00 p.m. After electric lighting was installed in Dawson Public School during the summer of 1902, the winter opening time was shifted forward to 9:30 and classes ran later into the afternoon. In fall and spring, classes started at 9:00 and ended in the mid-afternoon.[36]

School officials also ran into unexpected problems with the timing of the school year. "One of the most discouraging features of school affairs in Dawson," noted the *Yukon Sun* in June 1903, "is the practice of parents of withdrawing their children to take them outside or on the creeks during the last two or three weeks of school. This interferes with grading to a marked extent."[37]

A few weeks later the newspaper reported that there had been far fewer early withdrawals that year than in the past and that the change was "considered a good sign by the teachers as it indicates that the people here are beginning to conform themselves to ideas of permanent residence, doing everything they can to give their children a good education."[38] Nevertheless, the mid-August date for reconvening classes remained an issue, with many parents arguing that it should be shifted to later in the fall to accommodate family trips out of the territory.[39]

The creek schools faced both these problems, as well as a few that were unique to their location. In winter they were sometimes closed for anywhere from a day to several weeks because of the difficulty of heating poorly built schoolhouses and because severe winter weather posed a hazard for children who travelled long distances along the creeks to get to school. Temporary closures were also sometimes required in spring, when the trails became practically impassable. As a result, summer vacation was typically reduced to a few weeks in July.

In 1903 the government built a new schoolhouse in Grand Forks, but the green lumber from which it was constructed shrank as it dried and the building became draftier with every passing year. By the winter of 1906–07 the situation had become so intolerable that the school was closed for all of December and January. To make up for the lost time, classes were held right through the following summer, but the number of empty desks increased with every week as more and more families moved away. At the beginning of the 1906 school year, Grand Forks had had twenty-six pupils. By September 1907 there were only five, prompting the government to close the school.[40]

The few parents still living on Bonanza and Eldorado creeks begged the territorial commissioner to reconsider the closure. Their petition, sent that November, stated: "We cannot afford the expense of sending our children, and boarding them in Dawson, besides the great dangers, associate[d] with the fact, that they are not with us, but of necessity in the care of strangers." Among the children whose parents signed the petition were Jim and Ethel Kingsley and ten-year-old Teslin Hunter—Tessie to her friends—who was famous locally for having been born at Teslin Lake while her parents were en route to the Klondike.[41]

Although questioning why just five children had been showing up for school if there were ten who were eligible and eager to learn, as the parents claimed, the government agreed to reopen Grand Forks School in February 1908, after the worst of the winter cold was over, though only on an assisted basis. Whether it stayed open would depend on whether it could maintain the minimum number of pupils. After Jim and Ethel's mother died that January, shortly before classes recommenced, the school's precarious position may have influenced their father's decision to send them south in the spring. The loss of two more students did not bode well for the school, but it hung on for about another decade.[42]

When Grand Forks School had first opened in 1900, it immediately became apparent that no one had made plans for accommodating the dogs that provided essential transport for several of the students.[43] A shelter was promptly built to protect them from the elements during the day, and from then until the last creek schools closed, going to and from school by dogsled was standard practice for many Klondike children.

Victoria Faulkner was well accustomed to dogsled travel by the time she turned seven in 1904 and started attending school in the little settlement known as Last Chance at the junction of Hunker and Last Chance creeks. Her father had joined the stampede in 1897, just months after she was born in Tacoma, and she and her mother had come to the Klondike in 1901. John and Bella Faulkner and their four-year-old daughter spent that winter on Sulphur Creek, then moved to Hunker Creek the next spring.

The Faulkners' log cabin was three miles from Last Chance, and when there was no snow on the ground, the long daily trek between home and school was either dusty or muddy. Come winter, however, Victoria flew over the snowy trails in a sled pulled by two of her father's dogs and her own personal pet. She often picked up other students along the way. To combat the cold, Victoria wore felt boots, a fur-lined coat, and wool clothing, including one-piece undergarments known as union suits. The rule in her family was that "wool union suits . . . went on with the first frost."[44]

In 1907 Victoria traded her one-room log schoolhouse for the relative opulence of St. Mary's Catholic School in Dawson. There were many advantages to this move, including learning to play the church organ and to speak French, but it meant being away from her parents and her sister, Mary, who had been born in 1902. Victoria initially boarded with the Sisters of St. Ann, returning to her family on weekends and during school holidays. Then, in 1913, her parents and Mary moved to Dawson.[45]

A dogsled was still the most practical means of transportation up and down the creeks when the Murray family moved from Dawson to Number 26 Eldorado around 1911. In fall and spring, nine-year-old Irene Murray and her six-year-old sister, Grace, walked to Grand Forks to attend school. In winter they went by dogsled, with either their mother or Irene driving.

The Murrays' move to Eldorado Creek increased the number of names on the school roster to about a dozen and most likely pleased the other students, especially the girls. Children on the creeks inhabited a predominantly adult world and any newcomer was a potential friend. Despite the difference in their ages, one of Grace's favourite schoolmates was Teslin Hunter. Grace "loved going to her place," not only because Teslin "was so nice," but also because "she had a wonderful playhouse and lots of toys."[46]

Many Klondike children, especially those who lived on the creeks, became skilled mushers at an early age.

On Dominion Creek in wintertime Clemy Lung ran out to the government road every morning, tin lunch pail in hand, to catch the "sleigh-bus" to school in Caribou City.[47] If this service hadn't been available, he would probably have made the three-mile trip independently, for he was already learning to mush by the time he started school. To his mother's dismay, however, his time in the Klondike had also taught him some less desirable lessons. Velma discovered one of her son's new skills as they were returning home by dogsled one afternoon after visiting a friend. She and baby Ella were nestled in the sled. Seven-year-old Clemy, dressed in his usual winter outfit of a parka, wool mittens, and a red stocking cap, stood behind them on the runners.

What began as a pleasant ride suddenly exploded into chaos when a rabbit darted across the trail in front of them and the dogs took chase. Clemy and Velma screamed at them to stop, but to no avail. In wild pursuit, the team raced through the woods at full speed until the sled hit a rock and was brought to an abrupt halt. Ella flew from her mother's arms and landed headfirst in a snowbank, while Velma "was thrown just barely clear of the sleigh, landing under an avalanche of wadded diapers, wet snow, and yapping, quivering dogs."

Clemy quickly located his little sister, extracted her, and propped her up in the snow, then returned to the sled to try to help his mother free herself from the "awful, tangled mess of harnesses, dogs and everything else," but the more she struggled, the worse things got. Ella began to wail. Velma felt herself getting hysterical with desperation and fear that the dogs, who had not yet given up on catching their quarry, might "go completely savage." Clemy burst into tears. However, he kept pulling and tugging at the harness and even kicking the dogs, though they paid no heed.

"Then, all at once Clemy straightened. He rushed to the head of that frenzied heap of dogs and let loose torrents of terrible oaths that were indeed shocking to hear! His words were so bad they would have done credit to a profane old Sourdough." While Velma was speechless, "the effect of those impassioned, unprintable words was electric. To [her] amazement the dogs immediately calmed. Obediently forgetting the rabbit, they quietly let Clemy untangle them—and [her]—and right the sled. Actually, the animals appeared ashamed and as meek as lambs!"

As relieved as Velma was, she couldn't help wondering what her mother and friends in Tacoma would think if they ever heard her son using such vulgar language. That evening her husband, Ed, assured her that Clemy would refrain from using his new vocabulary when they returned south, but she was dubious.

That was not the last time Velma would question the effect of a Klondike upbringing on her children. In 1904 the family moved to a new claim and started taking their meals in the mess hall along with the labourers who worked for Ed. Though elated to be relieved of her cooking duties, Velma was appalled by the miners' eating habits and their effect on her son. "Clemy watched them with such admiration, aping their every mannerism! These Sourdoughs were absolutely perfect in his young eyes. They were his adored heroes and before I knew it he, too, was inhaling his soup and grabbing and snatching his food and loudly wolfing it down; also drinking out of his saucer, just the way they did."

Velma recognized that the men were of many nationalities "and with each nationality there was, no doubt, a wide difference in concept of table etiquette," but also despaired that "in the North, it seemed so very easy to slip away from the nice refinements of civilization and just go primitive!" Not wanting to raise a boor, she did her best to correct Clemy's sourdough table manners, though she tactfully abstained from rebuking him in front of the miners. Finally, when it became clear she was fighting a losing battle, the family went back to eating dinners in their cabin, a decision that greatly disappointed Clemy. Velma also laid down the law when she caught Clemy chewing a plug of tobacco in imitation of his idols, but she got no argument from him in that case, as the experiment left him feeling extremely ill.

In Dawson, concerns about the coarser elements of society and their effect on the town's youth were raised early on. In November 1899, a *Klondike Nugget* editorial denounced local tobacconists who were selling cigarettes to boys of twelve and under, in blatant disregard for the Canadian law prohibiting this practice. A "large measure of license" had been all very well when "these northern camps were made up exclusively of grown men and a few grown women," but times had changed. "We have a juvenile population growing up in our midst," the editors protested, and their presence called for "the restraints imposed in civilized communities."

The *Nugget* investigated the situation after "complaints from mothers . . . poured in." It determined that minors were unable to buy liquor because no dealer wanted to risk losing his licence, but "tobacco dealers [were] supplying young lads with tobacco and cigarettes in quantities only limited by the financial ability of the boys to purchase. The fumes of the demoralizing cigarette are seen rising from any gathering of boys one happens to run across, while the pale lips and sallow cheeks of many of the boys bespeak the devotee. Undoubtedly the mothers have not been far deceived and their complaints are well founded."

Since so many tobacconists seemed willing to flout the law, the newspaper urged local authorities to create a special ordinance carrying a heavy fine, arguing that "we [owe] this much to our growing metropolitan proportions and dignity." The police, however, probably felt there were more pressing issues of public order to be attended to first.[48]

Respectable Klondikers frowned on men who set bad examples for youngsters by cursing, selling them cigarettes, or appearing in public when drunk, and they took an even dimmer view of prostitutes and dancehall girls. The presence of these scarlet women couldn't be entirely ignored, but parents made every effort to ensure their offspring wouldn't be tainted by their immorality. The children, on the other hand, were invariably intrigued by them.

The Anderson children had their first encounter with a member of the demimonde on board the sternwheeler that carried them and their mother to Dawson in the fall of 1898. Five-year-old Ethel liked "the pretty lady" and thought she "smelled so nice," but her mother would have nothing to do with the woman and criticized her for laughing and joking with the male passengers and crew.[49]

When Ethel Russell moved to the Klondike at about age ten, she too saw "pretty ladies" in action, despite her mother's efforts to shield her from such sights. The Russells came to Grand Forks from Whitehorse around 1902, after Ethel's father, James, purchased the Vendome Hotel. James didn't tell his wife that the previous occupant of their cabin had been a prostitute, but he couldn't keep that information secret for long. In the middle of their first night in their new home, the Russells were awakened by a severely inebriated man pounding on the door and demanding to be let in for what was clearly not a genteel social visit. It took James a while to convince the caller he wasn't welcome and even longer to calm his distraught wife.[50]

The women who lived across the street from the Russells were of the same ilk as the cabin's former tenant. Ethel was completely ignorant of their profession, though she knew her father disapproved of the women coming to their house and that her mother didn't like her talking to them. What Ethel noticed about them was that "they were always so pretty and they had silk drapes in their windows. I was fascinated by all that silk."[51]

When her mother was needed at the hotel, Ethel looked after her younger siblings, often sitting in their cabin doorway with her little brother and sister on her lap. Since her mother wasn't there to see her, she could cheerfully exchange waves and greetings with her glamorous neighbours. Impressed by her helpfulness, or perhaps touched by her friendliness, some of the prostitutes wrote her mother a note asking if they could give Ethel a dress as a reward for being so good. In recounting the incident years later, Ethel didn't say whether her mother gave her approval.[52]

In the creek communities, families had little choice about living in close proximity to women of ill repute. This situation benefited the children of Grand Forks, who received discreetly delivered gifts from the town's prostitutes every Christmas. In Dawson, however, prostitutes were confined to a precisely defined red-light district as early as 1899. By 1904, when Ethel Russell and her younger siblings began attending St. Mary's School, those engaged in the sex trade were banned from living or working within the Dawson City limits and most had relocated to Klondike City, more commonly known as Lousetown. This residency rule, imposed in May 1901, was the last in a series of restrictions that had gradually limited the prostitutes' freedom to operate wherever and however they chose, with the protection of impressionable youngsters being one of the major justifications for the constraints.[53]

But banishing the scarlet women to the far side of the Klondike River wasn't enough to keep children from consorting with them. Like most of their peers, Dorothy and Bessie Miller were "absolutely forbidden" to go to Lousetown, which made sneaking across the bridge all the more enticing. The Miller sisters were no more than ten or eleven years old when curiosity finally trumped obedience and they made the first of numerous excursions to the prohibited zone. The women of Lousetown, whose professions kept them mostly isolated from children, made a great fuss over their young visitors.

Bessie and Dorothy soon came to regard the "fancy ladies" as friends, but they would also learn that such friendships could exist only on one side of the Klondike River. One day the girls met a couple of the Lousetown residents on the street in Dawson, "beautifully dressed and swishing along," and rushed up to greet them, only to be completely ignored. Hurt and puzzled—not understanding that the women were protecting them from public censure—the sisters watched them walk away. "I thought they were so beautiful,". Bessie later recalled. "I loved their clothes. I wondered why my mother didn't wear roses in her hair."

Despite being rebuffed on that occasion, Bessie and Dorothy continued to visit Lousetown. The women always welcomed them and plied them with treats, the best of these being oranges, which the girls devoured "skin and all." One day their friends gave each of them a little gold ring—a thin wire holding a single nugget for Bessie and a band with three nuggets for Dorothy. The girls were awed by these tokens of affection, but knew at once that it would be impossible to account for them when they got home. So, as they walked back across the bridge to Dawson, they reluctantly slipped the rings from their fingers and flung them into the Klondike River. Eighty years later, Bessie could still feel the pain of parting with such a precious and lovely gift.[54]

In Grand Forks, the Kingsley family lived right next door to a brothel. Perhaps because Jim was a boy, his parents seemed unconcerned about him associating with prostitutes. In fact, Jim's shopkeeper father often asked him to deliver merchandise to the red-light district. This wasn't much different from delivering orders of cigars, tobacco, and snuff to miners gambling in the town's hotels, except that in addition to giving him fifty-cent tips, the women always wanted to kiss him. Jim was happy enough to pocket the tips but "didn't like the kissing part."

His tolerance for this ritual was eventually stretched to the limit by "a coloured lady called Aunt Dolly who chewed tobacco [and] was the janitor for several of the hotels." One day, Aunt Dolly stopped to talk with Jim after meeting him on the street. He was politely enduring the conversation when she suddenly leaned over and kissed him. He responded immediately and instinctively by punching her in the stomach.

When Jack heard about the incident, he delivered the "one and only thrashing" he ever gave his son and demanded that he apologize to Aunt Dolly. Unharmed by the blow, she readily forgave him and the two "were great friends after that," but not everyone thought Jim had been in the wrong. "The affair nearly caused a riot at the time," Jim later wrote, "with great debates over whether I had the right to hit a woman who kissed me without a by-your-leave!"[55]

Bad influences may have been more prevalent in the Klondike than elsewhere, as some moralists maintained, but there were plenty of good ones to offset them, even at the height of the gold rush. Emilie Craig's parents and her Aunt Lulu, for example, mainly mixed with individuals who were not unlike their friends back in Colorado and Missouri. Social gatherings at their cabin, quaintly named the Birch Snuggery, featured erudite discussions and the music of violins, mandolins, guitars, and banjos. "We passed the time these long winter evenings in music and conversation on Art and Literature and the current topics of the day—or at least as far as we knew them," Lulu wrote. "The gentlemen brought their instruments with them and we all joined in the merry songs that resounded in our northern home."[56]

On the trail, Emilie's exposure to a much more varied array of humanity than she was used to had been an eye-opener and a lesson in tolerance and understanding. Lulu recalled that

> Day after day we were constantly thrown with men of all nationalities and all classes—men of all profession and of all trades—men of culture and education, as well as those of the ignorant, unrefined classes—men of baser natures, whose faces only too plainly told the tale of their evil lives. Yet by one and all were we most courteously treated and to all with whom we found it necessary to mingle, did we endeavor to give the kindly greeting that good breeding would always urge one to do, no matter to what class or station of life he might belong.[57]

The Reverend R. W. Hibbert was among those who considered the cultural diversity of the goldfields to be one of the advantages of a Klondike childhood. He observed that

> In addition to school work, the young people receive a broader education from contact with their older friends, among whom are men from all points of the compass. Since this circle of older companions embraces members of different nationalities, and customs, the young lad early learns the uselessness of national prejudice and imbibes his first lessons regarding the brotherhood of man. He listens to their stories, he studies their habits of thought, and by this contact with representatives of the different parts of the world, he prepares himself as a man of the world, even though the place of preparation be in a locality geographically retired.[58]

Just how cosmopolitan the goldfields were was confirmed in 1901 by the first federal census conducted after the start of the stampede. Although about forty percent of those residing in the Klondike in 1901 had been born in the United States and twenty-seven percent in Canada, the rest hailed from almost every corner of the earth. A majority of the latter group claimed either the British Isles or continental Europe as their birthplace, with most of the Europeans coming from one of the Scandinavian countries or Germany. Other places of origin included Australia, New Zealand, China, Japan, Brazil, Costa Rica, Mexico, the West Indies, Egypt, Palestine, Turkey, and Iceland. Many of the émigrés had lived in the United States or southern Canada for some time before the eruption of Klondike fever, but retained strong ties to their native lands.[59]

Klondike children were more likely than their parents to have been born in North America, but they were far from homogeneous in their mother tongues and the cultural traditions they followed. Hilja and Olga Ainaly, for example, had been born in South Dakota, while their younger sisters, Lili and Katri, were true Yukoners. All four learned Finnish from their immigrant parents, Abraham and Annie, but spoke English outside their home.

Abraham joined the gold rush in 1897 and started out working for another Finnish prospector on Bear Creek. Annie, four-year-old Hilja, and three-year-old Olga followed him north in 1898, and by 1901 the family had moved to 17 Below on Upper Dominion Creek. Other children living on Upper or Middle Dominion at that time included Danish sisters Neta and Mary Ann Nelson, age ten and four respectively; twelve-year-old Leon Very, who had come to the Klondike from France with his parents in 1898 and now had a one-year-old brother; Ralph Shoblad, the infant son of two Swedish-Americans; sixteen-year-old Alexander Smith, born in Wisconsin to a Canadian father and a German mother; Belgium native Aimee Gatin, age fourteen, and her three Canadian-born younger siblings; seven-year-old Mary Rendall, born in British Columbia to Scottish-Canadian parents; and a handful of other Americans and Canadians from half a dozen different states and provinces.[60]

Farther down Dominion Creek, around Number 7 Below Lower Discovery, was a small community known as Paris because most of its residents were francophones from Quebec and Europe, and the postmaster had been born in Paris, France. Children who lived in the Klondike's Paris spoke French with their families and neighbours and English at school in Caribou City. Events held at Paris's community hall, such as the annual children's Christmas concert, featured a medley of both languages.

There was also a close-knit francophone community in Dawson, which played an important role in the lives of Quebecois families like the Pepins. When Gédéon Pepin and his seven friends arrived in the Klondike in 1901, only he and one other member of the party spoke passable English. Gédéon initially found a labouring job at a mine on Dominion Creek, but a month later he eagerly traded it for the position of organist and gravedigger for St. Mary's Catholic Church. The young musician, a family man at heart, was desperately lonely for his wife and daughters and determined to save enough money to bring them to Dawson. It was a joyful day for him when Merilda arrived with four-year-old Imelda and two-year-old Blanche in the summer of 1903. Josette Marie Annette Pepin was born the following June and Marie Cecile Lumina joined the family in May 1906.

The Pepins and other transplanted French Canadians visited each other frequently and celebrated traditional holidays together. St. Jean-Baptiste Day in June was usually marked by a boat excursion to Moosehide or to an island in the Yukon River that was owned by the Sisters of St. Ann. These daylong outings featured elaborate picnics and were attended by two hundred to three hundred people.

When Merilda became ill in the winter of 1909 and then passed away on March 2, the French-Canadian community rallied around the Pepins. With a full-time job in the gold commissioner's office, Gédéon could not take care of his four daughters, so Sister Mary Zenon, the Superior of the Sisters of St. Ann, escorted Imelda and Blanche to a boarding school in Quebec. Annette and Cecile, as the two youngest girls were known, stayed in Dawson in the care of the Letourneaus, close family friends who had been their baptismal sponsors. They returned to their father's home when he remarried in 1910.[61]

Merilda and Gédéon Pepin and their four daughters were part of Dawson's vibrant francophone community.

The Klondike was equally diverse in terms of religious beliefs. The 1901 census recorded nineteen different religions among the area's residents, including Quakers, Mormons, Seventh Day Adventists, Buddhists, Confucians, and Free Thinkers. The Roman Catholic church was the single largest denomination, but adherents of various Protestant faiths were collectively almost three times more numerous. On the Protestant side, the

Presbyterians claimed the largest following, while the Anglicans, Methodists, and Lutherans also had strong representation.[62]

The Catholics and Anglicans were the first to minister to the stampeders' spiritual needs in Dawson, arriving in the spring of 1897, with the Presbyterians following close behind them. The Reverend R. J. Bowen had not been in town long, and the log building that would become St. Paul's Anglican Church was still under construction, when he was called on to perform his first baptism in the new parish. On June 17, 1897, he baptized George and Martha Cary's eight-month-old daughter, Georgia. Sadly, she died only five weeks later.[63]

The next couple of years saw the arrival of the Klondike's first Methodist clergyman, a Salvation Army brigade, and various missionaries and evangelists, including Lutherans, Christian Scientists, and Theosophists. By 1900 Dawson boasted four churches—St. Mary's Catholic, St. Paul's Anglican (also referred to as St. Paul's Episcopal), St. Andrew's Presbyterian, and First Methodist—and a Salvation Army hall. There were also places of worship on the creeks, with most communities having one Catholic and one Protestant church, usually Presbyterian or Methodist. In Grand Forks, the Catholics, Anglicans, and Presbyterians each had a church building.[64]

Among those looking out for the souls of young Klondikers was the Salvation Army.

By 1904, Sunday school was a well-established institution in Dawson. Pictured here are the Sunday scholars of First Methodist Church.

Dawson's small Jewish community held its first religious services in September 1898, when two Jewish merchants cleared the front room of their store and invited their brethren to join them in marking Rosh Hashanah. Forty worshippers, mostly of Russian or Polish origins, accepted the invitation, bringing their own prayer books and prayer shawls. Ten days later they convened again for Yom Kippur, this time meeting in the Yukon Pioneer Hall. After this beginning, Dawson's Jewish congregation continued to be active for many years, though no synagogue was built during the gold rush days.[65]

As in other parts of North America, Dawson churches typically held both morning and evening services on Sunday and one or more services during the week. By the fall of 1898 St. Paul's was also offering afternoon Sunday school, taught by the pastor's wife, Susan Bowen.[66]

When the Methodists started their Sunday school in August 1899, only about seven children showed up on the first few Sabbaths. Undaunted, Sunday school superintendent W. H. Burkholder "set to work energetically to secure new scholars" and appoint new teachers, and by Christmas, enrolment had risen to forty. By 1901 the town's burgeoning juvenile population had pushed the average attendance to sixty, with eight classes assembling at three o'clock every Sunday afternoon: two for boys and four for girls, as well as an infant class and a Bible class. The intermediate-level boys and girls also met every second Thursday evening for a church-sponsored Literary and Social Club.[67]

In June 1903, following the lead of Outside churches, Dawson's Methodists observed "Children's Day" for the first time, with sermons that focused on the congregation's young members. To mark the occasion they decorated the church with potted plants and wild flowers, and suspended canary-filled birdcages from the ceiling. The Sunday school pupils led the singing during the morning and afternoon services, accompanied by the canaries, which "trilled sweetest music during the service."[68]

Sunday school was a well-established institution in Dawson by the time Bishop Isaac O. Stringer and his family moved to Dawson in 1907, adding three more names to the Sunday school roster at St. Paul's Anglican Church. The Stringer children were all true Northerners: eleven-year-old Rowena and seven-year-old Herschel had been born on Herschel Island in the High Arctic, and four-year-old Alexander in Whitehorse. A pair of Klondike-born sons, Wilfred and William, also joined the family in the two years following their arrival in Dawson.

Despite the demands of caring for her growing family, Sadie Stringer actively supported her husband's clerical work. One of her traditions was to invite the Gwich'in women from Peel River to her home for a meal when the women and their husbands made their annual or semi-annual visits to Dawson to sell fresh game and furs. Sadie recruited girls from the Sunday school to assist her in serving up the repast. In retrospect, Bessie Miller wasn't sure how much help she and the other girls were, but she loved these occasions. When the women arrived, each one carried a baby on her back. They "would lean the papoose baskets up along the wall while they sat at the long table and were served moose meat and baked beans and Mrs. Stringer's famous blueberry pie, all observed by those black-eyed babies with never a cry from them—cutest things you ever could see!"[69]

Religious affiliations tended to be somewhat flexible in the Klondike, especially among Protestants and out on the creeks, where the frequency of services depended on the clergy's availability. If their church of choice lacked a local presence or was closed on a particular Sunday, many Klondikers made do with the closest substitute. In Grand Forks, for instance, Bonanza Presbyterian Church and St. Luke's Anglican held services on alternating Sundays, so families like the Kingsleys switched back and forth between them on a weekly basis.[70]

In Dawson, Dorothy Whyte attended Sunday school at both the Methodist and Presbyterian churches because her mother sang in both choirs. Between the two churches, Dorothy attended or participated in numerous concerts, basket socials, winter outings, and other events, but one pageant remained etched in her memory long after the details of the others had faded.

On that unforgettable occasion Dorothy was in a skit directed by church member Mrs. Alec McCarter. For the piece, the children were dressed entirely in white, with black sateen capes—representing their sins—overtop. At the climax they were to "shed [their] sins" in unison, but as the other performers released their capes on cue, Dorothy fumbled hopelessly with the knot that held hers fast. Mortified at being left as the only black sheep on the stage, she began "yelling and screaming about not being able to untie [her] string and drop [her] cape." Although the audience members undoubtedly were amused, Dorothy was certain she'd "spoiled the whole show" and Mrs. McCarter seemed to agree.[71]

Many of the churches on the creeks did double or triple duty as schools and social halls. The Gold Bottom Presbyterian Church was a hive of activity throughout the week, providing space for the public school during the daytime from Monday to Friday, hosting the Gold Bottom ping pong club three evenings a week, and housing a circulating library for literary-minded locals. This and other churches were also used as venues for a variety of events, from concerts and plays to dances and fundraising bazaars, though nothing risqué was allowed.

One popular diversion that was endorsed by the churches was formal debating. Dorothy Whyte was about fifteen when George Pringle, the itinerant minister for several of the Presbyterian churches on the creeks, invited her and three other girls to come to Gold Bottom and entertain the miners with a debate. Accompanied only by the stage driver, the four excited adolescents made the twenty-mile trip in an open, horse-drawn sleigh, singing songs and laughing all the way.

That evening, Dorothy, with her blond braids pinned up around her head in her usual demure style, took her place on the raised platform at the front of the church. The topic of the debate was "Courtship and Marriage," the negative position being "that anticipation [is] better than realization." Watching the four fresh-faced young ladies making their cases for and against this proposition, it is unlikely that any of the bachelors in the audience, including the Reverend Pringle, were persuaded to give up on matrimony.

A year or so later, after the Whyte family had left Dawson, and Dorothy was in England visiting relatives, she discovered that the minister had been "very sweet on [her]," despite being about twenty years her senior. She had been oblivious to his feelings for her until he sent her a letter saying, "I can't wait any longer for you. Your mother took you away and I'm marrying another girl." And so he did.

But this revelation was still far in the future as the four debaters headed home from Gold Bottom. Overnight, the temperature had dropped to forty below, so the driver removed the sleigh's seats and spread straw on the floor. Covered by buffalo robes and warmed by hot-water bottles and youthful exuberance, they managed to fend off the cold all the way back to Dawson.

There was nothing

but fun and noise.

Chapter 9

Thoroughly Enjoying
Themselves

When the Barrett family arrived in Dawson in the fall of 1897, Lawrence, Florence, and Freddy found few other children to play with and none of the kinds of activities that might have filled their days in Southern communities. Nonetheless, they discovered ways to have fun, even as winter cold and darkness descended on the Klondike. "We children played outdoors when it was [minus] forty, and thought nothing of it," Florence wrote. "We begged rides on dog sleds, chased scavenger ravens along the frozen river, and went 'bellybuster' on our sleds down the bank in front of the big log barracks of the Northwest Mounted Police."

Their favourite game was "racing along the streets looking up into the faces of the parka-clad men to see if their noses were white." When they spotted a frostbite casualty, they would loudly proclaim his plight. "'Say, mister, your nose is froze!' [they] would yell joyously, rushing up to the victim with a handful of snow" for him to rub on the frozen spot.[1]

That Klondike children were undeterred by winter weather was a source of amazement to many adults, though the youngsters themselves were relatively nonchalant about their hardiness. "Where else than in the Yukon will you see school children rolling and reveling in the snow when the mercury is on the shady side of 40° below, exulting in the keenness of the frosty air?" asked one observer.[2]

Of course, youth didn't make them entirely impervious to the cold. The Barrett children's own noses were frostbitten a few times, despite the protective bands of fur they wore over them, and most of their contemporaries had at least one experience of freezing some extremity during their childhood.

Margaret Strong marvelled at how, as a toddler, her Dawson-born son "would play outdoors at 20° below zero without seeming to notice the cold at all." However, her child-rearing techniques may have contributed to his robust constitution. During his second winter she regularly left his bedroom window cracked open to provide ventilation. Sometimes "in the morning there would be a rim of solid ice around the blanket where Charles had pulled it up halfway over his face as he lay in the crib. But that didn't hurt him at all!"[3]

Sometimes, however, the intense cold kept even the toughest children from playing outdoors, and when that happened, small, poorly lit cabins became more confining with every passing day. Even those who lived in more commodious frame houses with large, plate-glass windows began to feel shut in. Margery Wade, the daughter of prominent Dawson lawyer F. C. Wade, spent many winter hours scraping the thick frost from her home's windows with a little carving knife, in hopes of catching a glimpse of the sun when it made its brief appearance over the hilltops—though for much of December and January, it remained below the horizon. Long after she left the Klondike, the knife remained a treasured souvenir of her three years there.[4]

Toys were scarce in the Klondike during the early years of the gold rush, encouraging the kind of innovation that gave Ethel Anderson her prized collection of lions. Among the provisions Ethel's mother brought back from Seattle after her trip south in the summer of 1899 was a large stock of Lions Head coffee in bags bearing the brand's trademark leonine head in a circle. As the bags were emptied, Ethel carefully cut out the medallions and put them in a box. Before the end of winter she was in the enviable position of being able to "march out a long row of lions" whenever she wanted to mount a circus in their fourteen-by-twenty-foot cabin.

Ethel's other cherished toy was one she received for Christmas in 1898 from a family friend in Washington who sent a doll for each of the older Anderson children. Ethel's was two feet tall, with a kid-leather body, jointed arms and legs, curly hair, and big, blue eyes that rolled in its china head. Although Dewey's was smaller and its body was made of calico, it too had a china head and hands. No other Klondike child that Ethel knew had "real dolls" like theirs.[5]

With few human playmates around, a doll could be good company for any child, but a dog was even better. Olive Kinsey was one of the many children living on the creeks whose best friend was a dog. The daughter of photographer Clarence Kinsey and his wife, Agnes, Olive was born in Grand Forks in 1904. Four years later, she and her parents moved to Dominion Creek, where they lived until 1911, witnessing the departure of most other families from the area. Growing up, Olive's constant companion was a large, shaggy black mutt named Dick. He was so devoted to his little blonde mistress that he "would eat almost anything she fed him, including pickles, which he loved even though they made his eyes water."[6]

Grace Murray with her doll and carriage, around 1908.

This kind of relationship was no surprise, for dogs had held a prominent position in the lives of young Klondikers from the very beginning of the gold rush. In the winter of 1898–99, Lulu Craig frequently "met children of all ages from three to twelve years happy and gay in their glee, with their dogs and sleds. Sometimes a number would be piled on the Yukon sleds drawn by one or more dogs, attended or cared for by some older friend, though at times they would be in no one's charge, the older children driving the dogs, and calling out 'Mush on,' 'Gee there,' and 'Haw.'"[7]

In September 1900, journalist Faith Fenton Brown wrote about the bond between Dawson children and their dogs. "On the most extreme days of last winter, when the thermometer indicated over 50 deg. below, it was a common sight to see the little ones, wrapped until only their eyes peered out, racing up and down the streets with some pet dog attached to a small sled. The dog teams are a perpetual delight to the children in the Yukon."[8]

Mastering the art of mushing took practice, however, as Lulu Craig saw first-hand the day a thirteen-year-old friend named Josie invited her for a ride. Climbing onto the sled, Lulu asked the girl if she knew how to handle her two-dog team and was assured she did. No sooner were the words out of Josie's mouth than the dogs leapt into action, speeding downhill with the driver desperately trying to maintain control.

Well, they got away from her of course, as I might have known they would, and on they raced faster and faster, I laughing and calling to them; soon I saw a sawbuck for which they seemed heading. I quickly threw my arms up to protect my head and face if we struck it; fortunately we just grazed it and soon after the dogs turned off and the sled upset, I rolling down the incline. My young friend came rushing down in distress fearing I was hurt, and seemed so sorry that she had attempted to guide the dogs, but I soon relieved her by saying that I was not at all hurt and that I did not know when I had had such fun. After we got down on the river I got on again and then the dogs traveled nicely.[9]

The Miller family's dog, Bruno, was a huge but mild-mannered cross between a mastiff and a St. Bernard. He was powerful enough to pull all the Miller children or both their parents on a sled, and the children loved to hitch him up and go for rides around town. The only worry was whether they would encounter the laundry delivery sled, whose team of seven huskies was Bruno's nemesis. Every time he caught sight of the team, his hackles rose and he plunged into their midst. "Then pandemonium reigned with dogs snapping and growling and harnesses and sleds and packages of laundry all entangled and the laundry man cracking his whip and swearing and [the Miller children] on the sidewalk bawling at the top of [their] lungs."

One winter Bruno disappeared and, despite persistent searching, could not be found. The next spring, long after he'd been given up for dead, he showed up at the Miller house, reduced to skin and bones and barely able to drag himself to the door. It was then that the family realized he'd been stolen to work for some unscrupulous miner and let go once winter was over and he was no longer useful.[10]

The practice of turning dogs loose over the summer to avoid the expense of feeding them was so common that, in the spring of 1900, an estimated two thousand dogs roamed the streets of Dawson.[11] These uncontrolled animals posed a threat to everyone, children being the most vulnerable. During the winter of 1901, the NWMP killed several vicious strays in Dawson, and when rabies broke out that spring, they announced that they would shoot any dog that was not tied up. This edict was followed by a territorial government order that all dogs in town would have to be muzzled, tagged, and leashed. The canine population was significantly culled during this period, but there were no human deaths from rabies.[12]

These preventive measures did not completely eliminate the danger to children, however, as a dramatic incident in 1902 demonstrated. One December afternoon, a group of boys was playing outside Dawson Public School during their lunch break when a large yellow dog came along and suddenly attacked them "without any provocation or even any bother being paid to it." Moments later, three more dogs arrived on the scene in a pack and joined the fray. Eleven-year-old

Roy Porter bore the brunt of the assault, being "horribly bitten on his arms and legs," and eight-year-old Darrel Davis was also quite badly hurt.[13]

Out on Eldorado Creek, the Anderson children faced a different canine problem. The family dogs made good playmates, but when they got mange, so did Ethel, Dewey, and Clay. Their mother treated them by administering thorough scrubbings with carbolic soap and water and covering their sores with a homemade salve concocted from lard, sulphur, and carbolic acid—the same ointment that was used on the dogs. It was, according to Ethel, a "sure cure."[14]

Living in Bennett at the turn of the century, Hazel Hartshorn saw countless sled dogs coming and going on the winter trail to the Klondike, as well as many that were left to die because their owners had no more use for them. After her parents rescued one dog that was frozen onto the ice, he became Hazel's devoted pet and a "good playfellow" for the six-year-old. All winter long, even when the temperature dropped to sixty degrees Fahrenheit below zero, she and Jack played outside together, often spending the whole day tobogganing, a pastime he enjoyed as much as she did. Jack would pull the sled up the hill, then Hazel would unhitch him and they would both jump on and zoom down to the bottom. As soon as the sled stopped, Jack was ready to go again.[15]

Tobogganing was a favourite winter activity for many Klondike children, even those who didn't own sleds. Dorothy and Bessie Miller used their mother's baking pans in lieu of proper equipment, while Bessie's friend Grace Henderson simply slid down the hills on her coat, a practice that eventually wore the fur off its seat.[16] But unlike the first arrivals in the Klondike, they could also participate in more organized sports and recreational activities, including ice skating.

In November 1902 the Yukon commissioner's office received an unusual piece of correspondence. Neatly handwritten on lined paper, the first page read:

> Major Z. T. Wood, Acting Commissioner:
>
> We, the undersign[ed] coming generation and future voters and officers of the Yukon Territory, desire to call your attention to the fact that winter is now upon us, and such being the case, water congeals at 32 degrees above zero. Skating is a pastime indulged in by persons of all ages, but is more enjoyed by children of school age than at any other period.
>
> We would therefore ask that you, in conjunction with our good Mayor Macauly would prevail upon the Fire Department to flood a portion of the school grounds for skating purposes, and after it has frozen we shall try to keep it free from snow.
>
> We shall remain yours forever,
>   Yours respectfully,

An impromptu foot race at Gold Bottom.

The following four pages bore the signatures of eighty children with varying levels of penmanship.

The petitioners did not have to wait long for an answer. "Dear Lads and Lassies," Wood's reply began, "Of the many petitions which I have received, there is not one which will afford me more pleasure to act on than yours. When I lay this well-worded and well-written appeal, with so many signatures attached, before the Mayor and City Council, I am sure they will do everything in their power to assist me in meeting your wishes."[17]

Sure enough, just two days after Wood forwarded the request to the mayor, a member of the NWMP marched a pair of prisoners from the barracks over to the school and stood guard while they worked with picks and shovels, levelling the ground of the chosen rink site and building an embankment around it.[18] It was not until mid-December, however, that the fire department was able to flood the site and when the first group of eager young hockey players showed up the next day, they "found the ice a gently undulating plane with blisters from an inch to a yard in diameter all over it, through which their skates cut at the first impact."

Unwilling to wait, the boys went ahead with their game, playing on a ten-foot-wide strip of passable ice with "regular hockey sticks, some considerably the worse for wear, a regulation puck and two stones at either end [for] goal posts. Never was a league game played with more vim and desperation." A proper surface was eventually achieved after the prisoners did some more work on banking up the sides and the firemen returned to pump more water onto the ice.[19]

———

Although the public school rink was the first created exclusively for children, ice sports had been part of Klondike life almost from the beginning of the gold rush. At first, those who owned skates just cleared a patch of ice on one of the rivers or creeks. Later, they made more elaborate arrangements.

In 1901, during Emil Forrest's first winter in Dawson, four rinks were set up on the Yukon River and he made good use of them.[20] Emil and his family had been living in Grass Valley, California, in 1897 when they heard about the Klondike discovery. His father immediately quit his job as the foreman of a small gold mine and headed to San Francisco to sail north. Emil, his mother, and his sister went the other direction, back to their family home in Quebec, where Emil's two older brothers were attending school. The next fall, Emil's father met them there. He didn't bring "the bullion by the sack full" that they fully expected to see, but he was optimistic enough about the Klondike's potential that he took his eldest son, sixteen-year-old Paul, with him when he returned to the Klondike in the spring of 1899. Two years later, Emil, his mother, and his brother Albert joined them.

Emil hadn't learned to skate until he moved to Quebec, but he was far ahead of most of his Dawson peers. Many of his new friends were recent arrivals from coastal parts of California, Washington, and Oregon and had never donned blades until they moved north. Not only could Emil "lord it over" the other boys, he also gained skating privileges that were not normally open to thirteen-year-olds.

The largest of Dawson's 1901 skating venues was out in the middle of the Yukon River and was surrounded by a circular canvas wall, with tents for dressing rooms. The most modest was the "tin can rink," maintained by the Standard Oil Company and open to everyone, including novices. But the ice sheets that interested Emil were the two devoted to hockey: the civil service rink, built on the shore ice and surrounded by a wooden fence and benches for spectators; and the Northern Commercial Company's rink, which became the sole hockey rink after the shore ice settled and the civil service rink developed an impossible tilt. Emil was too young to join one of Dawson's competitive teams that winter and had to content himself with watching the games. Because of his skating prowess, however, he was "the only kid allowed on the ice during practices."

Cold temperatures, wind, snow, and the vagaries of river ice created problems for all the open-air rinks, so, in the summer of 1902, a group of townspeople formed the Dawson Amateur Athletic Association (DAAA) and erected a three-storey building that housed a regulation-sized hockey rink and two-sheet curling rink.[21] Unlike at the school rink and the tin can rink, skating at the DAAA was not free. In 1903, one-time admission was twenty-five cents for women and children and fifty cents for men. A child's season ticket cost $7.50 (compared to $10 for women and $20 for men), while a family season ticket, which covered one adult and any number of children, was $25. That year the management also decided that children under fifteen would be "positively forbidden the privilege of skating at night" since there had been "many complaints . . . regarding juveniles on the rink at night" during the previous winter.[22]

In addition to hockey, curling, and recreational skating, the DAAA hosted skating parties, carnivals, and sports nights, featuring a wide variety of skating races. The sports night that closed the skating season in April 1906 surpassed events of earlier years in the number of prizes offered and the size of the crowd. Children were given free admission and filled many of the seats in the stands, but they weren't there only as spectators. Five of the evening's twenty-two races were for children: one each for girls and boys aged fourteen and under; one for boys under twelve; and another two for "little" girls and boys. Children were also honorary competitors in the adults' Chilkoot Pass contest, in which each of the skaters "had to drag behind him a small boy on a sleigh. The boy was not allowed to put his feet to the ground or in any way to assist the racers . . . There were great cheers and much excitement all through this race."

One of the surprise winners of the evening was Phil Creamer, who took first place in the four-lap race for boys under twelve. His father, the manager of the DAAA, proudly noted that Phil had never seen an ice rink or skates before arriving in Dawson the previous fall. "They catch on quick, don't they?" he commented as he accepted congratulations on his son's behalf.[24]

As each year's new arrivals to the North made their first tentative glides across the ice of the DAAA rink, the Forrest brothers continued to hone their skills and cement their reputation as "the strongest combination of athletes and particularly hockey players ever brought out in the Klondike by one family."[25] Albert, a particularly strong skater and talented hockey player, won numerous prizes at DAAA sports nights throughout his teens and reached the apex of his athletic career in 1905 when he travelled to Ottawa with the Klondike All-Stars to compete for the Stanley Cup. Only eighteen at the time, he was the youngest player on the team and the youngest ever to have vied for the coveted trophy.

The Klondike All-Stars made a dismal showing at the championships, partly because of weariness and lack of practice after their twenty-three days in transit, but that didn't diminish sixteen-year-old Emil's pride in his brother's national fame. Emil also gained a measure of glory for himself when he was allowed to play goal for the All-Stars during a couple of local exhibition games before and after the team's trip to Ottawa.[26]

By the time Dawson got its first junior hockey teams in 1907, Emil was too old to join the lineup, but Phil Creamer and his fellow high school students impressed a *Yukon World* reporter by "play[ing] a good game and a fast game [and] being nimbler on their skates than some of the star players of the senior aggregations."[27]

While some Klondike children spent their free time passing the puck, others concentrated on practising their scales. One of the most popular music teachers was Arthur Boyle, and the annual recitals by his piano and voice students were well received. The 1902 recital, which brought "about 100 ladies with a sprinkling of gentlemen" to the Arctic Brotherhood Hall on a June afternoon, "was distinctly classical and the manner in which the youngsters acquitted themselves of the difficult parts assigned to them gave abundant evidence of the fact that they are receiving thoroughly capable instruction." Singled out for special praise were Lois Te Roller, whose "tiny fingers never went astray" as she played a piano duet with her teacher, and Daisy Scolan, whose piano solos were deemed "highly artistic for so youthful a player."[28]

Daisy also performed a Schubert sonata with violinist Elsie Larsen, a pupil of Professor A. P. Freimuth. In other towns, a man like Freimuth, who regularly played in the dancehalls, might not have been considered a suitable violin teacher for a young girl, but certain Klondike musicians seemed to be untouched by the usual prejudices.

Another resident who easily moved back and forth across the conventional boundaries of propriety was Gédéon Pepin, a civil servant by day and a musician at every other opportunity. His four daughters grew up listening to him play the organ on Sundays at St. Mary's Catholic Church and watching him direct the choir for midnight mass at Christmas, but were equally familiar with the lively ragtime numbers and other contemporary music he composed and performed in venues ranging from dancehalls to the governor's residence. Inspired by his example, his four daughters all made their musical debuts at an early age, appearing on stage at St. Mary's School and at the Palace Grand Theatre.[29]

Besides being the year that Dawson children got their own skating rink, 1902 was also when the *Klondike Nugget* added a Saturday Children's Department to its pages.[30] Featuring stories, poems, word puzzles, and numbers games, this section of the newspaper was a milestone of sorts, attesting to the growing number of children in the Klondike and recognizing their distinct needs for entertainment and leisure activities. However, it was not the first attempt to satisfy those needs.

In September 1898, Mr. E. E. Simons, the manager of the Combination The-ater, had begun presenting Saturday afternoon shows specifically for women and children. Not only were these family matinees "devoid of any feature that might offend the most sensitive," Simons also suspended liquor sales during the perfor-mances and created a private entrance to the theatre so patrons would not have to pass through the saloon at the front. His first program included a Western drama titled Brocky Morgan, a selection of songs, sketches, and dances, and a showing of stationary and moving pictures such as The Sinking of the Maine and The Battle of Manila.[31]

Unfortunately for Simons, presenting "good clean entertainment" was prob-ably not a lucrative venture. Even a year later, when the number of families in Dawson was considerably higher, a "clean and wholesome" Saturday afternoon matinee performance of The Two Orphans at the Opera House theatre attracted a meagre audience of only "about two dozen ladies and children." Although the thirty-five actors had donated their services, ticket sales were expected to barely "come near paying for the lights."[32]

It would be some time before commercial attempts to provide children's enter-tainment in the Klondike prospered. Community and church-sponsored activities, on the other hand, were successful from the start. The first major event of this sort was a children's Christmas party organized by Susan Bowen, the Reverend R. J. Bowen's wife and hardworking helper. Held at St. Paul's Anglican Church on December 27, 1898, the afternoon party attracted between thirty-five and forty children and a number of adults, including the territorial commissioner.

The log church was decked out for the occasion with flags, Japanese lanterns, "festoons of evergreens strung along the ceiling," and, of course, a Christmas tree. Thanks to Susan's persistence in asking the town's shopkeepers for donations, the tree was "beautifully decorated with strings of popcorn, sacks of nuts and can-dies, and other ornaments [and] illuminated with numerous wax candles. There was a present on the tree for every child in the house and in addition each one received a remembrance in the shape of a sack of candy." Adding to the festive atmosphere were several long tables, which "fairly groaned beneath their burden" of Christmas goodies.

After the feasting, Presbyterian minister Andrew Grant was recruited to play Santa Claus and distribute the gifts. Commissioner William Ogilvie then played some music on his gramophone, and the afternoon ended with a magic lantern show of biblical scenes presented by the Reverend Bowen, who tested the children's scriptural knowledge by peppering them with questions about the pictures.[33]

In following years, public Christmas celebrations in the Klondike increas-ingly involved children, both as entertainers and as the recipients of presents provided by munificent members of the community—ranging from toys and candy to nugget brooches and sterling silver souvenir spoons.[34]

A group of Dawson girls plays London Bridge, a popular children's game of the time.

The 1902 Christmas Eve festivities at St. Andrew's Presbyterian Church were typical of those hosted by Dawson's Methodist and Presbyterian churches after the turn of the century. With about fifty Sunday school students participating, the program of songs and recitations was long, but the spectators who filled the church hall vigorously applauded every child's contribution. "One of the prettiest numbers," according to a *Klondike Nugget* reporter, "was the dolly song by twelve little girls each with a treasure in her arms upon which a world of affection was lavished."

The climax of the evening was the arrival of Santa Claus bearing gifts for all the children. "Presently sleigh bells were heard and a driver's voice yelling 'whoa' to his reindeers came floating in through the open door. Then the well known features appeared, long gray beard, smiling eyes, pleasant voice and a pack on his back." In a classic Klondike twist, the long-awaited visitor announced upon entering the hall that he "had had trouble with his reindeers and wanted to trade off the team for some dogs. Who had a dog to trade or loan? Every hand whose owner possesse[d] anything in the shape of a dog went into the air."[35]

On the last day of school before the Christmas break, students at both the public school and St. Mary's entertained their parents and other guests with recitations, songs, essays, and dialogues. While the older children performed together, the "public school babies" in the kindergarten class had their own closing exercises in which they demonstrated their singing, marching, and craft-making abilities to their "fond mamas" and "doting papas."[36]

The Catholic children received their visit from Saint Nicholas at school, rather than at church, but Dawson's generous merchants ensured that the Christmas tree at St. Mary's School bore as many gifts as those at the Protestant churches, if not more. In 1901 the tree was weighed down with "several hundred dollars worth of Christmas store to say nothing of oranges, candy and nuts which Captain Starnes heaped on every child as it went forward at the call of its name by Mr. Claus . . . Every child present received from three to six or eight costly presents and all went home with full arms and happy hearts." In 1903 the St. Mary's Christmas tree "was laden with toys and costly presents, fully $300 worth being distributed among the pupils."[37]

Yuletide celebrations in the creek communities paralleled those held in Dawson. From the turn of the century onward, each settlement held its own Christmas party in a church, social hall, or other suitable venue, with gifts for the local children and often a recital. In 1903 the Yukon Sun observed that "[a] few years ago Christmas on the creeks meant a few drunks at a roadhouse, a dinner with a little extra beef and a rest from the routine of a miner's life. Today all is different. The little camps on the various creeks each had their Christmas tree with loads of presents, crowds of children as well as elders in attendance."[38]

That year the gathering at Caribou City was the largest and most lavish on the creeks, thanks to schoolteacher Laura Wilson, who "labored for six weeks in behalf of the little ones getting donations, teaching the children and doing a thousand little things to make a grand success of the affair." Knowing that many local families were struggling financially, Laura saw to it that "felt shoes, caps, hosiery and the like" were mixed in with the toys and other gifts given out during the party. Parents who had "a great, long poke [were] asked to put something on the tree for their own children, while for the other tots the [childless] men on the creeks [were] asked to contribute." Additional donations came from several Dawson firms.[39]

The other creek communities also marked the occasion in fine style. At Gold Run on Lower Dominion Creek, the "young folks held full sway and such a throng of eager faces was seldom seen." And in nearby Granville, the Bachelors' Club and two churches joined forces for an evening that included the customary tree, presents, and children's literary and musical recital, as well as a supper and dance.[40]

For Granville's celebration the Reverend George Pringle took it upon himself to go to Dawson and buy a Christmas gift for every child, "irrespective of creed." He made his purchases "not knowing whether he would be reimbursed. However, when he announced that a small collection to defray necessary costs would be taken up, it was responded to most liberally. The children, in whose honor the tree was planned, were so radiantly happy that the various committees that executed the work felt amply compensated."[41]

Winter weather limited the scope of Christmas festivities somewhat, confining them to indoor venues, but holidays that fell in spring and summer were celebrated exuberantly, with open-air revelry that often stretched over several days. The first big holiday of the year was Queen Victoria's birthday on May 24. After a long winter, even those who owed no allegiance to the British Crown were happy to join in the merrymaking. Then, just over a month later, Canadian Dominion Day and American Independence Day were combined into an extended holiday, which ran from July 1 to July 4 and was enjoyed by people of all nationalities.

During the first few years of the gold rush, children's involvement in these events was limited to being spectators who needed to stay alert to avoid being trampled by the throngs of unruly men. But from 1901 onward, they were active participants. That year, Dawson students opened the Victoria Day celebrations by

Young girls line up for a race, part of Dawson's 1904 Victoria Day festivities.

marching along First Avenue from the public school to the grandstand, accompanied by a "band composed of all the best musicians in the city." Once the students had taken their places next to the commissioner and other dignitaries, they listened to the booming twenty-one-gun salute fired by the NWMP and then launched into "God Save the King." Later in the program, they also sang "The Maple Leaf Forever" and "The Soldiers of the King."

Children took part in the grand parade, riding on a number of the floats, and for the first time in Dawson's history, there was a full program of races exclusively for the younger generation. In 1900, the only children's Victoria Day sporting event had been a race for boys under fifteen. In 1901, there were a dozen events. Cash prizes ranged from $5 for the winners of the boys' and girls' thirteen-and-over races to $1 each for the first four contestants to cross the finish line in the races for boys and girls under age six. In the sack races and potato races, the boys won pocket knives and the girls won sets of dolls' dishes.[42]

In 1902 several events were added to the children's sports program, including bicycle races, three-legged races, and long jump, high jump, and shot put contests. Best of all, the Victoria Day finance committee voted to spend a small portion of their funds on a "monster freezer of ice cream" to feed the participants after the sports events were over.[43]

By 1903 the children's part of the Victoria Day celebrations had grown into a separate Saturday event with an even wider variety of races and sports contests, a cake walk, a Highland dancing competition, and a military drill performed by the senior school pupils. Although there was no ice cream, shopkeeper Stanley Scearce donated a crate of oranges, and various businesses lent their wagons to transport the youngest children from the school to the police parade grounds where the event was held.[44] In the words of the Yukon Sun,

> It was a great day—the greatest day ever . . . From the time the gaily decorated wagons began the tour of the city filled with the children of Dawson, Col. McGregor with his arms full of little ones upon the seat with the driver of the first wagon, until after the last sport on the program was finished and 11,000,000 tired children, each with a dirty face, and the remains of an orange in their hand, toddled home to tea, there was nothing but fun and noise. Eleven million may be a high estimate of the number of children . . . but if sound goes for anything the shouts of the happy kids were of eleven million volume.[45]

Dawson's July 1 celebrations drew many people from the creeks, and starting in 1903, special excursions were organized to bring children from the outlying areas into town for the day.[46] However, some of the creek communities also marked the occasion with parades and athletic competitions. On his first Victoria Day in the Klondike, in 1903, nine-year-old Jim Kingsley rode in the men's horse race and looked like the favourite to win until the butcher "forced [him] into the sidewalk." Making up for that disappointment was his discovery that the miners who filled the streets of Grand Forks that day were eager to buy candy and other treats for every child they came across.[47]

The Klondike's July holidays—as well as special occasions, such as the coronation of King Edward VII on August 9, 1902—were commemorated in much the same way as Victoria Day, with speeches, parades, and sports, and buildings decorated with banners and bunting.[48] Only the location was different. An informal agreement worked out in the early days of the gold rush meant the principal Dominion Day celebrations took place in Grand Forks, while Dawson hosted the main Fourth of July festivities. Smaller events were also held at Granville and Caribou City.[49]

Besides enthusiastically participating in community celebrations of the major holidays, Klondike children also marked their own red-letter days, though at the beginning of the gold rush they mostly shared these occasions with adults.

A sumptuous feast awaits the young guests at this birthday party in the early days of Dawson.

Later, as the number of children grew, they enjoyed social events that were for them alone.

Emilie Craig turned ten while en route to the Klondike on June 3, 1898. She was the only child at her birthday party, held on the shores of Lake Lindeman, but her family made sure that their "June rose of ten summers" was properly fêted.

After preparing refreshments, Emilie's mother and aunt transformed their tent into "as much of a drawing room as possible," stretching a new tarpaulin across the floor and rearranging the china-press, bookcase, seats, and table to make more room for the guests. They then decorated the tent with bouquets provided by two stampeder friends who "had rowed across the lake that morning to a pretty spot where they found lots of wild flowers and had returned with their arms full." Lastly, they "selected a pretty pink flower to lay in garlands around the birthday cake upon which were placed ten lighted tapers."[50]

Emilie was again the youngest person present when she celebrated her eleventh birthday in Dawson. The "gay party of ladies and gentlemen" who joined the Craigs at their cabin in West Dawson to mark the occasion included six bachelors, one single woman, and a married couple. "A huge bonfire lit up the front of the house," reported the Klondike Nugget a few days later, "and the interior was tastefully and beautifully decorated with native flowers the variety and profusion of which were a revelation to those present." By then well accustomed to socializing with adults, Emilie "proved an ideal hostess," and the "array of nuggets and other presents attested [to] the high esteem in which the young lady [was] held by her friends."[51]

By 1902, children's birthday celebrations in Dawson were very different affairs. When Lena White turned ten in August of that year, she invited sixteen girls and seven boys to her party and "entertained her young friends from 2 until 5 o'clock in the afternoon [with] games and a birthday dinner."[52]

The following year, a half-page feature on "How to Entertain Children at Their Parties" published in the Yukon Sun raised the bar for Klondike birthday festivities. "It is not a difficult matter to make children have a jolly good time at a party if you go about it the right way," the article's author assured readers. Games like hunt the slipper, blindman's bluff, and London Bridge would have been familiar to most readers, but some mothers may have balked at suggestions such as serving "little cakes iced to represent dominoes" and orange jelly served in baskets carved from orange shells, or organizing the guests to dance "pretty german figures."[53]

Dawson may not have been ready for the kind of elaborate entertainment promoted by this article, but the Klondike had become a place where children were no longer relegated to the periphery of the social scene. On March 1, 1902, for example, the Klondike Nugget reported on two recent sleighing parties, one a "stag" event enjoyed by "a few of the prominent men of the city" and the other arranged by

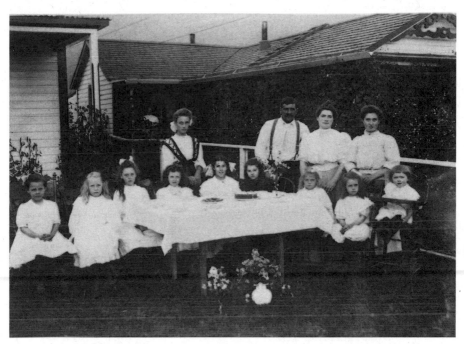

Ellie Ballentine celebrates her fourteenth birthday with family, friends, and neighbours.

fifteen-year-old Bennett James for several of his friends. Bennett's guests included a few boys his own age, as well as Paul Forrest and another nineteen-year-old. Their expedition out to Grand Forks was "greatly enjoyed" by all.[54]

A much larger children's sleighing party was held later that month when George Coffey, the manager of the Anglo-Klondike Mining Company, invited local youngsters to visit his operations at Fox Gulch. Eighty children and nine adult chaperones met at St. Andrew's Presbyterian Church in the morning and travelled up Bonanza Creek on sleighs furnished by several Dawson transportation firms. They reached their destination at three o'clock with "vigorous appetites" and were soon "attacking a feast of good things prepared by the mess house chef of Mr. Coffey's company."[55]

The Klondike's summer alternative to sleighing parties was paddlewheeler day trips on the Yukon River. In June 1901 the Northern Navigation Company volunteered one of its vessels to host what was billed as "the first excursion ever given in the Yukon for children only," though a number of adults, mostly women, went along to supervise.

The "palatial" steamer *Susie* cast off at two o'clock on a lovely Wednesday afternoon. As she "swept by the city her decks crowded with well dressed ladies and happy children it was a sight not to be excelled . . . and many a sour dough on the river bank was seen to pinch himself to see if he was really awake or only dreaming while others were heard to murmur something about further north, getting too metropolitan, etc. . . . All on board continued to wave their handkerchiefs and the children to cheer lustily until the steamer rounded the point above Klondike City."

The *Susie* went as far as the first island beyond Klondike City, then turned and headed downstream toward Fort Reliance, about six miles below Dawson. "As the steamer again swept by the city front she was greeted with cheer after cheer from the shore while the steamer Tyrell, which was the only steamer in port, and all the saw mills gave several salutes with whistles which were responded to by the Susie while the children aboard yelled so loudly that the whistles could hardly be heard and it was quite evident that all were thoroughly enjoying themselves."

Once they were on course for Fort Reliance, the crew brought out "a bountiful lunch which the thoughtful and genial manager of the company, Capt. Hansen, had provided." The repast concluded with ice cream and cake served by the ladies of the Catholic Guild and the mothers, after which the dining room was cleared for dancing to the music of the Savoy Orchestra.

On the return trip, the boat made a scheduled stop at Moosehide, "where the entire tribe of Indians arrayed in aboriginal costumes bedecked with feathers and faces made hideous with the regulation war paint . . . lined the bank chanting and dancing." After the excursionists went ashore, the men, women, and children of the village treated them to a half-hour display of traditional dancing. Chief Isaac followed the performance with a brief speech in which he reminded the visitors that his people had once "own[ed] all this country" and been much more numerous. They'd had "fine dance; hi-yu time" back in those happier days, he said, but they were still glad that their white neighbours liked to come see what they had to offer now. In appreciation for the entertainment, the Dawsonites took up a collection and presented it to the chief. Then they headed home, arriving back at the dock at 5:30 p.m.[56]

As time went on, the Klondike's fraternal organizations also got involved in arranging outings and throwing parties for Klondike youngsters. A special children's social given by the Freemasons in their Dawson hall in February 1907 was characteristic of these events, though the guest list was limited to members and their offspring. The one exception to this rule was Colonel MacGregor, "whose kindly face the children are so accustomed to see at all their gatherings that they would have felt a disappointment if he had not been included."

The evening began with a short program of recitations and musical numbers presented by several of the children. "Then followed a number of games in which the elders joined and became young again, after which the guests were seated at tables heaped with good things and were waited upon by the grown-ups. There

Adults and children alike enjoyed paddlewheeler pleasure trips on the Yukon River. This 1902 excursion was arranged by the *Klondike Nugget* for its staff and their families and friends.

were games after the feast, and then the tables were cleared away and the grown-ups had a jolly dance to end up with."[57]

On another occasion, four mothers rented the Masonic Hall for an evening gala for their teenage daughters. The 120 young people who attended the party played games conducted by the master of ceremonies and danced to a hired orchestra. Notable among the refreshments served at the end of the night was the homemade ice cream.[58]

For Klondikers, there were few events as prestigious as soirées at the commissioner's residence, so when nine-year-old Grace Henderson's father, Alexander, was appointed territorial commissioner in 1907, her classmates probably all hoped to be invited to a junior version of one of these affairs. Bessie Miller, who was the same age as Grace and frequently joined her in mischievous escapades, was one of the lucky ones. The afternoon functions that Bessie attended, along with about a dozen other children and a smattering of adults, were held in the residence's elegant dining room. The most interesting part of the proceedings, as far as she was concerned, was when the men taught the children how to play cards, standing behind their protégés and dealing out advice.[59]

For Dawson girls of all ages, tea parties—similar to the ones their mothers gave and attended—were popular, but the boys followed their fathers' lead when it came to socializing. In 1907 they even formed their own exclusive club, perhaps inspired by the numerous fraternal organizations that thrived in the Klondike. The boys' association was the Dawson chapter, or company, of the Order of the American Boy (OAB).[60]

Founded in 1901 by the publishers of *The American Boy*, the OAB was a "national non-secret society for American boys" that promoted "the cultivation of manliness in muscle, mind and morals." Membership was open to all subscribers to the magazine, provided their application to join was accepted by a local company. Each new member received a distinctive badge and a booklet of "perforated gummed stamps" to use "on his letterheads, envelopes, books, etc. to advertise the Order and show that he is a member in good standing." Those who distinguished themselves through "conspicuous heroism" or "good scholarship and excellence in school attendance" were awarded membership in the American Boy Legion of Honor and received another badge to wear.

While the members of the newly created Dawson OAB company were waiting for their copy of the official rulebook to arrive from headquarters in Michigan, they improvised with their own ideas of how to proceed. Motions passed during

A Dawson tea party. Identified in the back row are Dorothy Whyte (second from left), Gudrun Anderson (second from right), and Louise Forrest (far right). Beatrice Forrest is on the right in front.

the first weeks included one stating that "running the gauntlet shall be the initiation of this club till voted out" and another prohibiting smoking in the clubhouse. The group also approved the purchase of a punching bag and a pair of boxing gloves, as well as the card games "White Squadron," "Flinch," and "Bid." Funds to pay for these and other expenses, such as lamp oil, came from the members' monthly dues of twenty-five cents, as well as fines imposed for infractions such as using bad language or failing to bring firewood to meetings.

One of the Dawson company's first orders of business was setting up a library. During the fall and winter of 1907, the members also organized a boxing contest, a formal debate, and a party, to which each member brought refreshments worth $1, including sandwiches, pop, fruit, nuts, candy, cake, and the all-important ice cream. The number of members varied from about a dozen to nearly twenty. Phil Creamer, who was barely into his teens, was one of the youngest members, while nineteen-year-old Emil Forrest may have been the oldest. Most were about fifteen years old, but being of the right age didn't guarantee membership. For reasons that were not explained in the minutes, several applicants were "blackballed" and Samborn Brayton suffered the humiliation of being rejected twice.

In just ten years Dawson had changed from a place where children could hardly find playmates to one with so many young people that they could be fussy about who they chose as friends.

The Newman children will
appear in a delightful program
of specialties and farces.

Chapter 10

Picking Up the Coins

In the Klondike, as elsewhere, some children grew up more quickly than others, taking on adult responsibilities while they were still in their early or mid-teens. Bera Beatrice Beebe was one of them. Bera's troubles didn't begin in the Klondike, but she might have kept her innocence longer if her widowed mother hadn't contracted gold fever.[1]

When Iola Beebe decided to seek her fortune in the Klondike in 1898, she invested all her savings in furnishings and accoutrements for a hotel. Late that summer she loaded her outfit on a steamer and took it to St. Michael, where she left it to be shipped on to Dawson the next spring. Upon returning to the United States, Iola collected her daughters, fifteen-year-old Bera and nineteen-year-old Blanche, from their convent school in Portland and began making final preparations for the three of them to travel north. The one thing that worried her was that she knew no one in Dawson, so when a friend offered to introduce her to a well-connected gentleman who was in Seattle on his way back to the Klondike, she jumped at the chance.

Swiftwater Bill Gates had struck it rich in the Klondike in 1896 and spent the next few years wooing dancehall girls, living extravagantly, and speculating on various mining ventures. He showed up for his meeting with Iola fashionably attired in a black Prince Albert jacket and low-cut vest over a spotless white shirt, with neatly pressed trousers, patent leather shoes, and a four-karat diamond securing his silk tie. All smoothness and charm, he "spoke in a low musical voice, the kind of voice that instantly wins the confidence of nine women out of ten."[2] Iola was wary, but she couldn't afford to refuse either his offer to help her get established in Dawson, or his social overtures.

At Bill's insistence, Iola and her daughters joined him for dinner. That evening, Bera was, in her mother's eyes, "the very picture of beauty and innocence . . .

plump, with deliciously pink cheeks, great big blue eyes, regular features," and "wavy brown hair of silken glossy texture."[3] Bill, though exactly twice her age, couldn't take his eyes off her.

Over the following week, the dapper Klondiker sent flowers to the Beebes' apartment almost daily and took Iola, Blanche, and Bera to the theatre several times. Then, on the day he was due to head north on the *Humboldt*, Iola returned home to find the girls and most of their belongings missing. Bera had left a two-sentence note on the dresser: "We have gone to Alaska with Swiftwater and Mr. Hathaway. Do not worry, mama, as when we get there we will look out for your hotel."[4] It was 7:30 p.m. and the steamer was scheduled to sail at 8:00.

Iola raced down to the docks and arrived with just minutes to spare. Grabbing a brawny policeman for support, the incensed mother forced her way through the crowds and stormed up the gangplank, where she confronted the captain and informed him that he was not to cast off until her daughters were returned to her care. After much searching, the girls were located in a locked stateroom, and their abductor was extracted from his hiding place under a lifeboat.

Swiftwater Bill languished in a jail cell for a few nights but was released after Iola withdrew the kidnapping charge she'd laid against him. When they next met, about a month later in Skagway, Bill harboured no hard feelings toward Iola, but she was more suspicious of him than ever and would hardly let her daughters out of her sight. Yet somehow Bera and her ardent admirer managed to communicate, and one week after the Beebes arrived in Skagway, they slipped away. Bera's parting note was as brief as the previous one: "I have gone with Swiftwater to Dawson, Mamma. He loves me and I love him."[5]

Leaving Blanche to make her way back home, Iola took off after the pair, but by the time she caught up with them in Dawson it was too late. Bill's first words to her were, "Mrs. Beebe, we're married."[6] Then, as charming as ever, he invited her to their cabin for dinner. She not only accepted the invitation, she also moved in with her daughter and new son-in-law.

For a while, the three got along reasonably well. "Swiftwater during all that summer and winter in Dawson was the very soul of chivalry and attention both to Bera and myself," Iola later wrote. "There was nothing too good for us in the little market places at Dawson and a box of candy at $5 a box just to please Bera or to satisfy my own taste for sweetmeats was no more to Swiftwater than the average man spending a two-bit piece on the outside."[7] As the months passed, however, Iola and Bill began arguing.

The focus of their quarrel was the now-pregnant Bera. Bill wanted his child to be born at his claim on Quartz Creek, which he expected to yield a fortune that spring. Iola told him "he was talking arrant nonsense" and that travelling up there in late winter "would be the death of Bera in her condition." She also pointed out that there were plenty of qualified doctors in Dawson and none on Quartz Creek. Bill's response was to rig up a sleigh with a bed for Bera to lie on during the journey and to find a doctor who, for $2,000, would move to the claim for six weeks and deliver the baby. Bera settled the argument by siding with her husband.[8]

Despite Iola's fears, the baby arrived without incident. But Bill's anticipated prosperity did not materialize. Ever since his return to the Klondike he had been maintaining a precarious financial balancing act, and in the spring of 1900 it became clear that his safety net was in tatters. Three weeks after his son Clifford's birth, he told Iola he was going to Dawson to get supplies. Certain that he planned to abandon his family, she insisted that they would go with him, even though Bera was barely up to travelling.

After a harrowing two-day boat trip to Dawson via the Indian and Yukon rivers, the four reached town, "famished, cold, and completely exhausted."[9] Bill checked them into the Fairview Hotel, and a week later he and Bera pulled their third disappearing act, leaving Iola with an infant to care for and no idea of where his parents were. It was three days before she received any word from them, by which time they were well on their way to Nome.

Instead of opening a hotel when she arrived in the Klondike the previous year, Iola had sold her outfit and put most of the proceeds, nearly $40,000, into the Quartz Creek claim. Now, with no means of pursuing Bill and Bera, she settled

Newlywed sixteen-year-old Bera Gates stands behind her husband, Swiftwater Bill, outside their Quartz Creek cabin with her mother, Iola Beebe (seated left), and two unidentified Klondikers.

into their Dawson cabin and found work doing manicuring, hairdressing, and sewing to support herself and the baby. It was scarcely sufficient income, however, and when a man showed up with a deed for the cabin and evicted her, she had to go begging to the territorial government for assistance. When spring breakup came, Iola, lured by a telegram from Bill saying he would meet her in Nome and pay her back all the money he owed her, bundled up her grandson and boarded one of the first outbound steamers.

Bill was nowhere to be found when Iola arrived in Nome and she soon discovered why. On his way to Alaska he'd taken a shine to his fifteen-year-old stepniece and eloped with her, ignoring the fact that he was already married and had left his very pregnant wife in Washington, DC. A couple of months later, in August 1901, Bera gave birth to their second son, Freddie. Iola spent the next few years trying in vain to get Bill to support his family, but he avoided them assiduously until 1904, when the threat of being convicted of bigamy prompted him to come to Bera and plead for a divorce. Moved by Bill's argument that the boys would be disgraced if their father were thrown into prison, Bera agreed, but her own humiliation was irreversible. A year later, at the age of twenty-two, she committed suicide.

The year after romance brought Bera to the Klondike, it took another adolescent girl away from Dawson, at least temporarily. Sixteen-year-old Mabel Hummelin was the American-born daughter of Norwegian immigrants who ran a roadhouse on one of the creeks. The young man who won her affections, Joe Orton, was a Montana cowboy turned prospector. In late June 1899, the pair secretly left Dawson in a small rowboat, heading for Nome. When Mabel's parents learned of her flight, Alfred Hummelin hurried to town and demanded that the police issue a warrant for the arrest of his daughter's "abductor." He was "terribly angered" by the elopement "as he love[d] his daughter dearly, and was all the more incensed when investigation revealed that Orton had carried away other property belonging to him."[10]

The Klondike Nugget took a light view of the matter, comparing Joe to "young Lochinvar," the romantic hero of a Sir Walter Scott ballad, and describing Mabel as "his lady love," but as far as the law and her parents were concerned, she was the innocent victim of a wicked seducer. When a witness spotted the elopers in Forty Mile a few days later, they were summarily returned to Dawson. It seems they had not yet exchanged vows, and it's unclear whether their matrimonial ambitions were ever realized.[11]

One month later a story that, at first, seemed to leave no room for debate about victims and villains was splashed across the pages of the Nugget. The sordid tale became public knowledge on August 14 when R. Taniguchi, "a Japanese fellow of low character and unfilial disposition," was arrested and charged with "the heinous offense of forcing his little daughter, Kuni, to prostitution and himself living upon her earnings."[12]

Taniguchi and Kuni, an "extremely pretty" girl with long, black hair, had come to Dawson more than a year earlier, accompanied by two Japanese women, Ida and Gracie. From the time of their arrival, the four had lived together in a brothel known as the Yokohama House, yet the authorities seem to have been unconcerned about Kuni's presence there. Although at the time of the arrest she "look[ed] to be no more than 12 years of age," those who knew her said she was fifteen, and once a girl turned fourteen, having sexual relations with her was illegal only if she was "of previously chaste character."[13] Generally no one cared enough about girls like Kuni to bother trying to defend their virtue. Only when George L. Kershew, another Japanese man, accused Taniguchi of corrupting his own child did the police step in.

Kershew was the first witness to testify when the case came to trial on August 23, 1899. Describing Kuni as Taniguchi's stepdaughter and ward, he presented a heart-wrenching account of how she "used to complain to him of the sorrow she felt in being obliged to live the kind of a life she was. One night she ran to him in tears and he secured shelter for her at a lodging house known as the Gold City hotel, where he comforted her."

Then Kuni took the stand and denied every one of his claims. Taniguchi was her brother, she said, and Kershew, rather than being a benevolent protector, had tried to kill her. She told the court,

> Kershew met me at the A. C. Corner one night about two weeks ago. He had a pistol and he pointed it at me, saying, "I will shoot you if you do not marry me." I was much frightened. I went to a lodging house with him and remained until morning. He told me that I should say that Taniguchi is my step father; then he will be arrested and we will take his money and go away. I told Kershew I did not like him and he said he would shoot me if I did not; that he would kill me even if he had to kill himself.

With all the other witnesses—Ida, Gracie, and several Japanese men—supporting this version of events, the case against Taniguchi collapsed and the charge was withdrawn. He was, however, immediately rearrested on "a charge of vagrancy in that he was an idle person, living upon the avails of prostitution." A conviction on that charge earned him a $50 fine and a month in jail. What became of Kuni after the trial is not known.

There is no record of any other girl as young as Kuni working as a prostitute in the Klondike, but it is unlikely she was the only adolescent member of the local demimonde. In other late-nineteenth-century North American mining boom towns and frontier communities, most prostitutes were between fifteen and thirty years old.[14] It was similarly not uncommon for girls as young as fifteen or sixteen to be employed in dancehalls, whether as percentage girls, paid on commission for dancing and drinking with the male patrons, or as vaudeville performers on stage. Like prostitutes, however, they lived outside the bounds of respectable society, often falsified their names and ages, and left little documentation of their personal lives, so it's impossible to know how many of those who worked in the Klondike were chronologically closer to childhood than adulthood.

One of the few whose stories were not lost or intentionally obscured is Edna Radford, a high-spirited teenager who followed her older sister, Edith Neile— better known as the Oregon Mare—into the Dawson dancehalls in 1904.[15] Edna and Edith were born ten years apart in Yreka, California, but were always close to each other despite their age difference. Edna was only eight years old and still living in Yreka when their lawman father was killed in 1897, while eighteen-year-old Edith had already left home, married, and then separated from her husband. A year later Edith headed to the Klondike as a member of a theatrical troupe.

In Dawson, Edith quickly gained renown for her outlandish behaviour both on and off stage. Standing close to six feet tall, the "deep-voiced, magnificently proportioned brunette" was famous for her hilarious stage antics, which were invariably punctuated by long, loud, and highly convincing imitations of a whinnying horse.[16] Like many of the women with whom she shared the spotlights, Edith also spent time on the dancehall floor, entertaining the men more personally and encouraging them to buy liquor, though she herself was not a drinker. That much was expected of her, but the exchange of sexual favours for gold—a sideline that she is said to have pursued enthusiastically—was independent from her contractual obligations.

In 1903 Edith went home to California and found her mother at her wit's end trying to cope with Edna, who had grown into a wild and wilful fourteen-year-old. Marie Radford probably didn't know exactly what her eldest daughter had been up to in the Klondike or perhaps she was just happy to have someone else take responsibility for Edna for a while. At any rate, she allowed Edith to take Edna for a holiday in Mexico, which predictably did nothing to improve Edna's behaviour.

After the sisters came back from Mexico, Edith returned to the Klondike and Marie shipped Edna off to a convent in Spokane, which she endured for a short time before scaling the wall that surrounded the grounds and running away. There was only one place she wanted to go, and all it took to get there was a brief stint as a nurse's aid in a Spokane hospital so she could pay for her passage north.

With her youthful good looks and vivacious nature, it wouldn't have been difficult for fifteen-year-old Edna to find work in the Dawson dancehalls, even without an introduction from the Oregon Mare. Yet although she had Edith to teach her the basics, the Colt, or Little Filly, as she became popularly known, didn't have her sister's aptitude for the job. A few months after arriving in Dawson, she returned south.

By the time she turned eighteen, Edna had two marriages behind her and no promising prospects ahead, so once again she followed her adored sister's lead. Edith had by then moved to Fairbanks and opened a brothel, and for much of the next decade they worked together in the red-light districts of various Alaska towns. Edith seemed content with, or at least resigned to, this life, but Edna wanted something more. She left for a while and married a doctor in San Francisco, then went back north when that relationship also failed. As she approached the age of thirty, she may have despaired of ever leaving the path that she'd started down so young. In 1920, however, she finally retired from the trade for good and began a long and happy marriage to a civil engineer who had been recently widowed and left to raise his infant son alone.

Until about 1903 there was no discernible difference between dancehalls and theatres in the Klondike, regardless of what grand names these venues bore. Drinking, dancing, gambling, and licentious behaviour were all par for the course, and those who were offended by such activities were expected to stay away. Most men and women who worked in these entertainment venues were considered at least somewhat disreputable, but a few escaped censure and gained acceptance from even the more high-minded members of Klondike society. Amongst them were several children.

When the Snow family arrived in Dawson in 1897, many veteran prospectors who knew them from Juneau, Forty Mile, and Circle City were no doubt looking forward to seeing them on stage. George and Anna Snow had always prided themselves on being "legitimate" actors who staged bona fide theatrical productions, instead of the bawdy burlesques that most other companies presented, and their children were an integral part of their shows. From the moment that five-year-old Monte and three-year-old Crystal made their Northern stage debuts in Juneau in 1887, they were immensely popular. At the end of their numbers, audience members would shower the stage with silver dollars and gold pieces, some worth as much as $20, until the two siblings had to take shelter in the wings. "After the downpour, [they'd] bow, pick up the coins, and run to each other yelling, 'I could do this all night!'"[17]

But the Snow Family troupe apparently never performed in the Klondike, for George was too intent on digging his own gold directly from the ground. Since all the best ground was staked by the time he arrived, he took a lease, or lay, on a promising-looking bench claim on Bonanza Creek and got to work. For the Snows, as for all the early stampeders, the winter of 1897–98 was an endurance test.

Crystal and Monte Snow strike theatrical poses. The young performers were well known in the North before the Klondike gold rush but kept a low profile in Dawson.

Food, lamp oil, and candles were in short supply, and their hastily built and poorly furnished cabin offered little in the way of comfort. Come spring, however, the pile of dirt that George had laboriously accumulated from his subsurface mine shafts yielded between $75,000 and $78,000, enough for a triumphant return south after nearly eleven years away.[18]

After several months of visiting family and friends in California, George decided it was time to get back into show business. His new dramatic company was plagued with misfortune, however, and within two years all their hard-earned gold was gone. George's instinct was to join the latest gold rush to Nome, but sixteen-year-old Crystal wanted to live somewhere with a decent school, and since the only way they could afford boat tickets to Alaska was for her to pawn her prized gold-nugget necklace, she got her way. In 1900 George, Anna, and Crystal went back to Juneau, while eighteen-year-old Monte remained in Seattle to attend college, on his way to becoming a journalist.[19]

Although the Snows never performed as a family again, Crystal enjoyed a brief career as a professional singer in her early twenties, after graduating from high school and earning a teaching certificate. The Klondike finally enjoyed a taste of her talents in 1908, when she and a pianist named Dazie Stromstadt spent the summer touring towns and mining camps in Alaska and the Yukon, including Dawson. Their program of classical numbers was well received all along the way, and Crystal was praised for her polished stage presence and clear, expressive voice—a more mature and refined version of the one that had bravely rung out from the top of the snowy Chilkoot Pass fourteen years earlier.[20]

Although Monte and Crystal Snow didn't grace any stages during their family's time in the Klondike and had, in any case, almost outgrown their childhood roles, other youthful performers soon showed up to take their place. The most celebrated of these were the Newman children.

George, Willie, and Marjorie—better known as Margie—Newman arrived in Dawson with their parents at the height of the gold rush and began making a name for themselves almost immediately. One of their early appearances was at a "grand family entertainment" presented on August 12, 1898, at Belinda Mulrooney's sumptuous Fairview Hotel, under the auspices of the Mascot Theatre. Advertising for the event announced that the "celebrated Newman children will appear in a delightful program of specialties and farces," and that after the performances "Miss Mulrooney will tender her usual Friday evening social hop."[21]

At just under $3, tickets for the event weren't inexpensive, but for many of Dawson's more upright citizens it was an attractive alternative to dancehall entertainment. The rather straitlaced Clare Boyntan was among the many who were favourably impressed by the Newman children, writing in her diary the next day that they had done "several very clever turns."[22]

Some time in the next month the trio was engaged by the Monte Carlo, one of four prominent dancehall-theatres that vied for customers on Front Street. "The Newman children have added much to the popularity of the Monte Carlo," commented the *Klondike Nugget*, in the first of many glowing reviews. "The little girl is just about as sweet and clever as a child can be. The change from the comedy and farce of the usual run of variety performance to the innocence of childhood is grateful to the eyes and ears of the average Klondiker, as is demonstrated by the applause. Some of the songs by the little Newman girl have never been rendered in Dawson as cleverly and prettily."

Like most of its competitors, the Monte Carlo was simply a large tent with a wooden facade and frame. The main entrance was through the barroom, while a second bar inside the theatre allowed patrons to refill their glasses without missing any of the action on stage. The fifty-cent admission typically included a cigar or a drink, and as in other box houses, the audience sat either on movable benches on the dance floor or in raised boxes along the walls. Those who chose the boxes paid for the privilege indirectly, since they were expected to welcome percentage girls or actresses into their compartments and indulge them by spending lavishly on champagne.[23]

Although in the course of their work the Newman children undoubtedly witnessed scenes of impropriety, their reputations remained untarnished. Not long after they signed on with the Monte Carlo, they were among the star attractions of a "sacred concert" held at the Oatley Sisters' Concert Hall to raise money for Dawson's hospitals. The Sunday evening event, attended by "upwards of 40 ladies" and an unspecified number of gentlemen, was a decorous affair, featuring "recita-tions, songs, dances, impersonations and character-sketches" by both amateur and professional performers.

All three Newman children performed at the concert, but nine-year-old Margie was the clear favourite, a pattern that was to continue throughout their time in the Klondike. With her round face, and long, dark hair neatly parted in the centre and falling around her shoulders in fat ringlets, Margie's looks were in no way exceptional, but the combination of innocence and talent that she brought to the stage was irresistible to men and women alike.[24] "The charm of the little maid grows on one the oftener she is seen," the Klondike Nugget declared a few days after the hospital benefit. "She appears sometimes with her brothers, and they are both clever boys, but there is a natty neatness and grave conscientiousness about the little girl which has endeared her to the hearts of the big men who go so often to see her."[25]

In October 1898, the Monte Carlo changed hands and was rebuilt on a much larger scale, this time entirely out of wood.[26] The new owner "spared no expense in making the Monte Carlo a model place for lovers of amusement to secure a few hours of recreation," even going so far as to install seventy-five incandescent electric lights. In announcing the revamped theatre's grand opening, the Klondike Nugget reassured readers that the Newman children—especially Margie, who had "taken the house by storm" during the previous few nights—would "continue to please the crowds."[27]

The new Monte Carlo enjoyed packed houses throughout its opening week, and judging by the applause, Margie and her brothers were one of the biggest draws. But applause wasn't their only reward, for when it came to their favourite performers, Dawson theatregoers didn't stop at mere ovations. Like Crystal and Monte Snow, the Newman children took great pleasure in scooping up the gold that was flung their way. "It always provokes a genial laugh in the audience when the little maid drops her stage dignity and comes out to pick up the coins thrown upon the stage by her many admirers," the Nugget noted.[28]

In early January 1899 the Newman children moved over to the Tivoli theatre, where they continued to perform for many months.[29] They were also in great demand for appearances at community functions and charity performances, rang-ing from a "grand benefit" sponsored by the Benevolent and Protective Order of Elks in October 1898 to a gala Christmas bazaar held to raise funds for St. Mary's Hospital in 1899.[30]

The Elks event was aimed at boosting the brotherhood's fund for helping impoverished Klondikers pay their medical bills and burying those who died penniless. "Dawson's society simply turned out en masse" to support this worthy cause and to enjoy the impressive lineup of entertainment. The Newman children performed late in the evening, offering up "their pretty sailor songs and drill. Many of the large audience had never had the pleasure of seeing the children before and many were the expressions of approval, from the ladies especially."[31]

In December 1898 the Newmans were invited to provide after-dinner entertainment for a social gathering of the Tramp Shriners and Knights Templar, and from the moment they arrived at the Regina Hotel after the banquet Margie eclipsed her brothers.[32] Territorial Commissioner William Ogilvie, the event's master of ceremonies, gave her the seat of honour at his right-hand side and lavished attention on her throughout the evening.

After patiently sitting through a number of speeches and amateur offerings, the children finally had their turn to perform. First Willie and George "obliged with song and dance, in costume." Then Margie, appropriately dressed in a tartan outfit, sang her most popular vocal number, the Scottish ballad "Annie Laurie," and followed it with the Highland fling, widely considered to be "the prettiest and most finished of her many dances."

At the conclusion of Margie's act, Colonel Davis rose and proposed the only toast of the evening, saluting "Little Margie, the princess of the Klondike, and nearest to the hearts of every man, woman and child in the Yukon." The banqueters stood as one and drank the toast "with much enthusiasm." Ogilvie then lifted Margie onto the table, from where she confidently responded, saying, "Ladies and gentlemen, I did not prepare a speech; I didn't come to make a speech, but I thank you, everyone."

That Margie's success owed much to the scarcity of children in the Klondike was underlined by Colonel Davis's speech following the toast, in which he "spoke very feelingly of the loved ones at home" and how Klondikers "all deserved the very best at the hands of the country in return for this long deprivation of [their] families." Later, another member of the gathering made a brief address about distant kin and asked that everyone join him in offering up "a few words of silent prayer for the absent dear ones. The presence of little Margie had infected the heart-hungry absentees in a far land to strange degree with longings of their own little ones and all readily responded."

Despite the Newman children's popularity, their parents may have had difficulty making ends meet during their first months in Dawson. Shortly after the Shriners banquet, a benefit was held for the three youngsters at the Monte Carlo. A "host of volunteers" contributed to the program, donating their services "most willingly as a testimonial to the children who had done so much to give to Dawson clean, enjoyable amusement." Various amateur and professional performers, including John Estep, who had taught Margie the Highland fling, took the stage to sing, dance, and recite.

"Then came the little star of the evening . . . who simply re-entwined the love and affection existing in the hearts of all Dawsonites, by her childish grace and sweet rendition of sentimental and character songs. At the close of her number,

STREET SCENE, DAWSON CITY.

Mounted on banner-draped donkeys, Margie, Willie, and George Newman help advertise the Mascot Theatre's grand opening. One of the Newman brothers is mostly hidden by the moving donkey.

Captain Jack, carrying the little princess upon the stage in his arms, made a pretty little presentation speech and pinned to her breast a beautiful gold badge presented to her by admiring friends, while coins of all denominations, nuggets and boxes of candy rained upon the stage from admirers in the auditorium." After Margie finished cleaning up, George and Willie launched the second half of the program with "a characteristic darkey sketch . . . which was well-sustained" and were presented with two "handsome gold badges . . . as souvenirs of the occasion."[33]

Curiously absent from all newspaper accounts of the Newman children's activities in the Klondike is any mention of their parents, William and Mary. Neither of them seem to have been performers, though William may have worked in the same dancehalls as his children, as he was employed as a bartender for at least some of their time in Dawson.[34] Details of the children's life offstage are equally lacking, aside from the fact that George and Margie were enrolled at St. Mary's Catholic School in 1899.[35] In the spring of that year, George, "the clever little comedian," also merited a mention in the newspaper when he fell off a fence on which he was playing and broke his collarbone.[36]

At the time of the 1901 census, only the senior Newmans were living in Dawson. Most likely the children had gone Outside to attend school, but by 1904 they were back. When they appeared at the Auditorium theatre that April, Willie and George were given a more grownup billing as "the Newman Brothers" and fifteen-year-old Margie was promoted to the rank of "soubrette."[37] In June 1904 the entire family moved from the Klondike to Fairbanks and disappeared from the historical record.[38]

The only other young performer who came close to rivalling the Newman children's Klondike fame was Annie O'Brien, who was thirteen when she arrived in Dawson with her parents in the fall of 1899. Irish-born Eddie O'Brien, a veteran of the North American vaudeville circuit, had been hired as the Monte Carlo's new stage director, and the O'Briens took up residence above the theatre, typical lodgings for performers and dancehall girls.

Annie had undoubtedly lived in such places before but perhaps never one where so much tragedy had unfolded in such a short time. Since the building's construction in 1898, two murder-suicides and one solo suicide had taken place in the Monte Carlo's upstairs rooms.[39] Given this violent history and the dubious morals of many of the residents, most people would have said the Monte Carlo was an unsuitable home for a child, but the O'Briens weren't the only family living there. Another theatrical couple, Leo and Conchita, and their young children, Emily and Howe, were also tenants.[40]

During his first days on the job, Eddie "eliminated from the boards everything that hint[ed] at the rude and vulgar." New acts included "The Blackberry Hop," a sketch performed by the "smooth, clean and up-to-date . . . team of O'Brien, Jennings and O'Brien." Presumably one of the O'Briens was Annie's mother, Alice, a seasoned actress originally from Kansas. The program concluded with Eddie's version of *The South Before the War*, featuring "slaves, bloodhounds, snake whips and many other things which went to make up the furnishings of a Southern plantation 40 years ago." Given the large cast, Annie likely had a part in the play.[41]

At the beginning of January 1900 Eddie launched his latest headliner, a five-act drama titled *The White Slave*, in which Annie played a character named Paul.[42] The competition for customers required frequent changes to every theatre's program, so Annie, like all Klondike performers, had to be a quick study. During the week-long run of *The White Slave* she and the rest of the company also had to rehearse for their next production, *Buffalo Bill*, which opened on January 8. That play, however, was destined to have a very short run.

Just after three o'clock on the afternoon of January 10, one of the actresses who lived above the Monte Carlo noticed sparks falling from the ceiling of her room, close to the stovepipe. Knowing that many of her neighbours were resting in preparation for the coming night's work, she ran down the hallway, shouting and pounding on doors, while passersby who had spotted the fire from the street sounded the alarm and rushed in to help evacuate the building. Within ten minutes, the entire theatre was engulfed in flames, and by the time the fire was subdued, three hours later, it had wiped out more than $500,000 worth of property in Dawson's downtown core. The Monte Carlo and Opera House theatres, the Board of Trade building, the US consul's office, the Northern Trading Company building, several saloons and restaurants, and a handful of other businesses had all either burned to the ground or been torn down during the course of fighting the fire.[43]

Because the blaze spread so quickly, the Monte Carlo's tenants were forced to flee empty-handed and, in the case of many of the women, wearing only "their night dresses or other light and hastily donned clothing."[44] When the O'Briens took stock the next day they estimated the value of their losses at $2,000. The only other residents whose losses matched or exceeded this amount were the highly popular performer Gertie Lovejoy, who was left with little more than the diamond that sparkled between her two front teeth, and Rose Blumpkin, a winsome Monte Carlo ticket-taker, whose riches came from her lucrative after-hours work as a prostitute.[45]

Annie lost a number of precious possessions, including a gold bracelet set with jewels, but the only thing she cared about as she watched her home burn was her pet puppies, which no one had had time to rescue. By the time someone had the sense to remove her from the scene, she was hysterical with grief. Meanwhile, Conchita was in an even worse state, fearing that her little son, Howe, was also trapped inside the building. It was with great relief that she learned that a friend had taken him out for a sleigh ride earlier in the afternoon.

Although homeless and destitute, the O'Briens weren't out of work for long. Eddie was hired almost immediately as the stage manager for the Palace Grand, the only Dawson theatre that had escaped the conflagration, and most members of the Monte Carlo company transferred to the new venue. With Margie Newman gone from town, Annie's star was rising. In February, when the Palace Grand hosted a benefit for a fireman whose arm had been broken while fighting the Monte Carlo fire, she was among the most enthusiastically received performers. The Klondike Nugget reported that "Dawson's favorite, Miss Annie O'Brien, always welcome, was never more so than last night and her several sentimental songs only served to further endear the little lady to her hearers. Later, with her father, she assisted in the rendition of several excellent musical specialties."[48]

During the following year, the O'Briens continued to please audiences at the Palace Grand, but in the fall of 1901, with vaudeville's popularity in Dawson clearly waning, fifteen-year-old Annie and her parents moved on.[49]

Compared to the Newmans and Annie O'Brien, other children who were part of the Klondike's paid workforce attracted little attention. Nevertheless, their contributions to their families' incomes were often significant, whether their earnings went into their own pockets or were pooled with those of their parents, and a few were self-supporting.

Sixteen-year-old Tom Gibson and his fourteen-year-old brother, Elmer, arrived in the Klondike in the summer of 1898 knowing that they would have to pull their own weight. Joe Gibson had preceded his family by a year and had already realized that his Dominion Creek claim wasn't going to make them rich overnight. His letters home that winter had advised his wife, Ellen, to bring her sewing machine and clothes wringer so that she could help support the family. He also suggested that his sons could make some money by hauling freight between Dawson and the creeks. "The boys can get a dog team," he wrote, "and you and they can make more than I can."[50] Even though Joe's idea of his sons becoming dogsled teamsters went nowhere, his prediction about their earning power proved accurate.

Under Canadian law, an individual had to be eighteen or older to get a free miner's certificate.[51] However, that didn't prevent Tom from joining his parents in forming a mining partnership with another man in December 1898. A strapping six-footer with plenty of youthful energy, Tom helped work the group's claims on Dominion, Boulder, and Gold Bottom creeks that winter, but it took only a single season for him to become disillusioned with mining. Come spring, he moved into Dawson and found a job unloading cargo off incoming riverboats.

By the end of 1899 the whole family was living in town, and Ellen had purchased the Montana Steam Laundry. The business was a good investment, providing employment not only for Ellen but also for her sons, who assisted with the more strenuous tasks, such as wielding heavy polishing irons, as well as delivering laundry and collecting payment. Meanwhile, the boys were also busy with a new line of work.

Meat was a scarce and expensive commodity in Dawson, so Tom had taken to going out with his shotgun to keep down the family's food costs. After making a couple of sales when he brought home more game than they needed, he and Elmer decided to go into business as hunters. Starting with grouse and snowshoe hares as their main quarry, they extended their operations to hunting waterfowl and fishing after Ellen helped them purchase a canoe and some nets. The Montana Steam

Brothers Tom and Elmer Gibson contributed to family finances by selling the wild game they shot and working in their mother's steam laundry.

Laundry's location right on the banks of the Yukon River made it a convenient headquarters where regular customers could come and make their selections, though Tom and Elmer also sold directly to Dawson butchers.

Between the meat-supplying business, the laundry, and Joe's work as a hired mine labourer, the Gibsons had enough to get by and invest in a couple of rental cabins, but Joe and Ellen were increasingly at odds. She was still hoping to strike it rich with one of their own claims; he had abandoned such dreams and was content to work for wages by day and spend his evenings in the saloons. The marriage finally collapsed in 1902 when Ellen decided to follow the latest gold rush and Joe refused to go with her. Tom, by then an independent adult, followed his mother to Fairbanks the following year. Elmer had already left the Yukon, having returned to California in 1901 at the age of seventeen and enlisted in the army, but he came north again in 1903 to join his mother and brother in Fairbanks. Neither Ellen nor her sons ever found the fortune she'd been seeking, but by the time of her death in 1908 she had acquired some reasonably valuable real estate, which she bequeathed to her sons.[52]

Many children picked wild berries for their family's own consumption, but there were also willing buyers for their harvest. In September 1901 Dawson shopkeeper Joseph Clearihue wrote to his wife in Victoria that cranberries grew abundantly in the area and "quite a number of people, women and children, are making a very nice thing picking them, they sell them at 20¢ per lb. & they can pick 50 to 100 lbs. a day making from $5 to $10 per day and ready sale."[53]

A few years later, Finlay Whyte tried another type of provisioning business, keeping chickens in an empty cabin behind his family's Dawson home and selling the eggs for $3 a dozen. He gave up after one winter, however, as constantly stoking the wood stove to heat the makeshift henhouse was hard work, and during one particularly cold snap, the rooster's wattles froze and subsequently fell off.

Because of the Whyte family's tight finances, Finlay's two older brothers both worked from the time they arrived in the Klondike. Their father, John Whyte, had led the way to the goldfields, arriving in 1897 and finding a job working for Thomas Lippy. In 1899, the oldest son, sixteen-year-old Bert, followed his father north and was also hired on at the Lippy mine. A year later, they were joined by the rest of the family, except for thirteen-year-old Lily, who stayed in Washington to finish her schooling. Fifteen-year-old Harry initially worked as a cattle minder, then moved on to a job with the Alaska Commercial Company.

In 1908 fourteen-year-old Dorothy Whyte got a summer job working for Dawson dentist George Faulkner. Dr. Faulkner had not yet embraced the use of novocaine, so one of Dorothy's main duties was to stand behind the chair and hold the patient's head while Dr. Faulkner pulled teeth or performed other procedures. She was also tasked with melting $20 gold pieces and taking them to a jeweller who would roll the gold into thin sheets, which the dentist would cut to make gold caps. Having proved a competent assistant, Dorothy returned to the position with Dr. Faulkner for two more summers before her family moved south in 1910.[54]

During the first couple of years of the Klondike stampede, when there were more than enough failed prospectors and other frustrated gold seekers around to fill any job vacancy that came up in Dawson or on the creeks, it's unlikely that someone as young as Dorothy would have found work in a professional office. But as the gold rush excitement subsided, the number of jobless adults declined and employment opportunities for anyone who wanted or needed to work increased. However, that didn't stop teenagers John Kay and Fred Buteau from trying to make money the easy way.

In May 1902 the two boys were caught with a camera and photographic supplies that they'd stolen from a Bonanza Creek cabin. When they appeared in

An empty bottle holder and a big grin suggest that the 1900 Victoria Day celebrations were a success for this young pop vendor. Behind him, three girls (one covering her face with a flag) play on the empty grandstand.

court, the police testified that the pair had been "doing a wholesale business in the line of theft" for several weeks prior to their apprehension. Both pleaded guilty to a number of petty theft charges, but given their youth, Judge Macaulay had no desire to lock them up. Instead he arranged for Fred, a "half-breed Indian" from Holy Cross on the lower Yukon River, to be shipped back to his family. And he gave John a suspended three-month sentence, even though it wasn't clear where he would serve it.

According to John's father, the thirteen-year-old had been living with his mother in Vancouver before running away to Dawson. To the *Klondike Nugget* reporter he appeared "a bright and rather handsome boy," but Mr. Kay had little good to say about his son, explaining that he had been kicked in the head by a horse a few years earlier, "since which time his criminal instincts [had] rapidly developed."

The judge's preferred course of action was to return John to Vancouver, if someone would pay his way. In the meantime, he ordered him to report to Sergeant Smith at the Dawson police station every Monday and Thursday at noon. Since this requirement made it impractical for the boy to live with his father out on the creeks, the police were to see that he was provided with food and lodging at some place other than the jail until he could be sent south.[55]

In the end, John remained in the Klondike for the duration of his sentence and went back to living with his father, but he didn't stay for long. After running away again, he earned "a precarious existence by doing odd jobs here and there," including working in South Dawson for a man named Larsen and in a wood-cutting camp up the Klondike River. He also resumed his previous light-fingered ways, and by the middle of December he was back in court, facing more than twenty charges of theft.

When called to the stand, Mr. Kay "stated that he could do nothing with his son, that he would not obey and that he was incorrigible." However, John appeared remorseful, frequently wiping his eyes and blowing his nose on a ragged pocket handkerchief and breaking into sobs under Judge Macauley's stern but not unsympathetic questioning. For the sake of efficiency, the judge allowed John to plead guilty to just one charge, that of stealing a $16 rifle, and set the others aside, but with the boy's history of recidivism, that offence alone was serious enough to warrant harsh punishment.

When he heard that he was being sentenced to two years in prison, John's last vestiges of bravado disappeared and tears poured down his cheeks as he begged the judge to give him another chance. That, Macauley responded, was exactly what he intended to do. "I will make the sentence suspended and you will be sent to your mother at the earliest opportunity and if you are ever found in this territory again, the sentence will be strictly enforced. If there ever was a case for the reform school you are the one, and it is only because there is no such institution here that you are not in it."[56]

Macauley's approach was nothing new for the Klondike. The North-West Mounted Police had a long tradition of putting adult offenders on outbound steamers and warning them never to return. But John Kay and Fred Buteau may have been the first juvenile delinquents to receive a "blue ticket."

The year 1902 seems to have been a bad one for juvenile misbehaviour in the Klondike. In September, the same Sergeant Smith who had supervised John Kay's suspended sentence over the summer told the Dawson city councillors that "some steps were needed to keep many of the irresponsible youths of the city at home in their proper places."

"Some of them," it was reported, "combine in their diminutive bodies the very quintessence of cussedness, are impertinent, full of mischief, swear like a pirate, and a few of them will not stop at petty thieving if a good opportunity presents itself. Pop, fruit, and other articles displayed in the front of many stores are their principal graft and their boldness is so great that they have become a nuisance."

The known troublemakers must have been very young, since council responded by drafting a bylaw stating that no one under the age of twelve would be permitted to "loiter or stand as idlers" on any public street between 9 p.m. and 6 a.m., unless performing a service for a parent, guardian, or master. Once the new ordinance was passed, Smith assigned a constable to ring the fire hall bell every evening at nine o'clock "warning those of a tender age that it [was] time for them to be at home."[57]

———

In contrast to some of the youthful wrongdoing Sergeant Smith saw on the beat, Jim Kingsley's brief foray down the criminal path was inconsequential, but it permanently cured him of all larcenous tendencies and, surprisingly, helped temporarily bridge the gap that had opened up between him and his father during the six years they had lived apart.

Not long after Jim, Ethel, and their mother arrived in the Klondike in 1903, Jim pilfered some candy from a store and got caught. When his father found out, the nine-year-old was certain he was "going to get a thrashing." Instead, Jack delivered a solemn lecture on basic honesty and made him promise that he would never steal again. Still braced for punishment, Jim was astonished when his father ended the talk with an apology. He was sorry, he said, that he'd neglected to buy him any sweet treats. Then he took Jim out and bought two big glass jars of colourful candy to keep in the Kingsleys' Bonanza Clothing Store for Jim and his friends.[58]

Although Jack had told his son to just ask in the future if he needed anything, Jim was soon earning money of his own.[59] One of his first profit-making enterprises was hauling water in winter from Number 21 Above on Bonanza Creek to Grand Forks, where he sold it at twenty-five cents for four gallons. Jim transported the water in two small barrels set on a sled pulled by his three dogs. To keep the water from spilling, he dipped flour sacks in the water and secured them over the barrels with hoops. The covers froze solid in a matter of minutes and he never lost a drop on the trail. The young entrepreneur also used his dog team to travel up and down Bonanza and Eldorado creeks selling newspapers and magazines.

One summer the Grand Forks butcher bought about fifty head of cattle from a boatload that had come into Dawson. Knowing that Jim was a competent rider, he provided him with a mount and hired him to mind the herd. The job was "great fun" until the day his charges became restless for no obvious reason and suddenly raised their tails and started to run. Jim galloped after them, watching helplessly as they stampeded over the hill and down toward Hunker Creek, then gave up and returned to report to his boss. The butcher managed to round up all the cattle within a few days, but the incident apparently put an end to Jim's career as a cowboy.

Experience with horses did get Jim another job, however. He was only twelve years old when he became a part-time employee of the Door and Wright transportation company, driving a two-horse stage between Grand Forks and Quartz Creek every Sunday. While this responsible position earned Jim a hefty $4 a day, he was equally willing to take on smaller jobs, such as candling a shipment of eggs that had been exposed to freezing temperatures on the way from Whitehorse to Grand Forks. Customers wouldn't be happy if they discovered they'd purchased spoiled eggs at $4.25 a dozen, so the man who'd brought them in had Jim inspect them all, separating out the frozen ones to be mixed into dog rations.

Always a willing worker, Jim helped out with the family business in numerous ways, some of which gave him a rather adult view of Klondike life. He regularly made deliveries to prostitutes who felt uncomfortable venturing out among the respectable housewives to do their shopping. And after spring cleanup, when successful miners' pockets were filled with gold from their winter diggings, he made frequent visits to all seven of the town's hotels to deliver orders of cigars, tobacco, and snuff to men who were so fixated on gambling that they didn't leave the tables for days at a time. On his way to and from the gaming tables he encountered drinkers in various states of inebriation and percentage girls from the dancehalls that were part of most of the hotels.

One of the more surprising sights Jim saw while running errands for his father was not an illicit glimpse of a half-clad woman of ill repute but a revealing display of leg by Mrs. Garvey, the owner of a hotel and livery stable. Because Mrs. Garvey

A young entrepreneur with his laundry wagon outside the Gold Run Hotel.

always had plenty of cash around, Jack had sent Jim to her to get change for a $100 bill. She must have thought the boy was too young to require any modesty on her part, for when he handed her the $100 she hiked up her floor-length skirt and pulled a fat wad of notes from the top of her stocking. In the course of the transaction he determined that she had tens, twenties, and hundreds stashed in one stocking and ones, twos, and fives in the other. This extraordinary view of normally hidden lower limbs made less of an impression on him than the novel banking system; but after that, every time he saw Mrs. Garvey he wondered how she could walk carrying all those big rolls of bills.

Jack also entrusted Jim with far greater amounts than $100. During spring cleanup, some of the miners brought their earnings to the Bonanza Clothing Store to exchange for paper currency. It was Jim's job to take the gold to Dawson, travelling by stage with as much as a few thousand dollars' worth of gold dust and nuggets in his satchel. A friend of his father met him when he reached town and accompanied him to the bank to make his deposit and load up with cash, then saw him safely back onto the stage.

Some of the gold Jim handled was his own. He and his friends Norman Nelson and Hugh Cutting were given permission to rework the tailings on some of the miners' claims after they'd finished the cleanup. The boys used pans and rocker boxes to wash the gravel, and one spring they made enough to rent horses from the Garveys' livery stable. Several times they rode out of sight up the creek to stage exhilarating equestrian races, but after Mr. Garvey discovered their mischief, he refused to rent to them again.

Even with occasional spending on pleasures and treats, by the time Jim was sent south by his father after his mother's death in 1907, he had saved up $300. It was a substantial nest egg for a boy who just four years earlier had stolen candy because he couldn't afford to buy it. When he got to Vancouver, Jim went to visit his sister Ethel in the convent where their father had recently placed her and was dismayed to find her very ill. Showing a maturity beyond his years, the fourteen-year-old spent every penny he owned to pay the doctor and cover her other medical bills before he continued on to Victoria.[60]

I did not dig the dirt,

but men did that for me,

and I washed it out.

Chapter 11

Gold Nuggets and
Priceless Memories

Regardless of age or financial circumstances, it was almost impossible to spend any length of time in the Klondike during the gold rush years and not be tempted to try, at least once, to wrest from the ground some of the precious yellow metal that defined the place. In this respect, Klondike children were no different from Klondike adults.

The first spring that Clemy Lung lived on Dominion Creek, his father told the five-year-old about the pot of gold at the rainbow's end. As one spring shower after another moved through the valley, Clemy studied the colourful arcs and one day, when he was sure he'd pinpointed where one had touched down, he and his parents staked out his "Rainbow Claim."

Over the following weeks, with his dog, Nelly, keeping him company, Clemy spent hours industriously digging into the designated spot, never realizing that his father was salting the pile of excavated material when he wasn't watching. Ed had built him a small sluice box, and when Clemy's dump was big enough, Ed showed him how to wash the gravel using the meltwater that flowed down the hillside.

The day Clemy rushed home to show his mother a pan full of pickings sprinkled with gleaming specks, she cheerfully postponed supper so Ed could guide him through the process of separating and cleaning the gold. When they weighed the final result, he had exactly $1 worth of dust and nuggets, a fortune for someone his age. Best of all, his father declared him "a real miner."[1]

Florence, Freddy, and Lawrence Barrett also staked their own claim, a ten-square-foot piece of ground behind their father's cabin on Victoria Gulch. Martin built a small windlass for his children, and during visits from Dawson they "would mine there all day long, imitating everything [their] father did in his big shaft." One of their neighbours, a big, affable Swede, came over from time to time to watch and tease them about their efforts. He could also be talked into taking a turn at cranking the handle of the windlass, with a great show of grunting effort. It's not clear whether they ever brought up any pay dirt, but all of them, including the Swede, had fun.[2]

Many other children took their quest for gold very seriously. Like many of their peers who lived on the creeks, Ethel, Dewey, and Clay Anderson had their own child-sized rocker box and "soon learned to know pay dirt when [they] saw it." The miners were invariably generous with the youngsters in their neighbourhoods and would often let the juvenile prospectors scrape out any dirt that remained in cracks and knotholes in the long wooden troughs after they finished sluicing.

When the cleanup was in full swing the Anderson children operated their rocker almost daily and always captured at least a dusting of gold. On their best days, they made as much as $14. Their first-hand education in placer mining included seeing the "breathtaking beauty" of gold dust and nuggets collected in the bottom of the miners' sluice boxes after the water was shut off, sometimes lying an inch deep. They also learned that, contrary to the exaggerated claims made at the height of the stampede, "nuggets were not shaken from grass roots nor scooped up from the creek beds." Yet once, as the children were climbing over a pile of tailings, Dewey spotted a flat yellow rock about the size and thickness of a dollar, plastered to a piece of shale. They washed it in a puddle and found it was a genuine gold nugget. No doubt they walked with their eyes on the ground for many weeks after that.[3]

Hallie Heacock, who washed out his first pan of Klondike gold as a sixteen-year-old in 1898, spent the next few years working alongside his father on his Eldorado Creek claim and joined him in checking out the Nome goldfields. In 1901 Hallie went south to finish his interrupted high school education in Spokane, where his mother and siblings were living, but the classroom couldn't hold him. In March 1902 he headed north again to his father's new diggings on Bonanza Creek.

No longer an adolescent, Hallie did a man's work on the claim, but retained some of the privileges of youth. Hallie, his father, and his father's partner, Louis Arndt, spent two weeks painstakingly processing the sluice box takings, using a blower pan and mercury retort in the final stages. Then Hallie and Harry Arndt, Louis's twelve-year-old son, had a turn. The five-gallon can of black sand had already yielded more than $1,200 worth of gold; Hallie and Harry managed to extract another $30 worth, which was theirs to keep.[4]

Compared to children who lived on the creeks, young Dawson residents were at a disadvantage when it came to obtaining gold straight from the source, but that didn't deter Pearl Hall, the daughter of a prominent Klondike miner. During the school year, Pearl lived in Dawson, where her mother owned a hotel. In summer, she went out to her father's claim. When she left Dawson in 1905 to attend school in Vancouver, she had the satisfaction of being able to pay a portion of her educational expenses with gold she had panned herself.

Klondike children learned to recognize prize gold nuggets from an early age.

"I am especially proud of that fact," Pearl told a newspaper reporter, "because my father and mother are both amply able to pay my tuition, but I want to be as independent as possible. Part of the money I am going to use while in school I made by panning gold. I did not dig the dirt, but men did that for me, and I washed it out. If you are a miner you know that panning is often the hardest part of the acquiring of gold. I panned lots of it, and kept it to help defray my school expenses."[5]

Pearl's new Vancouver schoolmates were most likely impressed by her tales of Dawson life and moiling for gold on the legendary Klondike creeks. Although the gold rush had long since slowed to a trickle, the Klondike still held a special place in the popular imagination, and those who had been in the region long enough to see both freeze-up and breakup on the Yukon River enjoyed great prestige as Klondike sourdoughs. Children who could claim this status were an especially exclusive group, though they didn't necessarily realize the uniqueness of some of their experiences until they left the North.

When the Anderson family first moved back to Bellingham, Washington, in 1902, they relished the "aura of mystery and daring" that surrounded them and

Klondikers could call themselves sourdoughs once they had seen the Yukon River freeze in fall and thaw in spring. This massive ice block lingered onshore long after spring breakup, a reminder of winter's severity.

other Klondike veterans and couldn't resist showing off some of their wealth. At a minimum, most returned sourdoughs had a choice nugget attached to a watch chain. The Andersons "literally dripped nuggets." Emma wore "a long nugget watch chain which circled her neck and hung below her belt to loop back to the watch at her waist." P.B. sported a large nugget stickpin, as well as the requisite nugget watch fob. Ethel had a nugget necklace and both she and her mother wore nugget rings. As intended, this opulent jewellery attracted attention. When they walked down the street, people stared with amazement, and when they rode on streetcars, other passengers "drooled with questions as they eyed [their] nugget chains."[6]

The Andersons probably didn't continue displaying their Klondike souvenirs as everyday wear for long, though, if for no other reason than their sheer weight. Hallie Heacock certainly found his gold showpiece too much of a burden to be bothered with. When the Heacocks came out of the Klondike in 1901, Hallie's father had a watch fob made for him to drape across his vest. It featured ten $5 nuggets strung along the chain and a $14 nugget dangling from the end. Hallie wore this prize only once before deciding it was too heavy. At nineteen years old, he was more interested in having money to spend than in flaunting his

Klondike credentials, so he had the nuggets melted down and happily put the $64 he received for them into his pocket.[7]

When children who were born in the North, or who had moved there at a very young age, made their first trips Outside, much of what they encountered was as exotic to them as the Klondike was to Southerners. As the twentieth century gathered momentum, the novelties that greeted young Klondikers upon their arrival in places like Vancouver and Seattle included electric trolleys, towering skyscrapers, and "other marvelous things that pertain exclusively to the cities to the South."[8] When the Lungs returned to Tacoma in the fall of 1905, however, the sights that made the greatest impression on Klondike-born Ella, four and half years old, and Paul, two and a half, were much simpler.[9]

Leaving Ed to wrap up his mining operations, Velma and the children made their way south by steamer and train. Even though Velma eschewed any ostentatious display of gold, the family attracted attention on the last leg of the journey, when Paul and Ella discovered cows, pigs, chickens, ducks, and geese. Other children their age would have taken no notice of such common farm animals, but for the youngest Lungs these were mythical beasts. As the train rolled past the numerous farms along the route from Vancouver to Tacoma, the two little sourdoughs "went wild with ecstasy over each wonderful new sight and would screech and yell out their delight," much to the surprise and amusement of everyone else in the coach.

Their reaction to the livestock was not the only thing that made them a curiosity. When they passed an orchard, Ella, who had never seen fruit on trees, let loose a scream of excitement and urged everyone to look at all the "baked apples." Meanwhile, ten-year-old Clemy had found a receptive audience to admire his poke of gold and listen to his Klondike stories.

Leaving Dominion Creek also meant a change of attire for Ella, who had been dressed in boys' overalls for most of her life. Shortly before the family's departure, a group of local women gave Velma a parting gift of garments they had made for the children. When Ella saw the row of dainty little frocks laid out on the bed, some of them decorated with ruffles, ribbons, and bows, she "danced and skipped around the cabin . . . then grabbed the fanciest one and tried it on."

The Lungs' fourth child, conceived in the Klondike, was born in Tacoma in the spring of 1906. Worried about Velma's health, Ed had insisted she go south for the birth, a fortunate decision since she experienced complications and required the kind of medical care that wouldn't have been available in Dawson, let alone on Dominion Creek. Little Rowena was nearly six months old by the time

Some girls who grew up on the Klondike creeks were more accustomed to wearing overalls than frilly dresses.

Ed was reunited with his family, ending their final Klondike separation. He had sold his claim and brought out nine bricks of gold, each one worth about $9,000, enough money to invest in a business and live comfortably.

While Ella and Paul were too young to have real memories of the North, Clemy was old enough to hold onto his. As a skilled raconteur and the only child at his school who had been to the Klondike, he was in great demand during story hour, and some of his schoolmates were so eager to hear about his life in the goldfields that they would come home with him after classes and cut the grass, pile firewood, or pull weeds while he entertained them. Clemy's storytelling came to an early end, however, when he died at the age of seventeen from the crippling effects of polio.

When Mary Catherine Miller took her four children south in 1910, only the youngest, six-year-old Gladys, had never been Outside. Nevertheless, even

The Miller children around the time of their departure from the Klondike in 1910. Clockwise from left: Dorothy, Norman, Bessie, Gladys. The girl sitting centre front is probably their cousin Alfreda Thompson.

the older children were in for some surprises. In the eleven years since she had brought Dorothy and Bessie, one a toddler and the other a babe in arms, north to join their father, they had left the Klondike just once, in 1901. Their brother, Norman, had been a mere six weeks old when they left that fall to spend the winter in Seattle, so he recalled nothing of their time there.

Mary Catherine and the children said their final goodbyes to the Klondike under a cloud of sorrow.[10] Although Louis Miller's first years of mining had been profitable, his success had not continued. As his financial troubles multiplied, he took to drinking, and by 1909 he was no longer supporting his family. That Christmas was a grim one in the Miller's Dawson home. Louis was not around and Mary Catherine, a proud woman, found herself in the humiliating position of accepting charity. She couldn't refuse when one of the churches sent a Christmas dinner and a toy for each of the children but vowed to herself that the experience would not be repeated.

Perhaps Mary Catherine kept hoping Louis would reform, for she waited until the last moment to leave Dawson in 1910. On October 19, with the Yukon River starting to become choked with ice, she and the children boarded the last Whitehorse-bound boat of the year, on their way to Alturas, California, to seek refuge with her mother. Louis and the children's beloved dog, Bruno, came to see them off, and Louis "went to pieces" as they said their goodbyes. For twelve-year-old Bessie, the sight of her father forlornly standing on the pier as their steamer pulled away was never to be forgotten.

One of the first innovations the Miller children were introduced to when they went south was a bathroom with running water, which they encountered in a Portland hotel. Until then they had always taken their Saturday night baths in a tin tub on the kitchen floor. Indoor plumbing was so unfamiliar to Bessie that she couldn't figure out how to turn off the hotel bathtub's taps.

Although Bessie was very fond of her grandmother, she was terribly homesick for the Klondike during her first months in California. The children she met laughed at her Canadian accent, and some of the food her grandmother served up seemed strange. She and her siblings complained that the fresh eggs they got for breakfast were flavourless compared to the gamey but "delicious" cold-storage eggs they were used to. And fourteen-year-old Dorothy, raised on canned milk like all Klondike children, refused to drink milk "from a dirty ol' cow." However, the Miller children were entranced by the sight of orange trees laden with fruit. They picked the first ones they saw, even though they were still green, and pronounced them to be wonderful.

Of course, not all Klondike children left and took their memories with them. Some became Northerners for life, a hardy cohort, born "of rugged parents, the early pioneers who dared the hardships of the trail, who possessed the stamina to continue in the battle though oftentimes against overwhelming discouragement."[11] They were united by their bonds to a land that was not foreign, as it had been for their parents, but simply "home." Yet their paths diverged in all directions when they reached adulthood.

Victoria Faulkner, for example, graduated from St. Mary's Catholic School in 1916, twelve years after she started grade one in the little log schoolhouse at Last Chance. At nineteen years old and without ever having left the Klondike, she was a full-fledged graduate of St. Ann's Academy in Victoria, the mother school under which St. Mary's operated. She had "a very thorough grounding in the classics—in literature, . . . a wonderful knowledge of the world—of geography," and the ability to take shorthand in both French and English.

While several of Victoria's classmates left to attend universities in eastern Canada, she stayed in the Klondike and took a job as secretary for gold mining magnate Joe Boyle, working first at Bear Creek and later in Dawson. When Boyle left the Yukon in 1918, she began a forty-four-year career as a civil servant, starting as a stenographer in the gold commissioner's office. From there she went on to serve as secretary for nine consecutive territorial commissioners, eventually being regarded as one of the territory's most influential civil servants. Victoria moved away from the Klondike in 1953 only because Whitehorse replaced Dawson as the Yukon capital. Although she remained in Whitehorse from her retirement in 1972 until her death in 1981, she "never lost her love for life lived on the creeks" or her affection for Dawson.[12]

In contrast to those who pursued careers in business or the civil service, some Klondike children, like Ralph Troberg, carried on the search for gold that had brought their parents north. Ralph's father came to the goldfields from Finland and ended up staying and raising his family in the Klondike. Ralph, the second son, was born in Grand Forks in 1905. In 1910 fire ravaged the town, destroying more than sixty buildings as it burned for four straight days. Five-year-old Ralph watched the fire from a hilltop "where he and other children had been deposited while adults battled the blaze with a bucket brigade." After the fire, the Troberg family moved to Dawson, where Ralph entered school three years later and acquired his lifetime nickname of "Sox."

After graduating from high school at the age of seventeen, Sox began working in the goldfields. By then, dredges dominated the scene and for most of his mining career he was employed as a dredgerman. Periodically, however, he took time out to work his own claims the old-fashioned way, going broke as a miner five times. After marrying at thirty-five, Sox and his family spent some winters

Like these young Dominion Creek residents, photographed around 1898, many children living on the creeks did a little mining of their own.

with his in-laws in British Columbia, but his attachment to his birthplace never weakened. As a seventy-seven-year-old widower, he declared that he had no intention of ever leaving Dawson again. Of his nearly eight decades in the Klondike, all of them coloured by gold, he said, "It was a great life."[13]

Dorothy Whyte was sixteen when she moved south in 1910, leaving behind her childhood and the North at the same time. She had experienced the disappearance of her father when he joined the stampede in 1897 and had been among the flood of children who came north with their mothers in 1900—children who helped shape the Klondike over the next decade, even as it shaped them.

Although it would be nearly seventy years before Dorothy returned to Dawson, her memories of growing up there remained vivid all her life. The "crackling of the Northern Lights as they swept across the sky . . . mingling with the squeaking [of] wooden sidewalks" underfoot; the "joyful" sound of meltwater running in the ditches in springtime; and the repugnant odour of fish heads or horse meat being cooked up with rice or oatmeal for dog food. Her first encounter with frostbite, when she was six years old, and how the postmaster came out of the post office to rub snow on her frozen cheeks, a standard cure that was almost a rite of passage for new Northerners. School, church, community festivities, and private parties. Skating in winter, gathering crocuses for May Day baskets, and one long summer day when she and her best friend, Meta Miller, rode their bicycles all the way to Gold Bottom and back.[14]

Grace Murray moved to the Klondike as a pudgy two-year-old in 1907 and was raised in Dawson and on the creeks until her family left the North in 1918. She, too, was in her eighties when she made her first trip back. Returning released a flood of memories and made her realize what a strong hold the Klondike still had on her. As she wrote in a letter shortly after her nostalgic trip, "I have never got the 'Yukon' out of my system."[15]

Whether they remained firmly rooted in the North or departed when they were still young, nearly every member of her generation of Klondikers felt the same way: the Yukon, and more specifically the Klondike, was an indelible part of who they were. Most would also have agreed with the sentiment expressed by Ethel Russell, who moved to Grand Forks as a ten-year-old in 1902 and to Dawson a few years later. Interviewed at the age of seventy-five in the Seattle nursing home where she was living, she said simply, "I couldn't imagine a better place to be a little girl."[16]

Notes

❈ ABBREVIATIONS

ASL   Alaska State Library, Alaska Historical Collections, Juneau
BCA   Royal BC Museum, British Columbia Archives, Victoria
DCM   Dawson City Museum, Dawson City
LAC   Library and Archives Canada, Ottawa
SSA   Sisters of St. Ann Archives, Victoria
UW   University of Washington Libraries, Seattle
YA   Yukon Archives, Whitehorse

❈ CHAPTER 1: THE PRETTIEST LITTLE DAUGHTER
YOU EVER SAW

1. The information about Graphie Carmack and her parents comes from several sources, primarily: Julie Cruikshank, "Images of Society in Klondike Gold Rush Narratives: Skookum Jim and the Discovery of Gold," *Ethnohistory* (Winter 1992): 20–41; James Albert Johnson, *George Carmack* (Vancouver/ Toronto: Whitecap Books, 2001); and Rab Wilkie and the Skookum Jim Friendship Centre, *Skookum Jim: Native and Non-Native Stories and Views about His Life and Times and the Klondike Gold Rush* (Whitehorse: Heritage Branch, Yukon Department of Tourism, 1992).

2. Johnson, 111.

3. George Carmack to Rose [Watson], 28 July 1899, George W. Carmack papers, acc. 5176-1, box 1, folder 2, UW.

4. George Carmack to Rose [Watson], 25 July 1900, George W. Carmack papers, acc. 5176-1, box 1, folder 3, UW.

5. Kate Carmack to J. H. Durst, 15 Oct. 1900, George W. Carmack papers, acc 5176-1, box 4, folder 5, UW.

6. John H. Durst to Kate Carmack, 19 Oct. 1900, George W. Carmack papers, acc. 5176-1, box 4, folder 2, UW.

7. George Carmack to Rose [Watson], 15 Oct. 1900, George W. Carmack papers, acc. 5176-1, box 1, folder 4, UW.

8. George Carmack to Rose [Watson], 13 Nov. 1900, George W. Carmack papers, acc. 5176-1, box 1, folder 5, UW

9. George Carmack to Rose [Watson], 27 Nov. 1900, George W. Carmack papers, acc. 5176-1, box 1, folder 6, UW.

10. Most of the information about Daisy Mason and her parents comes from the same sources as for the Carmack family: Cruikshank; Johnson; and Wilkie.

11. C. W. Craig to Barbara McDougall, 12 Feb. 1980, Clarence Craig fonds, MSS 105 (80/26), YA.

12. Wilkie, 148.

13. Wilkie, 147.

❋ CHAPTER 2: ALL THOSE PEOPLE COME FOR GOLD

1. Ken S. Coates, *Best Left As Indians: Native-White Relations in the Yukon Territory, 1840–1973* (Montreal and Kingston: McGill-Queen's University Press, 1991), 9.

2. Tappan Adney, "Moose Hunting with the Tro-chu-tin," *Harper's New Monthly Magazine*, vol. C, no. DXCVIII (Mar. 1900), n.p.; Helene Dobrowolsky, *Hammerstones: A History of the Tr'ondëk Hwëch'in* (Dawson City: A Tr'ondëk Hwëch'in Publication, 2003), 3–4. The total population of the three Hän groups in the last quarter of the 1800s is estimated to have been about five hundred: Cornelius Osgood, *The Han Indians* (New Haven: Yale University, 1971), 32.

3. The Hän's traditional seasonal movements are described in Dobrowolsky, 3–11.

4. Dobrowolsky, epigraph n.p.

5. Osgood, 46–51; and Catherine McClellan, *Part of the Land, Part of the Water* (Vancouver/Toronto: Douglas and McIntyre, 1987), 191–208.

6. Osgood, 46–48.

7. Osgood, 48.

8. Osgood, 48–51; and Dobrowolsky, 196–207.

9. Dobrowolsky, 23; Developmental Studies Students of the Dawson Campus of Yukon College, *Moosehide: An Oral History* (Dawson City: Yukon College, 1994), 37.

10. Dobrowolsky, 3; according to Osgood, 17, Lucy Wood was born in 1887.

11. Julie Cruikshank, *Athapaskan Women: Lives and Legends* (Ottawa: National Museums of Canada, 1979), 48.

12. Mary Hitchcock, *Two Women in the Klondike* (New York: G. P. Putnam's Sons, 1899), 278–79.

13. Frederick Flewelling, "Canadian Yukon Diary of Frederick Fairweather Flewelling and his history as compiled by his eldest son, Reginald Halsall," diary entries 10 and 30 Nov. 1896, DCM.

14. Margaret E. Almstrom, *A Century of Schooling: Education in the Yukon, 1861—1961* (Whitehorse: privately published, 1991, revised edition), 56.

15. Almstrom, 69.

16. Dobrowolsky, 55.

17. Coates, 140.

18. This inequitable approach to education and the damage it did to Yukon Natives is described in Coates, 135–58.

19. Adney, 506.

❀ CHAPTER 3: KLONDICITIS

1. Emily Craig Romig, *A Pioneer Woman in Alaska* (Caldwell: Caxton Printers, 1948), 18.

2. "'A Woman' Who Helped Her Husband Dig $84,000 in the Klondike," *Seattle Daily Times*, 25 July 1897.

3. "Rests on Every Lip: 'Klondike' the 'Open Sesame' to a Dreamland of Wealth," *Seattle Post-Intelligencer*, 20 July 1897.

4. "A Winter of Terror at Dawson: The Excelsior Returns, After an Eventful Voyage, With Predictions of Tragic Moment," *San Francisco Examiner*, 16 Sept. 1897.

5. The other claimant for the title of first white child born at Forty Mile is Lee Henry Lindig, whose approximate date of birth is given as September 1895: "Local Brevities," *Klondike Nugget*, 27 July 1898.

6. Wesley A. Langlow, "The Langlow Family in Alaska and the Yukon," www.explorenorth.com/library/history/bl-langlow.htm (accessed 15 Nov. 2008).

7. "A Winter of Terror at Dawson."

8. "A Winter of Terror at Dawson."

9. "Langlow Bros.," *Klondike News*, 1 Apr. 1898.

10. "Langlow Bros."

11. Quote from "All Have Gold," *Seattle Post-Intelligencer*, 17 July 1897. Percy Lippy's story is related in Arnold and Helen Nelson, "The Dazzle of Gold at #16 Eldorado," in Virginia McKinney, ed., *The Alaska Journal: A 1981*

Collection (Anchorage: Alaska Northwest Publishing Company, 1981), 9–17; and Arnold and Helen Nelson, "Bringing Home the Gold," *The Alaska Journal* (Summer 1979): 52–59. Additional information comes from "The Early Yukon, Alaska and the Klondike Discovery As They Were Before The Great Klondike Stampede Swept Away the Old Conditions Forever, By ONE WHO WAS THERE Wm. Douglas Johns," Robert C. Coutts fonds, MSS 0092, folder 20 (78/69), YA, 104; and "Death Records from Green's Mortuary," DCM Pan for Gold Database.

12. Dorothy Whyte, interview by Kathy Jones, 1978, transcript, DCM; and Dorothy V. Whyte to Pierre Berton, 31 Aug. 1966, Dorothy V. Whyte biography file, DCM.

13. Ethel Anderson Becker, "Little Girl in the Klondike Gold Fields," *Alaska Sportsman*, Nov. 1962, 22–24, 34, 36–38.

14. Blanche (Pepin) Lambert, "Biography of Gedeon Pepin," Pepin Family fonds, MSS 61 (82/327), YA.

15. James Edward Kingsley, *Did I Ever Tell You About . . .* (Vancouver: privately published by George Kingsley Bryce, 1992).

16. Georgia White, "Diary of Mrs. Georgia White," MSS 4 (82/53), YA.

17. Melanie J. Mayer, *Klondike Women* (Athens: Swallow Press/Ohio University Press, 1989), 105.

18. White, diary entries 25 and 27 June 1898.

19. Martha Louise Black, *My Ninety Years* (Anchorage: Alaska Northwest Publishing Company, 1976), 19.

20. A. C. Harris, *Alaska and the Klondike Gold Fields* (publisher not identified, 1897; facsimile edition, Toronto: Coles Publishing Company, 1972), 213.

21. A. W. Moulton correspondence, Aaron Moulton fonds, MSS 204 (89/78), YA.

22. Carol Johnson [Aaron Moulton's granddaughter] to Dawson City Museum, 14 Aug. 1989, Aaron W. Moulton biography file, DCM.

23. Letters from Solomon and Rebecca Schuldenfrei, Solomon and Rebecca Schuldenfrei fonds, MSS 166 (84/47), YA; and letters to Solomon and Rebecca Schuldenfrei, provided by Robert Schuldenfrei.

24. Hallie C. Heacock, "Kid in the Klondike," *Alaska Sportsman* (June 1956): 22–25, 35–40.

⚜ CHAPTER 4: A STEEP, STEEP PLACE

1. Elizabeth Forbes, "Gold Rush Was Fun for Emilie," *Victoria Times*, 16 May 1973, 30; Irene Robertson, "Heap of Furs," *Victoria Daily Colonist*, 20 Sept.

1959, 11; and Lulu Alice Craig, *Glimpses of Sunshine and Shade in the Far North* (Cincinnati: Editor Publishing Co., 1900).

2. Information about First Nations use of the Chilkoot Trail is primarily from: Sheila Greer, *Skookum Stories on the Chilkoot/Dyea Trail* (Carcross: Carcross-Tagish First Nation, 1995); and David Neufeld and Frank Norris, *Chilkoot Trail: Heritage Route to the Klondike* (Whitehorse: Lost Moose, 1996), 22–48.

3. J. Bernard Moore, *Skagway in Days Primeval* (New York: Vantage Press, 1968), 46.

4. Frederick Funston, "Over the Chilkoot Pass in 1893," *Alaska Journal* (Summer 1972): 17.

5. The story of Monte and Crystal's early years in Alaska and trip over the Chilkoot Pass is related in several documents in the Snow Family papers, ASL: Anna Eades Rablan Snow, handwritten memoir and "Personal Record— Alaska-Yukon Pioneers," MS 38, box 8, folder 1; Crystal Brilliant Snow Jenne, handwritten and typewritten memoirs, MS 38, box 14, folder 1; and "George Snow," MS 38, box 26, folder 3. Additional details from "Crystal's Radio Interview," Crystal Brilliant Snow biography file, DCM.

6. Anna Snow, handwritten memoir, 2.

7. Crystal Jenne, handwritten memoir, n.p.

8. Anna Snow, handwritten memoir, 4.

9. Helen Dare, "The Child of the Chilcoot," *San Francisco Examiner*, 18 Sept. 1897.

10. "The Child of the Chilcoot."

11. Background information on the Barrett family comes from Nancy Warren Ferrell, *Barrett Willoughby: Alaska's Forgotten Lady* (Fairbanks: University of Alaska Press, 1994). Details of the family's Chilkoot Trail trip are from Barrett Willoughby, "I Went to the Klondike On My Father's Shoulders!" *The American Magazine* (June 1925): 42–43, 186–190.

12. Willoughby, 187.

13. A. B. Thompson, "Latest News from the Yukon," *Alaska Searchlight*, 5 June 1897.

14. Florence Hartshorn, notebook 4, Florence M. Hartshorn papers, acc. 570, box 1, folder 15, UW, n.p.

15. "Little Babies Buried Near Dyea Summit," *Fairbanks Daily Times*, 10 Nov. 1907; and Hartshorn, notebook 4, n.p.

16. "Little Babies Buried Near Dyea Summit."

17. "He Goes to Paris," *Yukon Sun*, 16 June 1903.

18. Hallie C. Heacock, "Kid in the Klondike," *Alaska Sportsman* (June 1956): 22–25, 35–40.

19. Willoughby, 188.

20. Willoughby, 189.

21. Willoughby, 189.

22. Martha Ferguson McKeown, *The Trail Led North* (New York: The MacMillan Company, 1948), 158–59; Hawthorne identifies the scow as Thomas Lippy's but doesn't name the woman or any of the other people on the scow. There is no evidence that the woman spotted was Salome Lippy. The wreck was reported by the *Klondike Nugget* ("Personal Mention," 16 June 1898), but the death is not confirmed and the passengers are not named.

23. Martha Grace Watson, "Diary from Dyea to Atlin, BC," and Bill Watson, biographical note, Watson Family fonds, MSS (80/12), YA.

24. Neufeld and Norris, 111.

25. Martha Watson, diary entry, 10 Mar. 1899.

26. Martha Watson, diary entry, 7 Apr. 1899.

❀ CHAPTER 5: BRING ME A STOCKING FULL OF GOLD

1. For a detailed account of the Edmonton routes, see J. G. MacGregor, *The Klondike Rush Through Edmonton, 1897–1898* (Toronto: McClelland and Stewart, 1970).

2. MacGregor (168, 263) identifies them as Mr. and Mrs. Sam Brown. Similarities between this couple and the stampeders that Emily Craig Romig knew as the Braunds were first noted by Melanie J. Mayer, *Klondike Women* (Athens: Swallow Press/Ohio University Press, 1989), 238. Most details of the Braunds' story are from Emily Craig Romig, *A Pioneer Woman in Alaska* (Caldwell: Caxton Printers, 1948).

3. Romig, 74.

4. Romig, 76.

5. Romig, 83.

6. Romig, 15, 82, 95; and MacGregor, 95, 135, 168–69, 263.

7. MacGregor, 79, 173.

8. A. C. Harris, *Alaska and the Klondike Gold Fields* (publisher not identified, 1897; facsimile edition, Toronto: Coles Publishing Company, 1972), 154–55.

9. Yukon Archives, "Black History of the Yukon," www.tc.gov.yk.ca/ archives/hiddenhistory/index.html, and "Outstanding Yukon Women!," www .tc.gov.yk.ca/archives/wc/outstanding/outstanding4.htm (both accessed 9 July 2009); and information provided by Peggy D'Orsay, Yukon Archives, 4 Oct.

2008. In 1901 the population of the Yukon was approximately thirty thousand, including ninety-nine black people. The 1901 census lists incorrect ages for Lucille and Teslin Hunter.

10. Audrey Loftus, "Lady Stampeder" [first of three parts], *Alaska Magazine* (Nov. 1977): 38–40.

11. Pierre Berton, *Klondike: The Last Great Gold Rush* (Toronto: McClelland and Stewart, 1972), 126.

12. Edith Feero Larson, interview by Melanie J. Mayer, 17 and 24 Sept. 1979, transcript, Melanie J. Mayer papers, acc. 4239, box VF2045a, UW.

13. Ethel Anderson Becker, "Little Girl in the Klondike Gold Fields," *Alaska Sportsman* (Nov. 1962): 22–24, 34, 36–38.

14. "Youthful Traveler," *Klondike Nugget*, 8 Nov. 1899.

15. "Young Boys Run Away," *Semi-weekly Klondike Nugget*, 13 July 1901; and "Will Ship Egan in Bond," *Semi-weekly Klondike Nugget*, 20 July 1901.

16. Becker, 24.

17. Becker, 24.

18. Sarah E. Hutchinson, *A Few Words From Grandmother* (privately published, 1991). The description of the Millers on the tram comes from a photograph belonging to Dorothy's daughter, Dorris Pooley.

19. Edith Murphy Reid, "Will Murphy, Here's Someone to See You!" *The Novascotian* (supplement to the *Chronicle-Herald* and *Mail-Star*), 16 Sept. 1989, F1 and F3; and Edith Murphy Reid, "Murphy Story" (1977), unpublished account, provided by John Gould.

20. "Like Doc Scharschmidt: Master Wells Refuses to Wear Mittens on the Trail," *Yukon Sun*, 10 Feb. 1904. The headline is probably a reference to P. F. Scharschmidt, a customs broker who worked at the Chilkoot Pass during the early days of the gold rush.

21. "Traveled in a Trunk," *Yukon Sun*, 6 Jan. 1904.

❋ CHAPTER 6: THE ARCTIC BROTHERHOOD OF BABYDOM

1. This account of Dawson Klondike Schultz's life is largely pieced together from the Dawson Klondike Hewitt fonds, MSS 48 (82/255), YA. Additional information comes from the newspaper stories cited below and from Benjamin F. Craig, handwritten account of "first white child born in Dawson," Craig Family fonds, MSS 199 (86/94), YA.

2. "Gone to Seattle," *Klondike Nugget*, 28 June 1898. According to other stories in this issue, the *Hamilton* left Dawson on June 24.

3. "Could Not Refund the Passage Money," *Klondike Nugget*, 6 Aug. 1898.

4. "Dawsie Schultz," *Semi-weekly Klondike Nugget*, 6 Jan. 1901. Charles did receive at least one letter from some "kindly people" in Seattle who were caring for Dawsie during this time: "Personal Mention," *Klondike Nugget*, 16 Aug. 1899.

5. "Dawsie Schultz: Her Father Needs Speaking To," *Yukon Sun*, 16 Mar. 1901.

6. "The Klondike and Indian River Divisions: Their Mines and the Men Who Operate Them," *Dawson Daily News*, Golden Clean-up Edition, 1902, 59.

7. "Dawson's First Baby Boy," *Seattle Post-Intelligencer*, 17 July 1899.

8. Frank Lynch. "Seattle Scene: In Which We Set Some Things Straight," Dawson Klondike Hewitt fonds, MSS 48 (82/255), pt. 1, folder 2, YA.

9. "Dawson's First Baby Boy."

10. 1901 census.

11. "Some More of Our Babies," *Dawson Weekly News*, 20 Sept. 1901.

12. "Baptisms St. Paul's Church, Dawson, Diocese of Yukon, from June 17, 1897. Copied 1925–26, Maude King, Dawson, YT," Anglican Church, Diocese of Yukon fonds, COR 1088, file 7, YA.

13. "Another Boy Baby," *Klondike Nugget*, 20 May 1899.

14. "Body of Baby Found," *Klondike Nugget*, 3 May 1899.

15. "Last Sad Service," *Dawson Daily News*, 10 Oct. 1906.

16. "Youngest Miner Out," *Semi-weekly Klondike Nugget*, 20 Sept. 1900.

17. Ella Lung Martinsen, *Trail to North Star Gold* (Portland: Binford & Mort Publishing, 1969), 195.

18. Martinsen, 201.

19. Martha Louise Black, *My Ninety Years* (Anchorage: Alaska Northwest Publishing Company, 1976), 45.

20. Black, 21.

21. Black, 43.

22. Black, 46.

23. Black, 44, 156.

24. Martha claimed Father Judge told her the bill would be $1,000 (Black, 44), but that figure seems erroneous.

25. Hal Guest, *A History of the City of Dawson, Yukon Territory 1896–1920* (Ottawa: Parks Canada, Microfiche Report Series No. 7, n.d.), chapter IX, n.p.

26. "Twins in a Dawson Home," *Dawson Daily News*, 24 Mar. 1903. The first names for Jennie Muir and Carl Lueders were obtained from the DCM Pan for Gold Database.

27. "Persecution Results in Death," *Klondike Nugget*, 17 Aug. 1898.

28. "Persecution Results in Death." Luella Day's involvement in Belle Conder's death is also discussed in letters to the editor, *Klondike Nugget*, 20 Aug. 1898.

29. The Grumanns' story is related in several documents in the Grumann Family biography file, DCM, including: Alice L. Sturzl, untitled Grumann family history, 1945; John Grumann, untitled account; and Pat Johnson, "Harold A. Grumann . . ." [title partially cut off on photocopy], *Gwinnett Sunday News*, 21 Jan. 1968. Edward and Theresa's second child, Myrtle, was born in the Hunker Creek cabin on 22 Sept. 1902.

30. Martinsen, 191.

31. Martinsen, 191.

32. *Dawson Daily News*, Special Mining Edition, Sept. 1899, 3.

33. "Yukon Census Returns," *Klondike Nugget*, 2 May 1900, 8.

34. Megan J. Highet, "Gold Fever: Death and Disease During the Klondike Gold Rush, 1898–1904" (M.A. thesis, University of Manitoba, 2008), 31. Charlene Porsild, *Gamblers and Dreamers: Women, Men, and Community in the Klondike* (Vancouver: UBC Press, 1998), 201, 206. Highet gives statistics for "Dawson proper." Porsild gives statistics for "greater Dawson." The numbers given here for the adjacent communities were calculated by subtracting "Dawson proper" from "greater Dawson."

35. J. S. Cruikshank, "The Early Yukon," RCMP *Quarterly* (July 1961): 30–32.

36. "In Family Propagation," *Daily Klondike Nugget*, 7 July 1902; and "Anton Vogee," biographical notes and "Certificate of Birth [Arthur Edward Vogee]," Anton Vogee fonds, MSS 122 (82/523), YA.

37. "Some More of Our Babies."

❀ CHAPTER 7: A PARTICULARLY HEALTHY PLACE FOR CHILDREN

1. NWMP, Annual Report for the Northwest Mounted Police, 1899, 351.74062 Nor 1899, YA.

2. Faith Fenton Brown, "The Dawson of Today," *Yukon Sun*, Special Number: The Dawson of Today, Sept. 1900, 1.

3. Ethel Anderson Becker, "Little Girl in the Klondike Gold Fields," *Alaska Sportsman* (Nov. 1962): 34.

4. Mrs. Albert [Florence] Hartshorn, "Along the Gold Trail [of the Yukon]," Ida Margaret Clarke Thompson fonds, MG 30, ser. D46, vol. 2, LAC, 16.

5. Hartshorn, 16.

6. Hartshorn, 18.

7. "Well Represented," *Daily Klondike Nugget*, 23 Aug. 1902. McCaul's occupation was obtained from the DCM Pan for Gold Database.

8. "Another Lonely Man," *Daily Klondike Nugget*, 23 Aug. 1902.

9. Becker, 37.

10. Becker, 37–38.

11. The Barrett family's Klondike experiences are described in Barrett Willoughby, "Thrilling Days in Dawson When the Klondike Rush Was On," *The American Magazine* (July 1925): 14–15, 68, 70, 72.

12. Willoughby, 70.

13. Willoughby, 70.

14. "St. Mary's School Register," St. Mary's School (Dawson City) fonds, COR 235 (82/462), YA; and Nancy Warren Ferrell, *Barrett Willoughby: Alaska's Forgotten Lady* (Fairbanks: University of Alaska Press, 1994).

15. Ferrell, 42.

16. Martha Ferguson McKeown, *The Trail Led North* (New York: The MacMillan Company, 1948), 203; and "The Klondike and Indian River Divisions: Their Mines and the Men Who Operate Them," *Dawson Daily News*, Golden Clean-up Edition, 1902, 31.

17. Lulu Alice Craig, *Glimpses of Sunshine and Shade in the Far North*, (Cincinnati: Editor Publishing Co., 1900), 71–72.

18. Craig, 71.

19. Elizabeth Forbes, "Gold Rush Was Fun for Emilie," *Victoria Times*, 16 May 1973, 30; Irene Robertson, "Heap of Furs," *Victoria Daily Colonist*, 20 Sept. 1959, 11.

20. "Her Daughter Dies at Tacoma," *Yukon Sun*, 4 June 1903.

21. Megan J. Highet, "Gold Fever: Death and Disease During the Klondike Gold Rush, 1898–1904" (M.A. thesis, University of Manitoba, 2008), 165.

22. Highet, 79, 124.

23. "Baby Is Dead," *Semi-weekly Klondike Nugget*, 13 Dec. 1900; and Dawson City Cemetery Database, Ed and Star Jones Collection, DCM.

24. Craig, 71.

25. Brown, 5.

26. "Register, St. Paul's Church, Dawson," Anglican Church, Diocese of Yukon fonds, COR 277, folder 9, YA.

27. Becker, 38.

28. Willoughby, 68, 70.

29. Ella Lung Martinsen, *Trail to North Star Gold* (Portland: Binford & Mort Publishing, 1969), 310. The number of dairies in 1899 is reported in the *Dawson Daily News*, Special Mining Edition, "Midsummer Number," Sept. 1899, 3.

30. Edith Murphy Reid, "Will Murphy, Here's Someone to See You!" *The Novascotian* (supplement to the *Chronicle-Herald* and *Mail-Star*), 16 Sept. 1989, F1 and F3; and Edith Murphy Reid, "Murphy Story" (1977), unpublished account, provided by John Gould.

31. Dorothy Whyte, interview by Kathy Jones, 1978, transcript, DCM, tape 1, 7.

32. Whyte, tape 1, 7.

33. Dawson City Cemetery Database, Ed and Star Jones Collection, DCM.

34. Highet, 100–22; and Hal Guest, A History of the City of Dawson, Yukon Territory 1896–1920 (Ottawa: Parks Canada, Microfiche Report Series No. 7, n.d.), chapter IX, n.p.

35. Sarah E. Hutchinson, A Few Words From Grandmother (privately published, 1991), 10.

36. Highet, 89–91; Guest, n.p.

37. Becker, 36.

38. "Register, St. Paul's Church, Dawson," Anglican Church, Diocese of Yukon fonds, COR 277, folder 9, YA.

39. The wreck of the Florence S was reported in a series of news stories in the Victoria Daily Colonist: "Victorians Lose Lives," 31 July 1900; "The Queen From Alaska," 4 Aug. 1900; "Wreck of Florence S," 7 Aug. 1900; "Aged Prospector Sentenced," 21 Aug. 1900; and "Body Found," 23 Aug. 1900. Additional information is from the Dawson City Cemetery Database, Ed and Star Jones Collection, DCM.

40. "Wreck of Florence S," 3.

41. The deaths of Whyner and Herman are listed in the Dawson City Cemetery Database, Ed and Star Jones Collection, DCM. The circumstances of Elton's death are described in "Elton M'Laren," Semi-weekly Klondike Nugget, 13 July 1901.

42. Bill Putnam, "Canadian Census Reports 1901," www.billputman.com/Canada%20Census%201901.htm (accessed 26 Mar. 2009); and DCM Pan for Gold Database.

43. "Residence Destroyed," Daily Klondike Nugget, 20 Mar. 1902; "Another Cabin on Hunker," Yukon World, 27 Jan. 1907.

44. Florence Bernsie's first name was obtained from the Yukon Archives Genealogy Research Database, www.yukongenealogy.com/content/ykgen_db.htm (accessed 1 July 2009).

45. "Burned in Death Trap," Yukon Sun, 7 Mar. 1903.

46. "Mother Makes Desperate Attempt to Save Child," Yukon Sun, 7 Mar. 1903.

47. "Work on Christian Lines," Yukon Sun, 14 Mar. 1903.

48. "Is Scene of Sorrow," Yukon Sun, 14 Mar. 1903.

49. "Last Sad Service," Dawson Daily News, 10 Oct. 1906.

50. "Take Body Outside," The Yukon Sun, 19 Nov. 1903; and "Death Records from Green's Mortuary," DCM Pan for Gold Database.

51. "Sad Occurrence on Sulphur," *Semi-weekly Klondike Nugget*, 18 Nov. 1900.

52. Dawson City Cemetery Database, Ed and Star Jones Collection, DCM.

53. "A Sad Death," *Klondike Nugget*, 7 Jan. 1899.

54. "Adopted the Child," *Klondike Nugget*, 18 Jan. 1899.

55. "Local Brevities," *Klondike Nugget*, 21 Jan. 1899.

56. "Baby's Night," *Klondike Nugget*, 25 Mar. 1899; and "Local Brevities," *Klondike Nugget*, 12 April 1899.

57. "In Memoriam," *Klondike Nugget*, 11 Jan. 1899.

58. "Historical Notes" regarding photo UW25866 ("People in front of home of Governor Ogilvie, 1899"), UW.

59. "Local Brevities," *Klondike Nugget*, 3 May 1899. Cyntha Daniels's first name was obtained from the DCM Pan for Gold Database.

60. "Young Wife and Mother," *Yukon Sun*, 24 Feb. 1904; and Dawson City Cemetery Database, Ed and Star Jones Collection, DCM.

61. Edith Feero Larson, interview by Melanie J. Mayer, 24 Sept. 1979, transcript, Melanie J. Mayer papers, acc. 4239, box VF2045a, UW.

62. Edith Feero Larson, interview by Melanie J. Mayer, 17 Sept. 1979, transcript, Melanie J. Mayer papers, acc. 4239, box VF2045a, UW.

63. James Edward Kingsley, *Did I Ever Tell You About . . .* (Vancouver: privately published by George Kingsley Bryce, 1992), 10.

✿ CHAPTER 8: THE NICE REFINEMENTS OF CIVILIZATION

1. "Women on Humboldt," *Seattle Daily Times*, 17 Aug. 1897.

2. Anna Fulcomer, "The Three R's at Circle City," *Alaska Journal* (Summer 1978): 217–21.

3. "Crystal's Radio Interview," Crystal Brilliant Snow biography file, DCM.

4. Crystal Brilliant Snow Jenne, handwritten and typewritten memoirs, MS 38, box 14, folder 1.

5. "Local Brevities," *Klondike Nugget*, 27 Aug. 1898.

6. "Letter to the Editor," *Klondike Nugget*, 23 Nov. 1898.

7. Lulu Alice Craig, *Glimpses of Sunshine and Shade in the Far North* (Cincinnati: Editor Publishing Co., 1900), 93.

8. "Dawson Needs a Public School," *Klondike Nugget*, 28 Sept. 1898.

9. "For a Public School," *Klondike Nugget*, 26 Nov. 1898.

10. "Dawson's First School," *Klondike Nugget*, 8 Nov. 1899.

11. Sister Mary Joseph Calasanctius, "Reminiscences of the Klondyke," file 569-7, SSA.

12. "Dawson's First School"; and Sister Margaret Cantwell, *North to Share: The Sisters of Saint Ann in Alaska and the Yukon Territory* (Victoria: Sisters of St. Ann, 1992), 90–92.

13. A letter written by the Dawson Committee on Education and Architecture states that a small number of students were "accommodated at a private school" in the fall of 1899: Geo M. Allen Charman et al. to the Trustees of the Board of Trade, Dawson, 15 Nov. 1899, Central Registry Files: School Building, Dawson, GOV 1615, file 505, YA. According to the *Dawson Daily News*, Special Mining Edition, "Midsummer Number," Sept. 1899, Dawson had three private schools at that time. No additional information about private schools in Dawson during this period was found.

14. Courtlandt Starnes to Commissioner [of] Yukon Territory, 28 Aug. 1900, Central Registry Files: School Building, Dawson, GOV 1615, file 505, YA.

15. G. P. McKenzie to J. H. Ross, n.d. (received 6 July 1901), Central Registry Files: School Building, Dawson, GOV 1615, file 505, YA.

16. Margaret E. Almstrom, *A Century of Schooling: Education in the Yukon, 1861–1961* (Whitehorse: privately published, 1991, revised edition), 83.

17. Almstrom, 82, 84.

18. S. S. Mitchell et al. to Members of the Yukon Council, 24 Oct. 1900, and D. G. Cock et al. to Commissioner Ogilvie, 15 Dec. 1900, Central Registry Files: Bonanza School, GOV 1925, file 364, YA.

19. Ethel Anderson Becker, "Little Girl in the Klondike Gold Fields," *Alaska Sportsman* (Nov. 1962): 36.

20. Anon. to Z. T. Wood, n.d. (received 24 Jan. 1903), Central Registry Files: Reports on Schools, GOV 1918, file 306, YA.

21. "Vacation is Ended," *Klondike Nugget*, 25 Aug. 1902.

22. John Ross to F. T. Congdon, 11 May 1904, and 4 Nov. 1904, Central Registry Files: School, Sulphur Creek, GOV 1620, file 1736, YA.

23. Edith Murphy Reid, "Murphy Story" (1977), unpublished account, provided by John Gould.

24. Almstrom, 110.

25. John Ross to F. T. Congdon, 13 June 1904, Central Registry Files: School Building, Dawson, GOV 1615, file 505, YA.

26. "News of the Creeks," *Yukon Sun*, 31 May 1903.

27. Almstrom, 96, 122–24; and Central Registry Files: School on Quartz, GOV 1925, file 366, YA.

28. "A Mother's Complaint," *Daily Klondike Nugget*, 31 May 1902.

29. "Yukon and Alaska Genealogy Centre: Historic Yukon and Alaska Hotels, Roadhouses, Saloons and Cafes Index," www.yukonalaska.com/pathfinder/gen/index.html (accessed 15 May 2009).

30. "Polks Gazetteer 1903 Directory," DCM Pan for Gold Database.

31. Acting Commissioner to S. T. Saylor, 27 Mar. 1903, Central Registry Files: School Building, Dawson, GOV 1615, file 505, YA.

32. "He Goes to Paris," *Yukon Sun*, 16 June 1903; and "A Successful Merchant," *The Northern Light* (July 1904): 29–30.

33. Almstrom, 88.

34. Cantwell, 95.

35. "Lanterns Not Now Required," *Semi-weekly Klondike Nugget*, 14 Dec. 1901.

36. "Vacation is Ended."

37. "School Grounds To Be Improved," *Yukon Sun*, 9 June 1903.

38. "School May End Friday Afternoon," *Yukon Sun*, 24 June 1903.

39. "To Enjoy Vacation," *Yukon Sun*, 28 June 1903.

40. Almstrom, 94–95.

41. A. Garvie et al. to Alexander Henderson, 15 Nov. 1907, Central Registry Files: Bonanza School, GOV 1925, file 364, YA. Teslin's nickname is from Kingsley, 6.

42. Central Registry Files: Bonanza School, GOV 1925, file 364, YA; and Almstrom, 94–95.

43. D. G. Cock et al. to Commissioner Ogilvie, 15 Dec. 1900, Central Registry Files: Bonanza School, GOV 1925, file 364, YA.

44. "Living With Yukon Winter," CBC radio program *Yukon Pot-pourri*, transcribed Aug. 1989, DCM, 5.

45. Joyce Hayden, *Victoria Faulkner: Lady of the Golden North* (Whitehorse: Windwalker Press, 2002); and Anne Tempelman-Kluit, "At Victoria Faulkner's House the 'King of the Klondike' Came to Tea," *Yukon News*, 25 Mar. 1977.

46. Grace McBride fonds, MSS 207 (90/2), YA.

47. The stories about Clemy in this section are all from Ella Lung Martinsen, *Trail to North Star Gold* (Portland: Binford & Mort Publishing, 1969), 207–09, 308, 321–22.

48. "Boys and Cigarettes," *Klondike Nugget*, 22 Nov. 1899.

49. Becker, 24.

50. Norm Bolotin, *Klondike Lost: A Decade of Photographs by Kinsey & Kinsey* (Anchorage: Alaska Northwest Publishing Company, 1980), 66. Ethel's age was obtained from the 1901 census.

51. Norman Bolotin, *A Klondike Scrapbook* (San Francisco: Chronicle Books, 1987), 82.

52. Bolotin, *Klondike Lost*, 66; and Bolotin, *A Klondike Scrapbook*, 81–83.

53. For a detailed discussion of the sex trade in Dawson, see Hal Guest, *A History of Ruby's Place, Dawson, Y.T. With Some Comment on Prostitution at the*

Klondike 1896–1962 (Ottawa: Parks Canada, 1983, Microfiche Report Series No. 91). Ethel, Leith, Catherine, and Altie Russell are listed in the "St. Mary's School Register," St. Mary's School (Dawson City) fonds, COR 235 (82/462), YA.

54. Sarah E. Hutchinson, *A Few Words From Grandmother* (privately published, 1991), 12; and Betty Neumiller interview by Michael Gates, 15 Aug. 1987, provided by Michael Gates.

55. James Edward Kingsley, *Did I Ever Tell You About . . .* (Vancouver: privately published by George Kingsley Bryce, 1992), 7.

56. Lulu Alice Craig, *Glimpses of Sunshine and Shade in the Far North*, (Cincinnati: Editor Publishing Co., 1900), 68.

57. Craig, 12–13.

58. R. W. Hibbert, "Children of the Yukon," *Dawson Daily News*, 17 Aug. 1913, 14.

59. Charlene Porsild, *Gamblers and Dreamers: Women, Men, and Community in the Klondike* (Vancouver: UBC Press, 1998), 203–04.

60. Information on the Ainaly family is from Dawson City Museum & Historical Society to Linda Richards, 23 July 2002, Manberg Family biography file, DCM, 2–3. Information on other children living on Dominion Creek is from the 1901 census and the Pan for Gold Database, DCM. Leon Very's younger brother, Ernest, died at 19 months old on 16 Feb. 1902: Dawson City Cemetery Database, Ed and Star Jones Collection, DCM.

61. Blanche (Pepin) Lambert, "Biography of Gedeon Pepin," Pepin Family fonds, MSS 61 (82/327), YA; and Pepin Family biography file, DCM.

62. Porsild, 208.

63. "Baptisms St. Paul's Church, Dawson, Diocese of Yukon, from June 17, 1897. Copied 1925–26, Maude King, Dawson, YT," Anglican Church, Diocese of Yukon fonds, COR 1088, file 7, YA; and Dawson City Cemetery Database, Ed and Star Jones Collection, DCM.

64. Porsild, 138–45; and Hal Guest, *A Socioeconomic History of the Klondike Goldfields, 1896–1966* (Ottawa: Parks Canada, 1985, Microfiche Report Series No. 181), 202.

65. Norton B. Stern, "The Jews in Yukon Territory and Their Cemetery," *Western States Jewish Historical Quarterly* (July 1982): 356–61; and Charles S. Rosener, "First Jewish Services at Dawson, Yukon Territory—1898," *Western States Jewish Historical Quarterly* (Jan. 1979): 145–46.

66. George Edward Gartrell, "The Work of the Churches in the Yukon During the Era of the Klondike Gold Rush" (M.A. thesis, University of Western Ontario, 1970), 155; "Church Notices," *Klondike Nugget*, 28 Sept. 1898; and Anglican Church of Canada, *Five Pioneer Women of the Anglican Church in the Yukon* (Whitehorse: Women's Auxiliary, Yukon Diocesan Board, Anglican Church of Canada, 1964), 4.

67. *First Methodist Church*, Albert E. Hetherington papers, MSS 201 (87/104), YA.

68. "Canaries Trill Sweetest Music," *Yukon Sun*, 16 June 1903; and "Sermon on the Mount," *Yukon Sun*, 31 May 1903.

69. Hutchinson, 9–10; and Neumiller interview.

70. Kingsley, 6.

71. Dorothy Whyte, interview by Kathy Jones, 1978, transcript, DCM, tape 1, 4.

72. Whyte interview, tape 1, 8, 19; and Dorothy V. Whyte, "Description of a Town," Dorothy V. Whyte biography file, DCM, 2–3.

❀ CHAPTER 9: THOROUGHLY ENJOYING THEMSELVES

1. Barrett Willoughby, "Thrilling Days in Dawson When the Klondike Rush Was On," *The American Magazine* (July 1925): 68.

2. R. W. Hibbert, "Children of the Yukon," *Dawson Daily News*, 17 Aug. 1913, 14.

3. Margaret H. Strong, "Dawson Days," Art and Margaret Strong fonds, MSS 122 (82/524), YA, 18.

4. Noel Robinson, "In the Brave Days of Gold," *Vancouver Province*, 14 Aug. 1948.

5. Ethel Anderson Becker, "Little Girl in the Klondike Gold Fields," *Alaska Sportsman* (Nov. 1962): 36, 38; and Ethel Anderson Becker, *Klondike '98: E.A. Hegg's Gold Rush* (Portland: Binfords and Mort, 1967), 95.

6. Norm Bolotin, *Klondike Lost: A Decade of Photographs by Kinsey & Kinsey* (Anchorage: Alaska Northwest Publishing Company, 1980), 63, 114.

7. Lulu Alice Craig, *Glimpses of Sunshine and Shade in the Far North* (Cincinnati: Editor Publishing Co., 1900), 69.

8. Faith Fenton Brown, "The Dawson of Today," *Yukon Sun*, Special Number: The Dawson of Today, Sept. 1900, 5.

9. Craig, 70.

10. Sarah E. Hutchinson, *A Few Words From Grandmother* (privately published, 1991), 9.

11. "The Dog Nuisance," *Dawson Daily News*, 23 May 1900.

12. Hal Guest, *A History of the City of Dawson, Yukon Territory 1896–1920* (Ottawa: Parks Canada, n.d., Microfiche Report Series No. 7), chapter IX, n.p.

13. "Cruelly Mangled," *Daily Klondike Nugget*, 8 Dec. 1902. Roy's and Darrel's ages are from the 1901 census.

14. Becker, 36–37.

15. Mrs. Albert [Florence] Hartshorn, "Along the Gold Trail [of the Yukon]," Ida Margaret Clarke Thompson fonds, MG 30, ser. D46, vol. 2, LAC, 19–20.

16. Betty Neumiller interview by Michael Gates, 15 Aug. 1987, provided by Michael Gates.

17. Lloyd Hawley et al. to Z. T. Wood, n.d. (received 21 Nov. 1902) and Z. T. Wood to Lloyd Hawley et al., 19 Nov. 1902, Central Registry Files: School Building, Dawson, GOV 1615, file 505, YA.

18. "Children's Rink," Daily Klondike Nugget, 21 Nov. 1902.

19. "Youngsters Indignant," Daily Klondike Nugget, 15 Dec. 1902; and "Sides Are Frozen," Daily Klondike Nugget, 20 Dec. 1902.

20. The Forrest family's Klondike story is related in Emil Forrest, "Sports," Emil Forrest fonds, MSS 127 (82/503), folder 3, YA. Paul's, Albert's, and Emile's ages were obtained from the 1901 census.

21. Forrest, "Sports," 1.

22. "Skating Rates are Announced," Yukon Sun, 6 Nov. 1903; "Skating Rink to Open Tomorrow," Yukon Sun, 13 Nov. 1903; and "Little Boys and Girls Must Keep Off the Ice at Night," Yukon Sun, 19 Nov. 1903.

23. Forrest, "Sports," 2.

24. "Splendid Night of Sport Witnessed by Hundreds at Rink," 6 Apr. 1906, clipping from unidentified newspaper, Emil Forrest fonds, MSS 127 (82/503), folder 4, YA.

25. "Emil Forrest Takes Trip Out," Oct. 1910, clipping from unidentified newspaper, Emil Forrest fonds, MSS 127 (82/503), folder 4, YA.

26. "Daffiest Stanley Cup Series of All," Weekend Magazine, vol. 8. no. 13, 1958; "Albert is Home," undated clipping from unidentified newspaper, Emil Forrest fonds, MSS 127 (82/503), folder 4, YA; and Forrest, "Sports," 3.

27. "Junior Hockey Players," Yukon World, 17 Feb. 1907.

28. "Pupils Recital," Klondike Nugget, 28 June 1902; and "Instruction in Music," Klondike Nugget, 12 Aug. 1902.

29. Blanche (Pepin) Lambert, "Biography of Gedeon Pepin," Pepin Family fonds, MSS 61 (82/327), YA.

30. "The Nugget's Department for Children," Daily Klondike Nugget, 4 Jan. 1902.

31. "The Family Matinee," Klondike Nugget, 7 Sept. 1898.

32. "The Opera House Matinee," Klondike Nugget, 25 Nov. 1899.

33. "Christmas for the Children," Klondike Nugget, 31 Dec. 1898; and Anglican Church of Canada, Five Pioneer Women of the Anglican Church in the Yukon (Whitehorse: Women's Auxiliary, Yukon Diocesan Board, Anglican Church of Canada, 1964), 4.

34. Dorothy V. Whyte, "Description of a Town," Dorothy V. Whyte biography file, DCM, 5.

35. "Santa Claus Appeared," *Daily Klondike Nugget,* 26 Dec. 1902.

36. "Precocious Youngsters," *Semi-weekly Klondike Nugget,* 21 Dec. 1901; "Christmas at School," *Daily Klondike Nugget,* 20 Dec. 1902; and "The Little Ones as Entertainers," *Yukon Sun,* 24 Dec. 1903.

37. "Sisters' School Exercises," *Klondike Nugget,* 28 Dec. 1901; and "Christmas in Dawson," *Yukon Sun,* 27 Dec. 1903.

38. "Christmas Cocktails," *Yukon Sun,* 27 Dec. 1903.

39. "Christmas Cocktails"; and "Christmas Tree on Dominion," *Yukon Sun,* 1 Dec. 1903.

40. "Christmas Cocktails."

41. "Christmas Echoes from the Creeks," *Yukon Sun,* 3 Jan. 1904.

42. "Children Tomorrow," *Daily Klondike Nugget,* 23 May 1901; and "Glorious Celebration," *Daily Klondike Nugget,* 24 May 1901.

43. "Children Invited," *Daily Klondike Nugget,* 26 May 1902.

44. "Children's Day," *Daily Klondike Nugget,* 29 May 1903.

45. "The Day of Days," *Yukon Sun,* 31 May 1903.

46. Hal Guest, *A Socioeconomic History of the Klondike Goldfields, 1896–1966* (Ottawa: Parks Canada, 1985, Microfiche Report Series No. 181), 209.

47. James Edward Kingsley, *Did I Ever Tell You About . . .* (Vancouver: privately published by George Kingsley Bryce, 1992), 7.

48. "Glorious Occasion," *Daily Klondike Nugget,* 5 July 1901; and "Observed in Dawson," *Klondike Nugget,* 9 Aug. 1902.

49. Guest, 210.

50. Craig, 40–41.

51. "Birthday Party," *Klondike Nugget* (Supplement), 7 June 1899.

52. "Birthday Party," *Klondike Nugget,* 4 Aug. 1902.

53. Edith Lawrence, "How to Entertain Children at Their Parties," *Yukon Sun,* 21 June 1903.

54. "Society Events," *Daily Klondike Nugget,* 1 Mar. 1902.

55 "Outing For Children," *Daily Klondike Nugget,* 31 Mar. 1902.

56. "It Was a Glorious Outing," *Daily Klondike Nugget,* 14 June 1901.

57. "Mason's Children's Social," *Yukon World,* 2 Feb. 1907.

58. Whyte, 4.

59. Betty Neumiller interview by Michael Gates, 15 Aug. 1987, provided by Michael Gates; and Sarah E. Hutchinson, *A Few Words From Grandmother* (privately published, 1991), 11.

60. Information about the OAB in Dawson comes from the official OAB rule book and an incomplete Dawson company journal, *Order of the American Boy,*

Dawson City Chapter fonds, COR 346 87/02, YA. Ages of some of the company members were obtained from the 1901 census.

❀ CHAPTER 10: PICKING UP THE COINS

1. Bera's story is related in Iola Beebe, *The True Life Story of Swiftwater Bill Gates* (privately published, 1908). Additional information about the Beebes and Swiftwater Bill is from Sherwood Eliot Wirt, "The Man From Eldorado [parts 1 and 2]," *Alaska Life* (July 1945): 34–43 and (Aug. 1945): 10–24; and Michael Gates, "The Many Wives of a Klondike King," *Up Here* (Oct.–Nov. 2008): 26, 28.
2. Beebe, 41.
3. Beebe, 44.
4. Beebe, 49.
5. Beebe, 57.
6. Beebe, 58.
7. Beebe, 58
8. Beebe, 61, 62.
9. Beebe, 66.
10. "The Klondike's First Elopement," *Klondike Nugget,* 1 July 1899. Mabel's surname is given as Nummelin in this account.
11. "The Elopers Are Brought Back," *Klondike Nugget,* 5 July 1899.
12. Kuni's story is related in three *Klondike Nugget* articles: "An Unnatural Father," 16 Aug. 1899; "Reads Like a Dime Novel," 23 Aug. 1899; and "Police Court News," 26 Aug. 1899.
13. Marilyn Pilon, *Canada's Legal Age of Consent to Sexual Activity* (Ottawa: Library of Parliament, Parliamentary Research Branch, 2001), www.parl.gc.ca/information/library/PRBpubs/prb993-e.pdf (accessed 8 June 2009).
14. Anne M. Butler, *Sisters of Joy, Daughters of Misery: Prostitutes in the American West, 1865–90* (Urbana and Chicago: University of Illinois Press, 1987), 15. According to Hal Guest, *A History of Ruby's Place, Dawson, Y.T. With Some Comment on Prostitution at the Klondike 1896–1962* (Ottawa: Parks Canada, 1983, Microfiche Report Series No. 91), 16, the recorded ages of women arrested for prostitution in Dawson around the turn of the century ranged from twenty to thirty-six.
15. Edith's story is related in Lael Morgan, *Good Time Girls of the Alaska-Yukon Gold Rush* (Fairbanks: Epicenter Press, 1998), 301–10.
16. Morgan, 299.
17. "Crystal's Radio Interview," Crystal Brilliant Snow biography file, DCM, 4.

18. Jane Rablen to Crystal Snow, 17 May 1898 (with notations added by David Kenway, July 1995), Crystal Brilliant Snow biography file, DCM, 2; and "George Snow," Snow Family papers, MS 38, box 26, folder 3, ASL, 415.

19. "Crystal's Radio Interview," 5; Alaska Department of Education, Division of State Libraries, Archives, and Museums, "The Snow Family of Juneau, Alaska: A Guide to the Papers and Photographs" (MS 38 and PCA 154), ASL; and Claire Rudolf Murphy and Jane G. Haigh, *Children of the Gold Rush* (Portland: Alaska Northwest Books, 2001), 12–19.

20. Gary L. Stevens, "Gold Rush Theatre in the Alaska-Yukon Frontier" (Ph.D. dissertation, University of Oregon, 1984), 341–3.

21. "Grand Family Entertainment," *Klondike Nugget*, 10 Aug. 1898.

22. Virginia P. Boyntan Nethercott, ed., *Klondike Tenderfoot: From the Diaries of Clare M. Stroud Boyntan Phillips* (Starrucca: privately published, 1992), 41.

23. Tappan Adney, *The Klondike Stampede* (Vancouver: UBC Press, 1994), 426–27.

24. One of the few known photographs of Margie Newman was published as part of a montage of photographs of girls in "The Dawson of Today," *Yukon Sun*, Special Number: The Dawson of Today, Sept. 1900, n.p.

25. "The Sunday Concert," *Klondike Nugget*, 21 Sept. 1898.

26. Chad Evans, *Frontier Theatre* (Victoria: Sono Nis Press, 1983), 236.

27. "Grand Opening of the Monte Carlo," *Klondike Nugget*, 5 Oct. 1898.

28. "At the Monte Carlo," *Klondike Nugget*, 8 Oct. 1898.

29. "The Tivoli" [advertisement], *Klondike Nugget*, 11 Jan. 1899; and Evans, 242–43.

30. *The Paystreak* [bazaar newspaper], Dec. 1899.

31. "A Social and Financial Success," *Klondike Nugget*, 26 Oct. 1898.

32. This account of the event is from "Tramp Shiners at the Banquet," *Klondike Nugget*, 7 Dec. 1898. The description of Margie's Highland fling is from "At the Monte Carlo," *Klondike Nugget*, 8 Oct. 1898.

33. "Benefit for Newman Children," *Klondike Nugget*, 10 Dec. 1898.

34. 1901 census.

35. "St. Mary's School Register," St. Mary's School (Dawson City) fonds, COR 235 (82/462), YA.

36. "Little Georgie Hurt," *Klondike Nugget*, 8 Apr. 1899.

37. "Auditorium" [advertisement], *Dawson Daily News*, 18 Apr. 1904.

38. "Clary Craig, post office worker list of people dying or leaving Klondike," Pan for Gold database, DCM.

39. "Dawson's Annual Fire," *Dawson Daily News*, 11 Jan. 1900; and "The Coroner's Inquest," *Klondike Nugget*, 24 Dec. 1898.

40. "Local Brevities," *Klondike Nugget*, 28 Oct. 1899; "Fire Notes," *Klondike Nugget*, 10 Jan. 1900; and "More Fire Protection," *Dawson Daily News*, 18 Jan. 1900. The newspaper accounts do not give Leo and Conchita's surname.

41. "At the Theatres," *Klondike Nugget*, 6 Dec. 1899.

42. "The Stage," *Dawson Daily News*, 2 Jan. 1900.

43. "Half Million Dollars," *Dawson Daily News*, 10 Jan. 1900; and "Dawson's Annual Fire."

44. "Half Million Dollars."

45. Morgan, 77–79.

46. "Fire Notes," *Klondike Nugget*, 10 Jan. 1900; and "Found in the Ashes," *Klondike Nugget*, 18 Feb. 1900.

47. "Palace Grand Re-opens," *Daily Klondike Nugget*, 15 Jan. 1900.

48. "Benefit for Matt Probst," *Klondike Nugget*, 1 Mar. 1900.

49. Robert Coutts, *The Palace Grand Theatre, Dawson City, Y.T.: An Interpretive History* (Ottawa: Parks Canada, 1981), Parks Canada Manuscript Report No. 428, 46–47, describes the end of the vaudeville era. The 1901 census lists the O'Briens as passengers on the outbound steamer *Dawson* on 20 Sept. 1901.

50. Audrey Loftus, "Lady Stampeder" [first of three parts], *Alaska Magazine* (Nov. 1977): 39.

51. William Ogilvie, *The Klondike Official Guide* (Toronto: Hunter Rose Co. Ltd., 1898), 146.

52. Loftus, "Lady Stampeder" [first of three parts], 38–40; Audrey Loftus, "Tom Gibson—Meat Hunter," *Alaska Sportsman* (June 1967): 18–21, 59; Audrey Loftus, "Lady Stampeder" [conclusion], *Alaska Magazine* (Jan. 1978): 87–89; and Bill and Sharon Gurney, *The Descendents of Joseph and Rosanna Smith: Pioneers of Wallace Township, Ontario*, (Kamloops: privately published by Bill and Sharon Gurney, 2004), provided by the Gurneys.

53. Joseph Clearihue to Annie Clearihue, 8 Sept. 1901, Add. MSS 698, vol. 1, file 4, J. B. Clearihue papers, BCA.

54. Dorothy Whyte, interview by Kathy Jones, 1978, transcript, DCM, tape 1, 3–7.

55. "Juvenile Thieves," *Daily Klondike Nugget*, 19 May 1902; and "Youthful Depravity," *Daily Klondike Nugget*, 29 May 1902.

56. "Youthful Offender," *Daily Klondike Nugget*, 18 Dec. 1902; and "Bad Boy," *Daily Klondike Nugget*, 20 Dec. 1902.

57. "Children Kept Home," *Daily Klondike Nugget*, 23 Sept. 1902.

58. Mary Kingsley, "Sadder but Wiser" (2009), unpublished account provided by Mary Kingsley.

59. Jim's entrepreneurial endeavours are described in James Edward Kingsley, *Did I Ever Tell You About* . . . (Vancouver: privately published by George Kingsley Bryce, 1992), 5–10; and Phyllis James, "Parksville's Jim Kingsley Remembers the Yukon," *Victoria Daily Colonist*, 29 Feb. 1976, 12–13.

60. Ethel did recover from her illness: George Kingsley Bryce, correspondence with author, 23 June 2009.

❀ CHAPTER II: GOLD NUGGETS AND PRICELESS MEMORIES

1. Ella Lung Martinsen, *Trail to North Star Gold* (Portland: Binford & Mort Publishing, 1969), 165–66.

2. Barrett Willoughby, "Thrilling Days in Dawson When the Klondike Rush Was On," *The American Magazine* (July 1925): 70.

3. Ethel Anderson Becker, "Little Girl in the Klondike Gold Fields," *Alaska Sportsman* (Nov. 1962): 36; and Ethel Anderson Becker, *Klondike '98: E.A. Hegg's Gold Rush* (Portland: Binfords and Mort, 1967), 95.

4. Hallie C. Heacock, "Those Wonderful Klondike Days," *Alaska Sportsman* (Sept. 1962): 30–34, 36–38.

5. "Panned Her Own Gold," *Victoria Daily Colonist*, 12 Aug. 1905.

6. Becker, "Little Girl in the Klondike Gold Fields," 38.

7. Heacock, 30.

8. R. W. Hibbert, "Children of the Yukon," *Dawson Daily News*, 17 Aug. 1913, 14.

9. The Lung family's departure from the Klondike and their life afterwards are described in Martinsen, 330, 335–38.

10. The circumstances of the Millers' departure and their reactions to life Outside are described in Sarah E. Hutchinson, *A Few Words From Grandmother* (privately published, 1991), 8–9, 14; and Betty Neumiller interview by Michael Gates, 15 Aug. 1987, provided by Michael Gates.

11. Hibbert, 14.

12. Joyce Hayden, *Victoria Faulkner: Lady of the Golden North* (Whitehorse: Windwalker Press, 2002), 17, 20–22; and Kevin Shakell, "Chapter in Yukon History Closes as Second Lady of the Territory Passes On," *Yukon News*, 26 Aug. 1981.

13. "Longtime Dawson Resident Remembers Bruised Kate," *Yukon News*, 11 Aug. 1982; and 1901 census.

14. Dorothy V. Whyte, "Description of a Town," Dorothy V. Whyte biography file, DCM; and Dorothy Whyte, interview by Kathy Jones, 1978, transcript, DCM.

15. Grace McBride to Lesley [no surname given], 17 Oct. 1989, Grace McBride fonds, MSS 207 (90/2), YA.

16. Norman Bolotin, A *Klondike Scrapbook* (San Francisco: Chronicle Books, 1987), 81.

Bibliography

❀ BOOKS AND ARTICLES

Adney, Tappan. *The Klondike Stampede*. Vancouver: UBC Press, 1994.

———. "Moose Hunting with the Tro-chu-tin," *Harper's New Monthly Magazine*, vol. C, no. DXCVIII, Mar. 1900, n.p.

Almstrom, Margaret E. *A Century of Schooling: Education in the Yukon, 1861–1961*. Whitehorse, privately published, 1991 (revised edition).

Anglican Church of Canada. *Five Pioneer Women of the Anglican Church in the Yukon*. Whitehorse: Women's Auxiliary, Yukon Diocesan Board, Anglican Church of Canada, 1964.

Becker, Ethel Anderson. *Klondike '98: E. A. Hegg's Gold Rush*. Portland: Binfords and Mort, 1967.

———. "Little Girl in the Klondike Gold Fields," *Alaska Sportsman*, Nov. 1962, 22–24, 34, 36–38.

Beebe, Iola. *The True Life Story of Swiftwater Bill Gates*. Privately published, 1908.

Berton, Pierre. *Klondike: The Last Great Gold Rush*. Toronto: McClelland and Stewart, 1972.

Black, Martha Louise. *My Ninety Years*. Anchorage: Alaska Northwest Publishing Company, 1976.

Bolotin, Norm. *Klondike Lost: A Decade of Photographs by Kinsey & Kinsey*. Anchorage: Alaska Northwest Publishing Company, 1980.

———. *A Klondike Scrapbook*. San Francisco: Chronicle Books, 1987.

Butler, Anne M. *Sisters of Joy, Daughters of Misery: Prostitutes in the American West, 1865–90*. Urbana and Chicago: University of Illinois Press, 1987.

Cantwell, Margaret. *North to Share: The Sisters of Saint Ann in Alaska and the Yukon Territory*. Victoria: Sisters of St. Ann, 1992.

Coates, Ken S. *Best Left As Indians: Native-White Relations in the Yukon Territory, 1840–1973*. Montreal and Kingston: McGill-Queen's University Press, 1991.

Coutts, Robert. *The Palace Grand Theatre, Dawson City, Y.T.: An Interpretive History*. Ottawa: Parks Canada, 1981, Parks Canada Manuscript Report No. 428.

Craig, Lulu Alice. *Glimpses of Sunshine and Shade in the Far North*. Cincinnati: Editor Publishing Co., 1900.

Cruikshank, J. S., "The Early Yukon," RCMP *Quarterly*, July 1961, 30–32.

Cruikshank, Julie. *Athapaskan Women: Lives and Legends*. Ottawa: National Museums of Canada, 1979.

———. "Images of Society in Klondike Gold Rush Narratives: Skookum Jim and the Discovery of Gold." *Ethnohistory*. Winter 1992, 20–41.

Developmental Studies Students of the Dawson Campus of Yukon College. *Moosehide: An Oral History*. Dawson City: Yukon College, 1994.

Dobrowolsky, Helene. *Hammerstones: A History of the Tr'ondëk Hwëch'in*. Dawson City: A Tr'ondëk Hwëch'in Publication, 2003.

Evans, Chad. *Frontier Theatre*. Victoria: Sono Nis Press, 1983.

Ferrell, Nancy Warren. *Barrett Willoughby: Alaska's Forgotten Lady*. Fairbanks: University of Alaska Press, 1994.

Fulcomer, Anna. "The Three R's at Circle City," *Alaska Journal*, Summer 1978, 217–21.

Funston, Frederick. "Over the Chilkoot Pass in 1893." *Alaska Journal*, Summer 1972, 16–24.

Gates, Michael. *Gold at Fortymile Creek: Early Days in the Yukon*. Vancouver: UBC Press, 1994.

———. "The Many Wives of a Klondike King," *Up Here*, Oct.–Nov. 2008, 26, 28.

Gould, John A. *Frozen Gold: A Treatise on Early Klondike Mining Technology, Methods and History*. Whitehorse: PR Distributing, 2001.

Greer, Sheila. *Skookum Stories on the Chilkoot/Dyea Trail*. Carcross: Carcross-Tagish First Nation, 1995.

Guest, Hal. *A History of Ruby's Place, Dawson, Y.T. With Some Comment on Prostitution at the Klondike 1896–1962.* Ottawa: Parks Canada, 1983, Microfiche Report Series No. 91.

———. *A History of the City of Dawson, Yukon Territory 1896–1920.* Ottawa: Parks Canada, n.d., Microfiche Report Series No. 7.

———. *A Socioeconomic History of the Klondike Goldfields, 1896–1966.* Ottawa: Parks Canada, 1985, Microfiche Report Series No. 181.

Gurney, Bill and Sharon Gurney. *The Descendents of Joseph and Rosanna Smith: Pioneers of Wallace Township, Ontario.* Kamloops: privately published, 2004.

Harris, A. C. *Alaska and the Klondike Gold Fields.* [Originally published in 1897.] Facsimile edition, Toronto: Coles Publishing Company, 1972.

Hayden, Joyce. *Victoria Faulkner: Lady of the Golden North.* Whitehorse: Windwalker Press, 2002.

Heacock, Hallie C. "Kid in the Klondike," *Alaska Sportsman,* June 1956, 22–25, 35–40.

———. "Those Wonderful Klondike Days," *Alaska Sportsman,* Sept. 1962, 30–34, 36–38.

Hitchcock, Mary. *Two Women in the Klondike.* New York: G. P. Putnam's Sons, 1899.

Hutchinson, Sarah E. *A Few Words From Grandmother.* Privately published, 1991.

Johnson, James Albert. *George Carmack.* Vancouver/Toronto: Whitecap Books, 2001.

Kingsley, James Edward. *Did I Ever Tell You About . . .* Vancouver: privately published by George Kingsley Bryce, 1992.

Loftus, Audrey. "Lady Stampeder" [first of three parts], *Alaska Magazine,* Nov. 1977, 38–40.

———. "Lady Stampeder" [conclusion], *Alaska Magazine,* Jan. 1978, 87–89.

———. "Tom Gibson—Meat Hunter," *Alaska Sportsman,* June 1967, 18–21, 59.

MacGregor, J. G. *The Klondike Rush Through Edmonton, 1897–1898.* Toronto: McClelland and Stewart, 1970.

Martinsen, Ella Lung. *Trail to North Star Gold.* Portland: Binford & Mort Publishing, 1969.

Mayer, Melanie J. *Klondike Women: True Tales of the 1897–1898 Gold Rush.* Athens: Swallow Press/Ohio University Press, 1989.

McClellan, Catherine. *Part of the Land, Part of the Water*. Vancouver/Toronto: Douglas and McIntyre, 1987.

McKeown, Martha Ferguson. *The Trail Led North*. New York: The MacMillan Company, 1948.

McKinney, Virginia, ed. *The Alaska Journal: A 1981 Collection*. Anchorage: Alaska Northwest Publishing Company, 1981.

Minter, Roy. *The White Pass: Gateway to the Klondike*. Fairbanks: University of Alaska Press, 1987.

Moore, J. Bernard. *Skagway in Days Primeval*. New York: Vantage Press, 1968.

Morgan, Lael. *Good Time Girls of the Alaska-Yukon Gold Rush*. Fairbanks: Epicenter Press, 1998.

Murphy, Claire Rudolf and Jane G. Haigh. *Children of the Gold Rush*. Portland: Alaska Northwest Books, 2001.

Nelson, Arnold and Helen Nelson. "Bringing Home the Gold," *The Alaska Journal*, Summer 1979, 52–59.

———. "The Dazzle of Gold at #16 Eldorado," in Virginia McKinney, ed. *The Alaska Journal: A 1981 Collection*. Anchorage: Alaska Northwest Publishing Company, 1981, 9–17.

Nethercott, Virginia P. Boyntan ed. *Klondike Tenderfoot: From the Diaries of Clare M. Stroud Boyntan Phillips*. Starrucca: privately published, 1992.

Neufeld, David and Frank Norris. *Chilkoot Trail: Heritage Route to the Klondike*. Whitehorse: Lost Moose, 1996.

Ogilvie, William. *The Klondike Official Guide*. Toronto: Hunter Rose Co. Ltd., 1898.

Osgood, Cornelius. *The Han Indians*. New Haven: Yale University, 1971.

Parr, Joy, ed. *Childhood and Family in Canadian History*. Toronto: McClelland and Stewart, 1982.

Porsild, Charlene. *Gamblers and Dreamers: Women, Men, and Community in the Klondike*. Vancouver: UBC Press, 1998.

Romig, Emily Craig. *A Pioneer Woman in Alaska*. Caldwell: Caxton Printers, 1948.

Rosener, Charles S. "First Jewish Services at Dawson, Yukon Territory—1898," *Western States Jewish Historical Quarterly*, Jan. 1979, 145–46.

Stern, Norton B. "The Jews in Yukon Territory and Their Cemetery," *Western States Jewish Historical Quarterly*, July 1982, 356–61.

Wilkie, Rab and the Skookum Jim Friendship Centre. *Skookum Jim: Native and Non-Native Stories and Views about His Life and Times and the Klondike Gold Rush*. Whitehorse: Heritage Branch, Yukon Department of Tourism, 1992.

Willoughby, Barrett. "I Went to the Klondike On My Father's Shoulders!" *The American Magazine*, June 1925, 42–43, 186–90.

———. "Thrilling Days in Dawson When the Klondike Rush Was On," *The American Magazine*, July 1925, 14–15, 68, 70, 72.

Wirt, Sherwood Eliot. "The Man From Eldorado [parts 1 and 2]," *Alaska Life*, July 1945, 34–43, and Aug. 1945, 10–24.

Yukon Tourism. *The Overland Trail: Whitehorse–Dawson City*. Whitehorse: Heritage Branch [1998].

❀ NEWSPAPERS

Alaska Searchlight
Dawson Daily News
Dawson Weekly News
Fairbanks Daily Times
Klondike News
Klondike Nugget (daily and semi-weekly)
The Northern Light
The Novascotian
San Francisco Examiner
Seattle Daily Times
Seattle Post-Intelligencer
Vancouver Province
Victoria Daily Colonist
Victoria Times
Yukon News
Yukon Sun
Yukon World

❀ UNPUBLISHED SOURCES

Gartrell, George Edward. "The Work of the Churches in the Yukon During the Era of the Klondike Gold Rush." M.A. thesis, University of Western Ontario, 1970.

Highet, Megan J. "Gold Fever: Death and Disease During the Klondike Gold Rush, 1898–1904." M.A. thesis, University of Manitoba, 2008.

Kingsley, Mary. "Sadder but Wiser," 2009, provided by Mary Kingsley.

Neumiller, Betty. Interview by Michael Gates, 15 Aug. 1987, provided by Michael Gates.

Reid, Edith Murphy. "Murphy Story," 1977, provided by John Gould.

Schuldenfrei Family. Letters to Solomon and Rebecca Schuldenfrei, 1897–1899, provided by Robert Schuldenfrei.

Stevens, Gary L. "Gold Rush Theatre in the Alaska-Yukon Frontier." Ph.D. dissertation, University of Oregon, 1984.

✸ ARCHIVAL SOURCES

Alaska State Library, Alaska Historical Collections, Juneau
    Snow Family. Papers.

Dawson City Museum, Dawson City
    Dawson City Cemetery Database, Ed and Star Jones Collection.
    Faulkner, Victoria. Biography file.
    Flewelling, Frederick. "Canadian Yukon Diary of Frederick Fairweather Flewelling and his history as compiled by his eldest son, Reginald Halsall."
    Grumann Family. Biography file.
    "Living with Yukon Winter," CBC radio program Yukon Pot-pourri, transcribed Aug. 1989.
    Manberg Family. Biography file.
    Moulton, Aaron W. Biography file.
    Pepin Family. Biography file.
    Snow, Crystal Brilliant. Biography file.
    Troberg Family. Biography file.
    Whyte, Dorothy. Interview by Kathy Jones, 1978.
    Whyte, Dorothy V. Biography file.

Library and Archives Canada, Ottawa
    Thompson, Ida Margaret Clarke. Fonds.

Provincial Archives of British Columbia, Victoria
    Clearihue. Papers.

Sisters of St. Ann Archives, Victoria
    Calasanctius, Sister Mary Joseph. "Reminiscences of the Klondyke." File 569–7.

University of Washington, Seattle
  Becker, Ethel Anderson. Papers.
  Carmack, George W. Papers.
  Hartshorn. Florence M. Papers.
  Mayer, Melanie J. Papers.

Yukon Archives, Whitehorse
  Anglican Church, Diocese of Yukon. Fonds.
  Central Registry Files: Bear Creek School.
  Central Registry Files: Bonanza School.
  Central Registry Files: Reports on Schools.
  Central Registry Files: School Building, Dawson.
  Central Registry Files: School on Quartz.
  Central Registry Files: School, Sulphur Creek.
  Coutts, Robert C. Fonds.
  Craig, Clarence. Fonds.
  Craig Family. Fonds.
  Finch, H. D. Fonds.
  Forrest, Emil. Fonds.
  Gibson, Albert Raymond. Fonds.
  Hetherington, Albert E. Fonds.
  Hewitt, Dawson Klondike. Fonds.
  McBride, Grace. Fonds.
  McLellan, Winifred. Fonds.
  Moulton, Aaron. Fonds.
  NWMP, Annual Report for the Northwest Mounted Police, 1899.
  Order of the American Boy, Dawson City Chapter. Fonds.
  Pepin Family. Fonds.
  Schuldenfrei, Solomon and Rebecca. Fonds.
  St. Mary's Catholic Church. Fonds.
  St. Mary's School (Dawson City). Fonds.
  Strong, Art and Margaret. Fonds.
  Vogee, Anton. Fonds.
  Watson Family. Fonds.
  White, Georgia. Fonds.

❄ WEBSITES

Dobrowolsky, Helene, Yukon Archives, and Yukon Council of Archives. "Outstanding Yukon Women" (entry on Lucille Hunter). *Yukon Women and Children.* www.tc.gov.yk.ca/archives/wc/outstanding/outstanding4.htm.

Friends of the Yukon Archives Society. *Yukon Genealogy Database.* www.yukongenealogy.com/content/ykgen_db.htm.

Friends of the Yukon Archives Society/Dawson City Museum. *Pan for Gold Database.* www.yukongenealogy.com/content/dawson.htm.

Langlow, Wesley A., ed. "The Langlow Family in Alaska and the Yukon." *ExploreNorth.* www.explorenorth.com/library/history/bl-langlow.htm.

Pilon, Marilyn. "Canada's Legal Age of Consent to Sexual Activity." Parliamentary Research Branch of the Library of Parliament, 25 Jan. 1999, revised 12 April 2001. www.parl.gc.ca/information/library/PRBpubs/prb993-e.pdf.

Putnam, Bill. Information on the Putnam family taken from the 1901 Canadian census reports as found on Ancestry.ca. www.billputman.com/Canada%20Census%201901.htm.

YukonAlaska.com. *Yukon & Alaska Genealogy Centre.* www.yukonalaska.com/pathfinder/gen/.

Yukon Archives, Cultural Services Branch of the Department of Tourism and Culture, Government of Yukon. *Hidden History: Black History of the Yukon.* www.tc.gov.yk.ca/archives/hiddenhistory/.

Photograph Credits

❀ ABBREVIATIONS

ASL Alaska State Library, Alaska Historical Collections
BCA Royal BC Museum, British Columbia Archives
BRBML Collection of Western Americana, Beinecke Rare Book
        and Manuscript Library
DCM Dawson City Museum
GA Glenbow Archives
LAC Library and Archives Canada
PC Parks Canada
UAF University of Alaska Fairbanks, Archives
UW University of Washington Libraries
YA Yukon Archives

Page number followed by source.
xx: YA, James Albert Johnson Fonds, 82/341 #22
3: YA, James Albert Johnson Fonds, 82/341 #15
5: YA, James Albert Johnson Fonds, 82/341 #22
9: YA, Their Own Yukon Project collection, 2000/37 #156 (with permission of the
    Council of Yukon First Nations)
10: YA, Dave Bohn Collection, 3/102 #4
12: UW, Special Collections, UW 17875
15: YA, Tappan Adney Fonds, Department of Rare Books & Special
    Collections, McGill University Libraries, 81/9 #45
18: UW, Special Collections, UW 28617z
19: UW, Special Collections, UW 17875
22: YA, Tappan Adney Fonds, Department of Rare Books & Special
    Collections, McGill University Libraries, 81/9 #123

24: DCM, 1994.257.02

27: From *The Klondike Official Guide* by William Ogilvie
    (Toronto: Hunter Rose Co. Ltd., 1898)

29: UW, Special Collections, UW 22084

32: Courtesy of George Bryce

35: UW, Special Collections, Hegg 2264

39: DCM, 1994.257.02

42: ASL, Winter and Pond Collection, ASL-P87-0664

44: Courtesy of John McTavish

48: DCM, 1993.257.10

52: ASL, Winter and Pond Collection, ASL-P87-0664

53: UW, Special Collections, UW 26629

57: UAF, Stereographic Library Collection, UAF-1975-0178-16

60: GA, NA-4412-20

69: GA, NA-4412-20

71: Courtesy of Mary Henderson

74: DCM, Frank E. Wolfe, photographer, 1991.51.10

76: YA, Martha Black Fonds, 82/218 #2

78: DCM, 1997.299.9

81: DCM, 1994.122.10

83: DCM, 1982.158.1

85: YA, Martha Black Fonds, 82/218 #2

88: YA, Arthur Campbell Fonds, 80/9 #1

90: UW, Special Collections, UW 28618z

92: UW, Special Collections, UW 28619z

96: YA, Adams and Larkin Fonds, 9127

98: DCM, 1990.43.108

101: UW, Special Collections, UW 28619z

103: UAF, Gibson Family Papers, UAF-1959-804-34

110: DCM, E. A. Hegg, photographer, 1998.22.645

113: Courtesy of George Bryce

114: UW, Special Collections, UW 26644

117: DCM, 1997.299.1

119: DCM, E. O. Ellingsen, photographer, 1984.221.8

120: DCM, 1990.43.24

121: UW, Special Collections, UW 26644

123: LAC, Henry Joseph Woodside, photographer, PA-016581

127: DCM, Frank E. Wolfe, photographer, 1991.51.53

134: YA, Pepin Family Fonds, 82/237 #5

135: DCM, 2004.614.7

136: DCM, 1984.17.26

140: LAC, Henry Joseph Woodside, photographer, PA-016714

143: YA, Grace McBride Fonds, 90/2 #6

146: YA, Betty Pierson Fonds, 79/49 #40

151: DCM, 1984.17.1.9
153: LAC, Henry Joseph Woodside, photographer, PA-016714
155: DCM, Larss and Duclos, photographers, 1984.212.7
157: DCM, Frank E. Wolfe, photographer, 1990.43.92
159: UW, Special Collections, UW 16634
160: DCM, 1998.17.1.18
162: UW, Special Collections, Hegg 556
165: LAC, C-014550
170: ASL, Snow Family Collection, PCA 154-243
174: UW, Special Collections, Hegg 556
178: UAF, Gibson Family Papers, UAF-1959-804-182
180: UW, Special Collections, UW 28616z
183: BRBML, 1052381
186: PC, Anita John Collection, YT-181
189: YA, Betty Pierson Fonds, 79/49 #3
190: DCM, 1990.53.3
192: PC, Anita John Collection, YT-181
193: Courtesy of Mary Henderson
196: UW, Special Collections, Hegg 3209

Index

Photographs are in bold.

About the Author

Frances Backhouse is a full-time professional writer with a passion for history. Her first book, *Women of the Klondike* (Whitecap, 1995), has become a Northern classic and was adapted for stage and performed by Theatre Erindale (University of Toronto) in November 2007. She is also the author of *Hiking with Ghosts: The Chilkoot Trail Then and Now* (Raincoast Books, 1999) and a contributor to *Castles of the North: Canada's Grand Hotels* (Lynx Images, 2001). Her stories of Canada's fascinating past have appeared in *British Columbia Magazine*, *Canadian Geographic*, *The Beaver*, *Canadian Living*, and *Up Here*.

Frances also writes about nature and the environment and is the author of *Woodpeckers of North America* (Firefly Books, 2005) and *Owls of North America* (Firefly Books, 2008), as well as numerous articles in magazines such as *Audubon*, *Canadian Wildlife*, and *Harrowsmith*. She lives in Victoria, BC, with her partner, Mark Zuehlke, and can be found on the web at www.backhouse.ca.